THE WAGES OF EMPIRE

TRANSNATIONAL FEMINIST STUDIES

KAMALA KEMPADOO, SERIES EDITOR

York University, Toronto, Canada

Books in the Series:

The Wages of Empire: Neoliberal Policies, Repression, and Women's Poverty
edited by Amalia L. Cabezas, Ellen Reese, and Marguerite Waller

Forthcoming:

Transformations: Feminist Pathways to Global Change
edited by Torry Dickinson and Robert Schaeffer

From Hollywood to Bollywood: The Cinema of South Asians Abroad
by Shoba S. Rajgopal

The Wages of Empire

NEOLIBERAL POLICIES, REPRESSION, AND WOMEN'S POVERTY

edited by
Amalia L. Cabezas, Ellen Reese, and Marguerite Waller

Paradigm Publishers
Boulder • London

Copyright © 2007 Paradigm Publishers

Published in the United States by Paradigm Publishers, 3360 Mitchell Lane Suite E, Boulder, CO 80301 USA.

Paradigm Publishers is the trade name of Birkenkamp & Company, LLC, Dean Birkenkamp, President and Publisher.

Library of Congress Cataloging-in-Publication Data

The wages of empire : neoliberal policies, repression, and women's poverty / edited by Amalia L. Cabezas, Ellen Reese, Marguerite Waller.
    p. cm. — (Transnational feminist studies)
    Includes bibliographical references and index.
    ISBN 978-1-59451-347-3 (hc : alk. paper)   ISBN 978-1-59451-348-0 (pbk.)
    1. Women–Economic conditions—Cross-cultural studies.   2. Women—Economic conditions—Developing countries.   3. Sex discrimination against women—Cross-cultural studies.   4. Globalization—Economic aspects.   5. International trade—Economic aspects.   I. Cabezas, Amalia L.   II. Reese, Ellen, 1969–   III. Waller, Marguerite R., 1948–
    HQ1381.W35 2007
    362.83086'942—dc22

2007014788

Printed and bound in the United States of America on acid-free paper that meets the standards of the American National Standard for Permanence of Paper for Printed Library Materials.

Designed and Typeset by Straight Creek Bookmakers.

11 10 09 08 07   1 2 3 4 5

Contents

❋

Acknowledgments

This book could not have come into existence without the support of many individuals, groups, and institutions. We are, first of all, deeply indebted to all our contributors, whose dedication and hard work in bringing together the textures, implications, and brute facts of the impact of neoliberal globalization on low-income women are the substance of this volume. We and they are even more deeply indebted to the many women around the world who have given of their time and allowed their experiences, analyses, and feelings to be represented here.

Financial support for this project was provided by the "Cloning Cultures" project, funded by a generous grant from the Ford Foundation and administered by the Center for Ideas and Society (CIS) at the University of California Riverside and the University of California Humanities Research Institute. In particular, we would like to acknowledge the crucial roles played by Piya Chatterjee and Emory Elliott of U.C. Riverside and Philomena Essed and David Theo Goldberg of the U.C. Humanities Research Institute, who conceptualized and administered the "Cloning Cultures" project. We also warmly thank Laura Lozon, director of the Center for Ideas and Society, who provided invaluable logistical and administrative support. The Ford Foundation grant also provided us the editorial and research assistance of three highly capable graduate students, Katrina Paxton, Michael Chavez, and Jenni Keys.

Marguerite Waller and Ellen Reese were in residencies at the CIS in 2003 and 2005 which greatly facilitated the development and exchange of our ideas for this volume. The original group included our UCR colleagues Manali Desai, Tracy Fisher, and Piya Chatterjee, with whom we read and talked extensively in the areas of gender and economics, feminist and women's activism, development, and neoliberal policy. Philomena Essed provided helpful feedback on our proposal for this volume, and the participants in the "Cloning Cultures" conference at the University of California, Irvine, organized by Philomena Essed, Piya Chatterjee, and Emory Elliott, offered us extremely useful responses to early drafts of several of the essays. The 2004-05 and 2005-06 UCR Mellon Foundation Workshops in the Humanities also financed several series of presentations by scholars and activists whose ideas shaped our thoughts on this topic in significant ways. We thank Thomas Scanlon, Ian Chambers, Vonnie Tessier, Tina Stavrapoulos, Kenneth Barr, Christine Petit, and Linda Kim for their support and assistance in organizing these events.

Amalia Cabezas is grateful for the love and encouragement of Alfredo Cruz, Deena J. González, and Ramona Sliva. Ellen Reese would like to thank especially Edna Bonacich, Scott Coltrane, Christopher Chase-Dunn, Rebecca Giem, Christine Gailey, Vincent Geidraitis, Kamala Kempadoo, Ernest Savage III, Eric Vega, and Robin Whittington. Marguerite Waller would like add to her thanks to Steve Cullenberg, Mary Cummins, Eric Field, Sandra Harding, Kathleen Hartford, Emily Hicks, Amy Kofman, Corinne Kumar, Ethan Nasreddin-Longo, Ruth Wallen, and other colleagues, friends, and family members too numerous to name for their guidance, questions, insights, and mindfulness. All three editors join in thanking the librarians at U.C. Riverside for their advice, research assistance, and support for this project.

Not least, we are deeply grateful to our publisher, Dean Birkenkamp, to his managing editor, Melanie Stafford, and to all the others at Paradigm whose commitment and thoughtful guidance have brought this book to completion.

I
The Policies and Ideologies
of Neoliberal Globalization

Introduction

❋

LOOKING BACKWARD: FROM BEIJING TO BRETTON WOODS

We doubt that it was the intention of the statespeople and economists who convened the UN Monetary and Financial Conference in Bretton Woods, New Hampshire, in July 1944, to base the economic "growth" of corporate capital in the late twentieth and early twenty-first centuries on the superexploitation of women, particularly women of color.[1] Nevertheless, by 1995, when the UN Fourth World Conference on Women was convened in Beijing, China, the two institutions that loomed as the biggest contributors to women's poverty, and as the most intransigent obstacles to improving women's health, education, participation in civil society, and general well-being, were the International Monetary Fund (IMF) and the International Bank for Reconstruction and Development (now known as the World Bank). These two financial institutions, created at Bretton Woods, have largely orchestrated the transnational economic restructurings known in the 1970s and 1980s as "development" and, more recently, as "globalization." The General Agreement on Tariffs and Trade (GATT) of 1947 evolved into a complementary third institution, the World Trade Organization (WTO), in 1995, the very year that women were meeting at the UN Conference in Beijing to protest the catastrophic economic policies of the World Bank and the IMF, both of which had, by that time, inflicted malnutrition and starvation, unimaginable violence, and devastating environmental degradation on vast numbers of the world's people—with low-income women and children taking the brunt of these effects.[2]

The two major concerns at Bretton Woods were the economic reconstruction of Europe after World War II and the prevention of another global crisis on the

3

order of the Great Depression of the 1930s. The World Bank was to make loans available for reconstruction projects, and the IMF was to bail out economies suffering from potentially destabilizing downturns and shortfalls. The term *Development* in the original name of the World Bank was an afterthought (Stiglitz 2002, 11). Many of the countries in which the World Bank and the IMF are now most active were, at the time when these institutions were founded, colonies of Europe or the United States; their economies, physical infrastructures, and legal systems were therefore considered the responsibility of their colonial occupiers. (In the mostly independent countries of Latin America, the United States nevertheless pursued colonial-like economic and political policies. It tended to see the region as its "backyard," and to support, militarily and otherwise, regimes that gave North American corporate interests free rein.)

The IMF and the World Bank were to see to it only that the industrialized nation-states in existence at the end of the war remained economically "healthy," keeping supply up and unemployment down, and maintaining a favorable international trading environment. Along with the GATT, these financial institutions were to moderate market forces. Following the thinking of British economist John Maynard Keynes, the Bretton Woods paradigm did not assume that the market always worked well. Rather, it assumed that collective governmental control was essential for stable economic growth (Rapley 2002, 7–9; Stiglitz 2002, 12). By contrast, the neoliberal paradigm (sometimes known as "the Washington Consensus"), upon which the chapters in *The Wages of Empire* are focused, envisions market forces as working best without governmental control.

One further outcome of Bretton Woods has proved decisively significant in the roughly sixty-year history of development and globalization: The voting arrangements in the World Bank and the IMF are based largely on the distribution of power and wealth at the end of World War II, with the United States being both the largest contributor and the most powerful voice in the collective of nation-states. Neither institution is answerable to any elected official; they both report to the ministries of finance and the central banks of participating governments (Stiglitz 2002, 12). It is the U.S. dominance of these institutions, along with the willingness of the U.S. government to deploy its armed services in defense of the financial interests of these entities, that has led to the perception of a new form of imperialism. According to some analysts, the new "Empire" is administered not by a nation-state, as the nineteenth- and twentieth-century British and French empires were, but by a transnational consortium of financial interests and corporations (Hardt and Negri 2000; Perkins 2004).

The rapidity and scale of transnational trade, investment, and financial transactions and the role of global governance institutions are certainly novel. However, as in previous eras, power and wealth remain highly concentrated within a few nation-states (among them, currently, the United States, Japan, dominant members of the European Union, and China). U.S. hegemony, and efforts to maintain that hegemony through military force, shape the current dynamics of Empire in fundamental ways (Chomsky 2003; Eisenstein 2004). The title of this volume refers to this contemporary form of Empire. Our contributors bring to light the diverse but comparably immiserating conditions that neoliberal economic policies, and the repression that backs them up, have created for low-wage, urban, rural, and migrating women.

Many economists, anthropologists, sociologists, novelists, and filmmakers have grappled with the complicated histories of the impact of World Bank and IMF policies on people living in poverty, itself a multifaceted, disparately experienced position. Particularly in the years since 1973, when World Bank president Robert McNamara announced a reorientation of the Bank's activities toward poverty alleviation, there has been an outpouring of volumes signaling that something was going terribly wrong. Among these are *The Devil and Commodity Fetishism in South America* (Taussig 1980), *Banking on the Poor* (Ayres 1985), *Underdeveloping the Amazon* (Bunker 1985), *Staying Alive: Women, Ecology, and Development* (Shiva 1988), *Storm Signals: Structural Adjustment and Development Alternatives in the Caribbean* (McAfee 1991), and Philippine director Kidlat Tahimik's film *Perfumed Nightmare* (1979). These have been followed by the distress signals of a new generation of commentators, whose titles and metaphors cohere with those of their predecessors: *Dream Jungle* (Hagedorn 2003), chapters called "Dreamland" and "Nobody Listens to a Poor Man" in Timothy Mitchell's *Rule of Experts: Egypt, Techno-Politics, Modernity* (2002), *Disposable People* (Bales 1999), *Confessions of an Economic Hit Man* (Perkins 2004), *World on Fire* (Chua 2003), and *Globalization and Its Discontents* (a title adopted by both Stiglitz 2002 and Sassen 1998a).

Despite divergences among institutions and internal changes in policy and philosophy (Ayres 1985; Rapley 2002; Stiglitz 2002), the conceptual frame of economic policymaking has not fundamentally changed. What is commonly referred to as the "free market" continues to be taken as an absolute—as the only measure of, and means to, prosperity—by economic planners. None of the financial and trade institutions has ever wavered in its commitment to protecting capitalist economic development (commonly equated with "growth" and "prosperity") and the financial elites who administer it (Jacobs 2000; Waller 2006).[3]

NEOLIBERALISM, STRUCTURAL ADJUSTMENT PROGRAMS, AND MULTILATERAL INSTITUTIONS

Economic crises in industrialized nations in the 1970s and 1980s, and the demise of Communist rule in the Soviet Union and Eastern Europe in the late 1980s and early 1990s, spurred the intensification of "development" and the "globalization" of trade. In understanding these changes it helps to contextualize them in relation to the circumstances out of which they arose. The "Marshall Plan" (the name given to the economic policies that allowed the rapid reconstruction of Western Europe after World War II) fueled an economic boom in the United States, and the outbreak of the Korean War in the early 1950s extended the already considerable postwar military presence of the United States in Asia. By the late 1960s and early 1970s, however, the Cold War arms race with the Soviet Union and the ongoing "hot" war in Vietnam were draining the U.S. budget. In order to fund the arms race and the war in Vietnam and to cover mounting trade deficits, the United States went off the gold standard in 1971–1972, compromising the Bretton Woods agreement for which gold had been the basis. The value of U.S. dollars in circulation far exceeded the amount of gold held in reserve, resulting in currency instability. When, in 1973, the Organization of Petroleum Exporting Countries (OPEC) was formed and raised the price of oil fourfold, a worldwide energy crisis ensued, catalyzing recessions in both industrialized and "developing" nations (Rapley 2002, 34). The impact of recession, though, was dramatically different for nations indebted to Western banks than it was for the nations that controlled these financial institutions. With the increase in oil prices, OPEC countries realized tremendous profits, which they deposited in Western banks. In turn, Western banks loaned money, often at variable interest rates, to fund development projects, many of which were ill-conceived. A second oil shock in 1979 and the tight monetary policies of lender governments led to drastic increases in interest rates. These increases and the world recession left many developing countries unable to meet even the interest payments on their loans. Nor could they sell their products in the global market.

Intensifying this economic double-bind was the fact that lenders, such as the World Bank, turned from development strategies to debt recovery as the value of their loans rose. OPEC crises in combination with increased lending to "developing" nations thus not only brought about the reformulation of rela-tionships—economic as well as political—among the "first," "third," and, more recently, the "second" (formerly communist, Central European) worlds but also transformed class, racial, ethnic, and religious relationships within nations. We turn now to the intellectual development of this reformulation, commonly known as *neoliberalism*.

Neoliberalism represents a conjunction of political and economic theories going back to the eighteenth-century Scottish founder of modern economic theory, Adam Smith (1723–1790), whose *Inquiry into the Nature and Causes of the Wealth of Nations,* published in 1776, argued for free markets, unfettered by government regulation (though Smith favored government activity in many nonprofitmaking spheres). An extreme or "fundamentalist" version of the market theory of economics, today's neoliberalism rejects the Keynesian notion of market fallibility in favor of a notion of the market's infallible goodness. In its current incarnation, this ideology privileges the expansion of the "free" (without regula-tion and tariffs) market and the global integration of economies. It proposes the abolition of government intervention in economic matters and radical cutbacks in social services, including education, healthcare, housing, agricultural subsidies, and nutrition. The emphasis by lending institutions and the WTO on breaking down barriers to international trade has also meant that previously protected industries and economic sectors are now subjected to intense competition.

Loan conditions widely imposed by the IMF, known as "structural adjust-ment policies" (SAPs), have had disastrous consequences in Africa, Asia, Latin

America, and the Caribbean, undermining democratic political processes as well (Assié-Lumumba 2000; Bank Muñoz, Karides, and Esbenshade in this volume). A typical structural adjustment program includes the devaluation of a country's currency and the privatization of utilities and services such as water, electricity, transportation, healthcare, and education. SAPs also entail the lifting of trade tariffs and agricultural subsidies, the reduction of civil service jobs, and other measures aimed at enforcing fiscal austerity. Theoretically, the purpose of an SAP is to balance the national budget and restore a country's capacity to make interest payments on outstanding debts. In practice, however, these programs have intensified unemployment, political instability, the proliferation of street vending and other forms of contingent work, and international labor migrations (Assié-Lumumba 2000). Universally imposed as a kind of "one size fits all" prescription, regardless of the diversity of circumstances in which they are implemented, SAPs have led to the massive transfer of public assets into the hands of local elites and/or multinational corporations, resulting in the devastation of economies that, in many cases, were relatively strong before the IMF intervened (Karides in this volume).[4] Through the use of lending as a tool to manipulate domestic policies, these outside entities have also influenced internal politics, undermining democratic processes and reorienting government policy according to neoliberal principles (Assié-Lumumba 2000). Meanwhile, nation-states in the global North, often encouraged by corporate-sponsored think tanks, have embraced neoliberal policies, including privatization, social service cutbacks, and the rollback of labor rights and environmental regulations (Peck and Tickell 2002; Reese in this volume).

Some critics argue that neoliberalism involves not only "rollback" processes, in which previously established labor rights and economic regulations are weakened or eliminated, but also "rollout" processes, through which paternalistic and disciplinary control is exerted on the poor and other disadvantaged groups (Peck and Tickell 2002). Thus, although neoliberal policies have weakened the capacity of the state to redistribute income and provide social services, they often involve "coercive, disciplinary forms of state intervention in order to impose market rule upon all aspects of social life" (Brenner and Theodore 2002, 5). Examples of "rollout" neoliberalism would be the criminalization of poor people's survival strategies, including street vending, sex work, subsistence farming, crossing borders in search of jobs, and living in spaces that cost little or nothing (Brenner and Theodore 2002; Cabezas 2005; Parenti 1999; Peck and Tickell 2002). Domestic populations around the world are suffering increased police and military repression as unpopular neoliberal policies are implemented, inequality grows, environments degrade, and economic hardships ensue (Eisenstein 2004; Ezeilo in this volume; Harvey 2003; Perkins 2004; Roy 2004; Shiva 2002).

The rise of neoliberalism has also been accompanied by military invasions and occupations. The militarization of foreign policy is particularly evident within the United States, where neoconservatives embracing the Project for the New American Century successfully championed the invasions of Iraq and Afghanistan, leading to an unprecedented rise in national military expenditures (Chomsky 2003;

Eisenstein 2004; Harvey 2003). Other, less visible occupations are also in progress in such disparate locations as Aceh, Ecuador, and the Niger River Delta. These widely differing campaigns have in common the goals of maintaining access to oil and other resources, suppressing resistance to neoliberal policy, and increasing the control by multinational corporations—most of them based in the United States or Western Europe—of the global marketplace (Ezeilo in this volume; Perkins 2004; Siapno 2006). For the U.S. elite, militarism is also a strategy for maintaining global political domination.

LOOKING FORWARD: NEOLIBERALISM AS A FEMINIST ISSUE

Policymakers themselves often seem to know very little about the effects of their decisions (Waller 2006). As contributor Caitilyn Allen argues, what seem like minor shifts in government or economic policy in the industrialized world can create disasters in distant communities, which go completely unnoticed at their source. The unpredictability, pervasiveness, and violence of neoliberal empire are a telling index, though, of a force that is highly "political" even if it has not been legislated by, or even particularly visible to, many of its practitioners. In this volume the feminist analyses of low-wage women's exploitation by, and resistance to, contemporary global capitalism, and the militarism that accompanies it, moves from the financial and cultural policymaking end of globalization processes to an illuminatingly diverse selection of receiving ends. Whereas globalization scholarship has largely been conducted in gender-neutral terms, we have taken our inspiration from a growing body of feminist scholarship that explores the intersecting politics of gender, race, and class in the ideologies and consequences of imperial globalization (Eisenstein 2004; Enloe 2004; Lionnet et al. 2004; McClintock 1995; Moghadam 2005; Naples and Desai 2002; Rowbotham and Linkogle 2001; Rowbotham and Mitter 1994; Waller and Marcos 2005). Here, we focus particularly on the effects of neoliberal theory and practice on labor by women who are socially marginalized. Neoliberal reforms tend to worsen the conditions of already-vulnerable groups, such as low-income single mothers, the indigenous, and those disadvantaged by racism. Although there are many causes and consequences of women's poverty, and the term *low income* can have very different meanings depending upon the context, these diverse situations, seen in transnational perspective, offer a fresh and deeply disturbing lens through which to assess the short- and long-term consequences of neoliberal economic restructuring.

There is already plenty of evidence to suggest that macroeconomic adjustment policies formulated to open free markets have heaped disproportionate burdens on poor women and brought increases in poverty, malnutrition, and lack of access to healthcare and education. The precise ways in which these burdens are shifted onto women are constantly changing, and they vary greatly from one social and political context to another. Virtually all of the chapters in this volume testify, however, to the urgent need for further investigation and action. Already, declines in jobs, wages, and the public sector have resulted in dramatically lower employment rates for men and the deterioration of women's ability to meet day-to-day needs. Whatever the makeup of the household, women's traditional responsibilities toward children and elders have expanded with the elimination of social services (Misra and Merz in this volume). In many contexts, because the civil service has been the principal employer of women, they have lost both their source of income (as nurses, teachers, social workers, office workers) and their social services (healthcare, education, public transportation, food and fuel subsidies) at one stroke. Increased family responsibilities are then compounded by long hours spent on low-paid wage work (if available) and informal sector activities. And the increased workload, in turn, often means that daughters and grandmothers must take greater responsibility for household chores and childcare (Sharma 2000). With lower state support for education and higher school fees, low-income children, especially girls, are more likely to drop out of school or attend only sporadically. Budget cutbacks and user fees have also led to sharp declines in prenatal services and primary healthcare. With fewer resources in households and the decrease in or elimination of food subsidies, caloric intake has deteriorated, resulting in malnutrition, disease, and increased infant mortality. The hyperexploitation of women's labor, much of it unpaid—as well as the unacknowledged dependence upon women, especially socially marginalized women, to sustain social and community infrastructure—can no longer be seen, we maintain, as accidental or temporary consequences of the intensification of economic globalization.

These circumstances are virtually identical to the circumstances in Palestine and Iraq, for both men and women, studied by contributor Jennifer Olmsted. Currently living under stringent military occupation, these populations, Olmsted argues, are impoverished by their rigorous *exclusion* from the global economy. The striking parallel between the lives of low-income women living under structural adjustment policies and those of men and women living under military occupation calls attention to the hierarchies and exclusions effected *internally* by neoliberal economic policy itself. The chapters in this volume that focus on globalization's labor practices and the working conditions of low-income women depict a systematic enforcement and exploitation of gender, racial, ethnic, and national hierarchies. Neoliberal theory and practice have yet to deal with, or even to acknowledge, the illogic of trying to create a fully integrated economic/political system grounded in the exclusionary, win/lose logic of competition and capital accumulation. Over and over again, so-called poverty alleviation campaigns, particularly those directed toward women, consist of ever more inventive ways of enlisting low-income women's time, labor, and resources to feed the growth of business and financial institutions (Roy in this volume).

Increased repression is also reshaping the lives of women in many countries. Women's livelihoods are abruptly being disrupted or eliminated due to a "war on terror," the demand for oil, or simply the drive for higher profits. Although Afghanistan, Iraq, and Palestine are better known in the global North as theaters of war, less visible campaigns are also being waged—using not only bullets but sexual harassment, rape, disease, dislocation, and starvation—with the backing of state- and corporate-sponsored armed forces (Allen, Chatterjee, Esbenshade, Ezeilo, Kolhatkar, Useche and Cabezas, and Olmsted in this volume).

This repression is compounded by the circumstance that low-income people of color and disadvantaged whites in the United States—many trapped in multigenerational patterns of poverty and disenfranchisement—are enlisted to fight wars overseas against other colonized, racialized, extremely impoverished people. The intensification of empire-building has also meant that practices recently associated only with corporate regimes, such as subcontracting, are now used to contract soldiers from countries experiencing internal displacement and terrorism, such as Colombia, into the "war on terror." With only a few exceptions, furthermore, the allies assisting the United States in the occupation of Iraq are considered low-income countries within the international community. Thus, the very constitution of the armed forces is contributing significantly to a class schema in which the poor fight the poor to enrich the multinational corporate sector.

RESISTING EMPIRE

Women are playing visible roles in opposing neoliberalism and militarism through activist groups such as Women in Black, the Zapatistas, the Courts of Women, the Revolutionary Association of the Women of Afghanistan, Black Laundry, Code Pink, as well as many antiwar organizations, labor unions, and political groups.[5] Activists in the labor, environmental, feminist, and human rights movements have also cooperated transnationally through conferences, cross-border labor struggles, organizations, and lobbying campaigns, coordinating global protests such as the demonstrations that disrupted the 1999 meeting of the WTO in Seattle and the 2004 meeting of the WTO in Cancún (Moghadam 2005; Smith 2004a). The year 2003 witnessed millions-strong marches against the invasion of Iraq, and rising resistance to militarism and neoliberal global capitalism has been reflected not only in the impressive growth of the World Social Forum (WSF)[6] but also in the power gained by socialist parties in a number of countries, including Argentina, Bolivia, Brazil, Chile, Ecuador, Uruguay, and Venezuela.

Although transnational feminist networks have lobbied officials in the United Nations, WTO, IMF, and World Bank, and organized mass protests, these global governance institutions have a track record of ignoring such demands. At best, they grant their critics symbolic victories designed to co-opt, rather than to respond to, protest (Moghadam 2005). Nevertheless, such actions attest to the vibrancy of organized feminist resistance to Empire. The World March of Women coordinated a series of actions in 2005, including marches, vigils, lobbying, conferences, and cultural celebrations, in which women's groups from fifty nations participated. Kicked off by a demonstration drawing 30,000 women into the streets of Sao Paolo, Brazil, on March 8—International Women's Day—and ending with a gathering of 5,000 participants from 25 countries in the West African nation of

Burkina Faso on October 17, this global relay highlighted a transnational demand for an end to women's exploitation, poverty, and oppression under patriarchal capitalism (World March of Women 2005). Also on International Women's Day that year, organizations affiliated with the Global Call to Action Against Poverty issued a powerful press release headlining the fact that "two-thirds of the world's 1.3 billion desperately poor are women, living on less than one dollar a day" (Millennium Campaign 2005). Later in the same year, at the United Nations' Fifth World Conference on Women, held ten years after the historic 1995 conference in Beijing, the Women's Environment and Development Organization (WEDO) publicized its report, *Beijing Betrayed*, which called attention to the worsening conditions experienced by many women across the world during this ten-year period following the Beijing meeting. It called on government officials across the globe to put into practice the commitments they made in 1995 to promote women's rights (Kyriakou 2005; Pollitt 2005).

Given the repressive conditions under which many low-income women work and live, their resistance must sometimes take subtler and more covert forms. For example, Carolina Bank Muñoz's interviews in Tijuana reveal that women factory workers resist exploitation by disrupting the labor process—specifically, by taking long bathroom breaks or showing up late for work. Impoverished women have also been at the forefront of numerous organized actions against militarism and neoliberalism, as when peasant women in Guatemala helped to lead peaceful protests, under highly repressive conditions, against their government's signing of a free trade agreement with the United States (Forster 2005). Piya Chatterjee, Joy Ngozi Ezeilo, and Sonali Kolhatkar in this volume contribute to the new and theoretically original literature on grassroots women's activism for global and economic justice. The depth and extent of women's resistance to neoliberal empire are, at this point, as little known in the industrialized world as the effects of neoliberal globalization itself, but these examples suggest that grassroots activity is diverse and widespread (see also Cabezas, Reese, and Waller 2006; Waller and Marcos 2005; Waller and Rycenga 2001).

OVERVIEW

We have organized the chapters in this volume into four sections, though the issues they raise are densely interrelated, and we encourage readers to cross reference them freely. Part I, "The Policies and Ideologies of Neoliberal Capitalism," examines the ideological underpinnings of neoliberalism as they have worked to legitimate rollbacks in labor and welfare rights, the spread of free market trade policies, and the rise of export processing zones. Such policies have significantly shifted the balance of power both within countries and across them, giving wealthy nations and multinational corporations even more power to exploit women workers and their countries' resources. Bernardo Useche and Amalia Cabezas follow a series of connections that lead from neoliberal policy to the current HIV/AIDS pandemic. Ananya Roy performs a detailed and critical analysis of the promotion of alternative microcredit schemes as antidotes to women's poverty; she rigorously uncovers the biases in their construction of the "Third World Woman" and "gender empowerment," and explores the potential for radically altering the terms of the debate. Jennifer Lynn Stoever, taking the women's fashion magazine *Marie Claire* as her example, shows how the mainstream media appropriate an activist idiom to sell upper-middle-class American readers an enhanced version of self at the expense of other "women of the world," reinscribing a fundamentally colonial mentality under the guise of modern feminism. (The mobilization of this version of feminism to enlist support for the war in Afghanistan is treated by Sonali Kolhatkar in Part IV).

Part II, "Impacts of Neoliberal Policy and Ideology: Case Studies," examines the effects of recent shifts in state policies, from trade liberalization and structural adjustment policies in the global South to welfare reform and citizenship in the global North. Drawing from field research, survey data, interviews, and activist involvement, the four chapters in this section show how women have been robbed of social services, employment, and life itself. Piya Chatterjee traces the devastation of the lives of women tea pluckers in North Bengal to the policies of international food conglomerate Unilever and the Indian government's capitulation to the recolonization of India's tea plantations. Marina Karides compares the response to neoliberalism by the governments of two former British colonies, the Republic of Cyprus and the Republic of Trinidad and Tobago, finding that Cyprus, which rejected neoliberal reforms, has also provided greater economic security for women. Her research, together with Chatterjee's, suggests that national governments have a large role in determining the effects of globalization on women. Focusing on the export of U.S.-style "welfare reform" to other industrialized countries, Ellen Reese explains how the "Wisconsin model" of coercing low-income mothers into the workforce plays into a broader effort by economic elites to cheapen labor within the global economy. Tracy Fisher then explores the ways in which such dismantling of the welfare state in Britain has catalyzed changes in notions of citizenship. In an illuminating analysis of the involvement of grassroots organizations in the provision of services previously offered by the state, she argues that poor, working-class, largely immigrant women are recreating citizenship, not in terms of identity but in terms of their exercise of novel forms of political agency.

Part III, "Laboring Under Corporate Globalization: Case Studies," provides detailed analyses of how neoliberal globalization processes have displaced rural workers, forced women to toil under sweatshop conditions inside multinational factories, and instigated vast international migrations of domestic workers. Joya Misra and Sabine N. Merz show how policy decisions and neoliberal values have shaped a system that requires the emigration of poor women workers to provide domestic care in wealthier countries. Acknowledging the policy facet of this international division of care, these authors argue, is essential to organizing resistance and creating more equitable care arrangements. Carolina Bank Muñoz also connects working conditions with policy. She links the vulnerability of Mexican factory women to exploitation, sexual harassment, and racial discrimination with their husbands' loss of agricultural land and jobs and their migration out of the country, which followed in the wake of the North American Free Trade Agreement. The militarization of the U.S.–Mexican border and lax enforcement of labor protections under the Mexican constitution have further weakened the position of women workers. In the Colombian flower industry, low wages and short-term contracts with no benefits are compounded by ongoing exposure to high concentrations of toxic pesticides. Cynthia Mellon analyzes the interrelated stresses to which this multibillion-dollar industry subjects women workers, labor standards, and the environment. Jill Esbenshade's case study of the garment industry in El Salvador, where the IMF and the World Bank have promoted the growth of Export Processing Zones (EPZs), strongly corroborates the need to focus on policy. The EPZs she studies employ tens of thousands of women and teenagers in sweatshops where they, too, are both harassed and denied basic labor rights. Esbenshade persuasively argues that the decline in labor protections in El Salvador's EPZs contributes to the worldwide pattern of decline in working conditions among garment workers, most of whom are women.

Part IV, "War and Military Repression," opens with plant pathologist Caitilyn Allen's startling story of how new U.S. "biosecurity" laws have combined with the outsourcing of agricultural production to destroy the livelihood of 600 Guatemalan flower workers. We have been surprised, in fact, to discover the many ways in which neoliberal policies are rendering low-income women just as economically vulnerable as the subjects of military occupation. Jennifer Olmsted's groundbreaking analysis of the economic impact of occupation on low-income populations in Palestine and Iraq argues further that it is just as important in assessing the implications of globalization to look at its effects upon those who are excluded from its processes as it is to consider how it is affecting the lives of those whom policymakers target as potential workers, consumers, or users of financial services. The inability to distinguish, in many cases, between inclusion and exclusion, between opportunity and oppression, constitutes a very significant dimension of neoliberalism—a dimension that warrants further theoretical and empirical study (Ovalle 2005).

Nigerian women's human rights lawyer Joy Ngozi Ezeilo and feminist activist radio host Sonali Kolhatkar conclude the volume with two instances of women's active resistance to imperial globalization. Both the "Amazons" of the Niger Delta and the Revolutionary Association of the Women of Afghanistan (RAWA) have openly challenged the legitimacy of the national and international collaborations among patriarchal institutions that have intensified women's vulnerability in their regions. Powerful collusions among governments, oil companies, and multilateral financial institutions have devastated the largest delta region in Africa, now designated by the United Nations as the most endangered delta region in the world. The indigenous women who depended on the rivers and mangrove forests of the Niger Delta for their food, fuel, housing, and income have demanded an equal place at the conference table with the executives of Exxon, Chevron, and Shell.

RAWA recognizes no current administration in Afghanistan or the United States as having legal or moral authority over Afghan women. It is perhaps an aspect of Empire's vulnerability that it chooses to deny these votes of no confidence, as if it had already achieved the hegemony for which it is reaching. We take with great seriousness the realities of the lives of the many women who have entrusted our contributors with their experiences and insights, and we encourage our readers to do likewise as they work to find their own agency in a volatile world.

Amalia L. Cabezas
Ellen Reese
Marguerite Waller

NOTES

1. As Anne McClintock points out, though, in her landmark *Imperial Leather: Race, Gender, and Sexuality in the Colonial Contest,* the gendering of nineteenth-century imperialism, upon which economic globalization builds, was neither accidental nor superficial, but "fundamental to the securing and maintenance of the imperial enterprise" (McClintock 1995, 6–7).

2. Even proglobalization economist Joseph Stiglitz agrees that poverty has worsened. Stiglitz writes, "Despite repeated promises of poverty reduction made over the last decade of the twentieth century, the actual number of people living in poverty has actually increased by almost 100 million. This occurred at the same time that total world income increased by an average of 2.5 percent annually" (Stiglitz 2002, 5).

3. See Jacobs (2000) for a critique of this equation.

4. Against the argument that the goal of economic prosperity justifies the means, even the data from internal and external reviews of IMF policies are unfavorable (see Ismi 2004; Naiman and Watkins 1999). While SAPs have not been successful in creating sustainable economic growth, they are efficient in facilitating the transfer of wealth to the rich, possibly for generations to come.

5. Women in Black is a movement that has inspired groups of women in different parts of the world to stand in their own towns and cities for one hour per week, dressed in black, silently protesting the many forms of violence that are increasingly becoming intrinsic to everyday realities in different cultures and communities. It began with Palestinian and Israeli women, was inspired by the Mothers of the Plaza de Mayo in Buenos Aires, Argentina, and became a significant presence during the wars in the former Yugoslavia during the 1990s (Waller and Marcos 2005, 196–197). The Zapatista movement is an indigenous organization based in Chiapas, Mexico, that, since the implementation of NAFTA in January 1995, has been demanding a constitutional amendment that would recognize the rights and values of indigenous people within the national boundaries. Zapatista women are widely known and admired for their innovative participation as combatants, spokespeople, organizers, and policymakers in this movement. Over a dozen Courts of Women have been organized since 1992 by the Asian Women's Human Rights Council (AWHRC) in Bangalore, India, and by El Taller, an NGO based in Tunis. The AWHRC organized the World Court of Women on Violence Against Women in Huairou, China, as part of the NGO Forum of the Fourth United Nations Conference on Women in 1995. All the Courts are located in the global South. They hear and respond to testimony about crimes for which there currently exist no national or international legal remedies, exposing interconnections among forms of personal and public violence against women, especially those that have arisen in the context of the "new world order" (Waller and Marcos 2005, 192–196). Black Laundry is a joint organization of Israeli and Palestinian activists who are united in their opposition to Israel's occupation of Palestine, militarism, and other forms of social oppression. Originally founded by lesbians, it now includes a broad range of participants. Code Pink is a

female-led movement that opposes war and seeks to redirect military resources to meet unmet social needs. Formed in 2002 by U.S. women activists in the global justice movement, it claimed more than 250 local groups in the United States and worldwide in 2006. Mocking the U.S. government's code system to alert the public of terrorist threats, the organization has called "a code pink alert signifying extreme danger to all the values of nurturing, caring, and compassion that women and loving men have held." Dressed in pink, its participants combine protest tactics with humor and femininity.

    6. Initially organized by the Brazilian labor movement and the landless peasant movement, the WSF was intended as a forum for grassroots movements from all over the world. It is open to all those opposed to neoliberal globalization but excludes groups that openly advocate armed resistance (Patomaki and Teivainen 2004). The first meeting of the WSF, in 2001, reportedly drew 5,000 registered participants from 117 countries; the 2005 meeting drew 155,000 registered participants from 135 countries. Though a lack of resources prevents many, especially the most disadvantaged, from participating, the WSF and the rise of local, national, regional, and thematic social forums around the world have helped activists make connections across borders and movements, learn from each others' experiences, strategize, coordinate protests, and bring global attention to the hardships associated with militarism and neoliberal global capitalism (Byrd 2005; della Porta 2005; Patomaki and Teivainen 2004; Smith 2004c).

I

The Vicious Cycle of AIDS, Poverty, and Neoliberalism

Bernardo Useche and Amalia L. Cabezas

❂

World maps illustrating areas of high poverty largely overlap those of high HIV/ AIDS prevalence. It's no coincidence that both poverty and the HIV/AIDS pandemic have run rampant in these last two decades of neoliberalism, as the root causes of both can be found in the economic model.[1] The most recent UN figures show the true magnitude of the tragedy: Approximately 40 million people are currently living with the human immunodeficiency virus (HIV) or are suffering from illnesses associated with acquired immunodeficiency syndrome (AIDS). In 2003 alone, 5 million people joined the list of those who tested HIV-positive, and nearly 3 million others died from complications associated with AIDS.

Faced with a tragedy of epic proportions, the United Nations' World Health Organization (WHO) and UNAIDS launched a plan to provide antiretroviral medications to 3 million AIDS patients in the next two years—approximately half the patients currently estimated to need this kind of treatment. The WHO strategy incorporates plans recently proposed by the World Bank and the U.S. government. At first glance, this global strategy appears to be a humanitarian gesture as well as a decisive intervention by the international health organizations and the White House to control this devastating disease. However, to thoroughly understand the true dimension of the AIDS pandemic and the possible scope of the WHO/World Bank/Bush government plans, it is essential that we consider the socioeconomic world context in which the disease has been gestating over the last two decades.

This context continues to be defined by the priority given to the interests of multinational pharmaceutical companies above those of the patients who are supposed to benefit from their medicines. Neoliberal economic policies in recent decades have created conditions in which it has proven impossible to control or reduce the number of infections, despite the efforts of scientists, the investment of billions of dollars, and the work of innumerable organizations in prevention programs.

EPIDEMICS AND ECONOMICS

Social epidemiology, defined initially as "the study of the role of social factors in the etiology of an illness," grew out of Friedrich Engels' study of the living conditions of English workers in the nineteenth century. Today, this area of public health looks at how historical, political, and economic tendencies influence the dissemination of an illness among different populations and how social forces and factors affect individuals' bodies and generate pathologies.

In the case of HIV/AIDS, researchers point out that neoliberal policies such as the North American Free Trade Agreement (NAFTA), economic austerity programs, environmental degradation, and increases in social disparities in health are of particular concern (Krieger 2001, 2003; Lurie, Hintzen, and Lowe 1995). The study of the effects of health service organizations and coverage as well as drug production and marketing systems on a specific society's most vulnerable population is also important to epidemiology and social medicine.

Researchers agree that the AIDS pandemic is concentrated in the poorest countries and among the poorest sectors of wealthy countries. But very few studies analyze the close relationship between the causes of the affected nations' socioeconomic reality and the as yet uncontainable advance of the epidemic during the last two decades. With a few very valuable exceptions, most research simply describes the situation without clearly defining the fundamental responsibility of the economic globalization model imposed on nations in these times of AIDS.

British epidemiologist Thomas McKeown (1979) demonstrated that progress in controlling a population's illnesses cannot be attributed to vaccines, antibiotics, and improved medical treatments alone, given that socioeconomic conditions and their effects on nutrition constitute an essential health factor. Without denying the importance of advances in biomedicine, epidemiological studies currently confirm that health expectations are directly associated with quality of life, which in turn is determined by environmental health, nutritional status, water quality, housing, education, working conditions, and emotional and psychological factors that benefit human development throughout the life cycle.

Health in a given country depends not only on inhabitants' income but also on the degree of equality within the society. Health expectations are greater in countries with relatively less income and social inequality among the population. This explains the differences in life expectancy and other health indicators among industrialized countries. Sweden, Switzerland, and other developed countries, for example, have better health rates and higher life expectancy than the United States, a country that despite having the most powerful economy on earth also has abysmal social inequalities, with 46 million citizens currently unprotected because they cannot afford health insurance.

BLAMING THE VICTIM

The undeniable link between health problems and social inequalities presents an ideological dilemma. Are the sick to blame for their illnesses, or do they result from social inequality? The social history of AIDS has largely been one of apportioning blame to the victims. At the beginning, AIDS was even defined as the disease of the four *H*s: homosexuals, Haitians, hemophiliacs, and heroin addicts—to which one could more recently add "hookers." All these categories carried implicit derogatory social connotations.

Blaming the victims hides the fundamental role that socioeconomics plays in generating and propagating illnesses, instead placing the "cause" on the victims and saddling them with the responsibility for prevention and treatment. The state's obligation to care for its population's health is obscured. Yet the true causes are closely interlinked to social factors beyond the victims' control. Poverty often creates the alienating conditions that lead to a culture of intravenous drug use. And in the concrete case of Haiti, Paul Farmer (1992) established that, contrary to the widely disseminated stigma that blames Haitian immigrants for introducing the AIDS epidemic to the United States, it was the sexual tourism of U.S. citizens to Haiti—fueled by the poverty that left Haitians with no other means of livelihood—that started the AIDS epidemic on the island.

As a result of viewing AIDS transmission as essentially a problem concerning the individuals involved, prevention efforts during the first twenty years of the pandemic focused on trying to modify individual risk behaviors and attitudes. This unilateral approach, which ignored the socioeconomic factors behind AIDS, predictably failed in stopping the epidemic. But it succeeded in blocking in-depth debate on the responsibility of the neoliberal economic model implemented throughout the world during this period, and the social consequences provided a breeding ground for the epidemic's progress.

NEOLIBERAL FAMINES AND THE SPREAD OF AIDS

Neoliberalism is the set of economic theories and policies developed by contemporary monopoly capital to consolidate its global expansion and achieve control of the world markets it needs to survive. The distribution of the HIV/AIDS infection matches the current world socioeconomic order. In this era, health problems have been polarized along with distribution of wealth, as born out by Farmer's (1992, 1996, 2001) theory that the health of the world's poor is affected primarily by infections and violence, whereas the rich suffer from chronic illnesses associated with aging. The twenty-one nations with the highest AIDS prevalence in the world are found in sub-Saharan Africa, where dramatic poverty has resulted largely from neoliberal measures imposed by the structural adjustment programs of the International Monetary Fund (IMF) and the World Bank.

Famine and AIDS go hand in hand on the African continent. As elucidated by Steven Lewis, UN Special Envoy for HIV/AIDS in Africa, when the body has no food to consume, the virus consumes the body. When the body's immune system is weakened by lack of food, the illness progresses much more quickly and people die faster. The main cause of the recent famines, with their inevitable malnutrition and death, are not the droughts and other natural disasters that frequently afflict Africa but, rather, the elimination of agricultural subsidies, privatization of public services, and complete opening up of the economy—measures that are an integral part of the structural adjustment programs demanded of the African nations by international agencies since 1986.

Zimbabwe: A Tragic Case

Zimbabwe sadly illustrates the point. According to various studies, the average real economic growth in Zimbabwe during the 1980s was 4 percent per year (Ismi 2004; Naiman and Watkins 1999). During those years, food security developed somewhat and the manufacturing sector was strengthened, contributing to a diversification of exports. At the same time, health services increased and life expectancy rose from 56 to 64 years of age, and child mortality fell from 100 to 50 live births.

In 1991, Zimbabwe received a U.S.$484 million loan conditional on the structural adjustment of its economy. The demands of the adjustment included reducing public spending, deregulating the financial market, eliminating manufacturing protections, liberalizing the labor market, reducing the minimum salary, and eliminating labor stability, all to guarantee reduction of the fiscal deficit. Zimbabwe's economy entered into recession a year later, and between 1991 and 1996 per capita private consumption fell 37 percent, salaries fell 26 percent, unemployment rose, and food prices skyrocketed.

The IMF's recipe, which required the Zimbabwean government to slash spending by 46 percent—above all, by cutting health workers' salaries—had disastrous effects on public health. The vast majority of the population was left without access to health services and medicine. Malnutrition and the incidence of illnesses such as tuberculosis rose dramatically. Life expectancy is currently down to 38 years of age. Between 5 million and 8 million people—around 70 percent of the population—depend on international food aid to survive, and 2,500 people die of AIDS every week. Even so, the IMF has initiated procedures to expel Zimbabwe for not having consistently accepted all of the economic reforms it "recommended."

Social Catastrophes Feed the AIDS Epidemic

The situation is similar in the other African nations. Zambia, where AIDS left some 600,000 children orphaned in 2001, liberalized its economy, including agriculture, in 1991 under World Bank–imposed conditions. It is currently in its fourth consecutive year of food crisis, and more than 3 million inhabitants have nothing to eat. Malawi and Mozambique are also suffering from chronic food insecurity.

In 1991, the Malawi government had placed grain deposits in even the most remote parts of the country and was able to sell cheap food, saving a large part of the population from famine. The IMF "recommended" selling part of these food reserves to guarantee payments on the country's foreign debt, at the same time enriching private traders. Ten years later, food cost ten times more and, with the elimination of agricultural subsidies, the price of maize rose by 400 percent between October 2001 and March 2002. Peasants started eating unripe maize, resorting once again to the diet responsible for the disease pellagra, and there was generalized famine. In 2002, 7 million of Malawi's total population of 10 million suffered from pellagra. Between 2001 and 2005, an estimated 125,000 children under the age of 5 died of AIDS in Malawi.

Even in the United States, where neoliberal measures also increase social inequalities, new HIV infections are concentrated among African Americans and Latinos. In neoliberal Russia an estimated 3 million people are intravenous drug users—one of the most important AIDS risk factors—and half that number are infected with HIV. In Latin America and the Caribbean, the lack of social and economic equity provides a favorable context for the AIDS epidemic to reach disastrous proportions in the coming decades, according to the United Nations' adviser for Colombia, Ricardo García. The worst cases so far correspond to the region's most economically depressed countries or regions. In Colombia, it is predicted that 1.6 percent of the population will be infected with HIV by 2010.

The Current Anti-AIDS "Crusades" of the IMF, World Bank, WHO, and Bush Administration

Today, 95 percent of AIDS cases occur in the pauperized Third World. In response, the U.S. government and the World Bank, which are the main bodies responsible for the neoliberal reforms that have destroyed national economies and starved vast sectors of the world population, have launched a worldwide campaign to combat the pandemic. In January 2003, President Bush announced a U.S.$15 billion program to provide antiretroviral drugs to 2 million people infected with HIV in twelve African countries, Haiti, and Guyana. For its part, the World Bank began financing projects and developing an AIDS policy in 1986. In 2000, the World Bank and the IMF jointly decided to incorporate their anti-AIDS plans into their development assistance programs, arguing that AIDS is increasingly delaying economic growth by reducing productivity and the workforce. At that time, the Bank illustrated its point using the case of Zimbabwe, a country whose 1 percent drop in economic growth was attributed to the fact that 25 percent of its adults were HIV-positive.

In December 2003, the WHO urged that these projects be coordinated with the UN Global Fund to Fight AIDS, Tuberculosis, and Malaria, established in 2001, and launched an initiative known as "Treating three million by 2005." As its name suggests, this WHO campaign proposed providing antiretroviral medicines to 3 million AIDS patients in the next two years. It is worth analyzing the origin, philosophy, and political and economic content of these anti-AIDS crusades to assess whether they will indeed translate into relief for the people and regions in the grip of the epidemic.

Is AIDS the Cause of Poverty?

World Bank Director General Mamphela Ramphele categorically stated on June 1, 2003, that "our dream is a world free of poverty. But we now know that that mission will remain only a dream until the world is free of AIDS." Paraphrasing the title of Doctor Rambphele's speech that day—"HIV/AIDS: Turning Adversity into an Opportunity"—one could say that the adversity of the AIDS tragedy has represented an opportunity for the agencies of international capital to blame the epidemic for the poverty caused by their own policies. Worse still, they have attempted to postpone any hope of economic recovery in impoverished nations until AIDS has disappeared from the planet.

Such words are not isolated. World Bank documents have been insisting on this idea for some time now. One stated that although it is still not clear whether poverty increases the probability of HIV infection, there is strong evidence that HIV/AIDS causes and increases poverty. The U.S. government also defends the idea that AIDS is a cause of poverty. As U.S. Secretary of Health Tommy Thompson recently stated, "Poverty, unfortunately, is a common symptom of AIDS." Given these tendencies, it's no surprise that the introduction to the document in which the WHO set out its strategy establishes that "HIV/AIDS is destroying families and communities and sapping the economic vitality from countries. The loss of teachers through AIDS, for example, contributes to illiteracy and lack of skills. The decimation of civil servants weakens core government functions, threatening security. The burden of HIV/AIDS, including the death toll among health workers, is pushing health systems to the brink of collapse. In the most severely affected regions, the impact of disease and death is undermining the economic, social, and political gains of the past half-century and crushing hopes for a better future." Clearly, the champions of "free trade" seek to blame economic ruin, loss of political conquests, illiteracy, destruction of health systems, and social problems on a biological agent—the virus—rather than on their imposed structural adjustments, privatization programs, and other reforms.

A WORLD OF CLIENTS, NOT PATIENTS

Hundreds of millions of poor people in the world suffer and die from infectious diseases for which there are almost no cheap and effective medicines, despite the existence of the scientific and technological knowledge to develop them. Likewise, whereas North America, Europe, and Japan consume 82.4 percent of the medicines produced in the world, Asia and Africa consume just 10.6 percent of those available on the market, despite accounting for two-thirds of the world's population.

Patrice Trouiller (2001) and colleagues have documented the reason for this criminal inequity: In the neoliberal economy it is not the population's health needs but, rather, the financial interests of the large-scale pharmaceutical industry that influence both the research to develop new drugs and the production and marketing of available medicines. In a world with no patients, just clients, and in which the state is abandoning its public health responsibility, the drug transnationals simply do not invest in medicines to treat illnesses affecting poor people with no money to pay for them; instead, their production and sales strategies focus on the market sector from which they can obtain greater profit margins. Although there is currently no cure for AIDS, anti-HIV medicines can delay the disease's progress and reduce mortality by up to 80 percent. The "free trade" policies that have allowed the drug-producing corporations to make record profits off these medicines have also intensified the misery of people who need them. In the case of the AIDS pandemic, neoliberalism has been responsible for exacerbating to the extreme one of the basic contradictions of the capitalist economy: It created an immense potential market for the new antiretrovirals—42 million people with HIV/AIDS—among a population without the capacity to buy them.

Of the 6 million AIDS patients who currently require medicines to improve their health, only 8 percent have access to antiretrovirals—a figure that in countries such as South Africa is as low as 1 percent. It is estimated that the current cost of treating a person with HIV/AIDS in the United States is about $20,000 a year, including the value of antiretroviral therapy, lab tests, medical visits, and medicines to prevent or treat opportunistic illnesses.

WHO believes this situation can now be resolved: "The prices of antiretroviral drugs, which until recently put them far beyond the reach of low-income countries, have dropped sharply. A growing worldwide political mobilization, led by people living with HIV/AIDS, has educated communities and governments, affirming treatment as a human right. The World Bank has channeled increased funding into HIV/AIDS. New institutions such as the Global Fund to Fight AIDS, Tuberculosis, and Malaria and ambitious bilateral programs, including the United States Presidential Emergency Plan for AIDS Relief, have been launched, reflecting an exceptional level of political will and unprecedented resources for the HIV/AIDS battle. This unique combination of opportunity and political will must now be seized with urgent action."

In the neoliberal economy, it is not the population's health needs but, rather, the financial interests of the large-scale pharmaceutical industry that influence both the research to develop new drugs and the production and marketing of available medicines.

But despite all this "political will," a fundamental obstacle remains—the pharmaceutical patent monopolies. Since 1995, the Trade-Related Aspects of Intellectual Property Rights (TRIPS) Agreement established by the World Trade Organization (WTO) has backed up the patents of the transnational pharmaceutical corporations, guaranteeing them a market monopoly and exorbitant profit margins. As is the norm in neoliberal strategies aimed at eliminating competition by national products to benefit big capital, mainly from the United States, the WTO initially allowed its member-countries to produce generic medicines during the first years after intellectual property rights came into force. A few countries, including South Africa, India, and Brazil, used this regulation to start producing generic versions of medicines used to treat AIDS and demonstrated that companies run by the state or national capital could substantially reduce prices and generate profits while at the same time attending to the health needs created by the epidemic in their own countries.

The U.S. government and representatives of the pharmaceutical companies soon started pressuring for "respect" for the patent monopolies. In 2000, thirty-nine companies sued the South African government. During the 14th International AIDS Conference in Barcelona in 2002, there were mass protests rejecting transnational corporations that profit from these medicines as millions of poor people throughout the world die without access to them. On August 30, 2003, in a measure to forestall a repeat protest at the WTO meeting in Cancún, México, the Bush administration and the large-scale pharmaceutical industry agreed that poor countries could temporarily continue buying generic medicines, but added a clause stipulating that all member-countries would soon be able to buy only medicines patented by the transnational companies. In the words of South African Finance Minister Trevor Manuel, there is a risk that most of the budgeted $15 billion announced by Bush to fight AIDS will end up directly in the coffers of U.S. pharmaceutical companies.

THE BUSH PLAN: BIG BUSINESS FOR THE TRANSNATIONAL CORPORATIONS

At the same time it is promoting its own commercial interests in the WTO, the United States is continuing to push bilateral agreements and regional treaties such as the New Partnership for Africa's Development (NEPAD), the Central American Free Trade Agreement (CAFTA), and the Free Trade Area of the Americas (FTAA) for Latin America as a whole. This ongoing attempt to impose its neoliberal policies includes increased patent protection. President Bush's anti-AIDS initiative was launched independently of the existing Global Fund to Fight AIDS, Tuberculosis, and Malaria with the evident aim of directly controlling both the project's philosophy and the money that Washington will invest in the campaign.

Bush named Randall Tobias to run the program in Africa. Tobias had no experience either working in that region or managing AIDS-related programs, but he is a major Republican Party contributor and former general manager of Eli Lilly, a powerful pharmaceutical company. In Bush's plan, the U.S. government will subsidize capital investments in anti-AIDS medicines by buying up the medicines the companies can't sell to the impoverished nations of Africa and the Caribbean due to their high prices. Given Finance Minister Manuel's above-stated concern about misdirection of the $15 billion budgeted for fighting AIDS, it is no surprise that big laboratories such as Bristol-Myers Squibb, which controls the patent of the antiretroviral drug Stavudine (Zerit®), support the initiative and are competing to obtain their share of the $15 billion, or that the giant corporations that produce anti-HIV drugs are financing lobbying of Congress to support the White House anti-AIDS plan. Under this plan, 130 transnational companies have joined the Global Coalition Against AIDS.

The Bush administration's fight against AIDS is governed by its policy of globalizing the free trade agreements that benefit its own interests. This was made clear by former U.S. Trade Representative Robert Zoellick, when he stated that the administration is not thinking of discussing new economic development models for African countries; they are simply looking at how to apply development based on market laws in very poor regions. The aid dedicated to the fight against AIDS will be conditioned on these nations' acceptance of the economic measures prescribed by the World Bank and the IMF.

Washington's initiative to take antiretroviral medicines to countries in Africa and the Caribbean also contains a strong ideological component that promotes sexual abstinence as the basis for HIV prevention. In May 2003, the U.S. Congress introduced an amendment to the Bush initiative obliging it to invest one-third of the millions earmarked for prevention into projects whose only objective is chastity. This is yet another of the neoliberal paradoxes: The very promoters of economic policies that leave millions of people unemployed and force many women into prostitution are now the standard-bearers of a sexual morality that the vast majority of the population finds impossible to fulfill in real life. But this does not stop them from proclaiming it as the most effective way of combating the AIDS pandemic. Any attempt to illuminate the reasons behind the promotion of sexual abstinence as a means of prevention must first clarify certain questions about how sexual life affects HIV transmission.

With a few exceptions, scientists believe that the main form of HIV transmission is via sexual relations with an infected person. Since the virus was discovered, it has been insisted that the highest-risk behavior is anal intercourse between homosexuals or heterosexuals and that in vaginal intercourse the virus is most easily transmitted if the infected person is male. Researchers further believe that the number and concurrence of sexual partners and the frequency of sexual activity with new partners play an important part in increasing the probability of transmission.

In the United States, the AIDS epidemic was initially identified among male homosexual drug users. Not until 2003 was it estimated that heterosexual contact produced one-third of all new infections in the United States and Canada, and that intravenous drug users' sharing of infected needles caused one-quarter of them. In Africa, by contrast, the epidemic was associated from the start with heterosexual transmission. Lately, other possible means of transmission are being examined, such as use of needles and other medical instruments and equipment that do not comply with basic biosecurity norms due to the deteriorating health services and terrible conditions in which they are provided.

The problem with the abstinence approach to AIDS control is that it doesn't work. In sex education classes offered to young people in the United States, current programs promote abstinence, despite the lack of any definitive demonstration of their effectiveness. A systematic evaluation of this issue by Douglas Kirby (2000) concluded that abstinence-only programs do not postpone sexual intercourse.

HOW THE AIDS VIRUS INCUBATED IN INEQUITY

Neoliberalism expresses the interests of big capital concentrated in the giant monopolistic corporations. Based on the thinking of neoclassic economics, it proposes reduction of the state including eliminating or privatizing many public services, public-sector workers, and government housing, education, food, and health programs. In recent decades, the U.S. government and its allies have promoted globalization under neoliberal principles and "free trade" economic policies and imposed them on the nations of the world mainly through the international agencies under their control—the IMF and the World Bank—as a supposed panacea for all social problems.

World Bank and IMF structural adjustment programs have devastated Latin America, Africa, Asia, and the Caribbean over the last twenty years. Promoting privatization, fiscal austerity, deregulation, market liberation, and the cutting back of the state, these programs have increased and globalized poverty, migration, unemployment, and temporary work contracts, and produced extremely polarized income and living conditions across the world to the benefit of big capital.

AIDS was incubated and has been propagated in this system of social inequity, and efforts to prevent and combat it effectively will fail if they don't go after the conditions that are generating the pandemic. The anti-AIDS initiatives implemented by the Bush administration and the World Bank are set within the U.S. government's strategy of neoliberal globalization, a strategy that also guides the projects of the United Nations and the WHO. The central purpose behind all of these plans is to create funds for channeling money donated by the governments of developed countries and philanthropic organizations attached to the big corporations to be used mainly to purchase and distribute antiretroviral medicines and to fund AIDS prevention programs that promote sexual abstinence. These anti-AIDS programs also serve to reinforce the implementation of neoliberal policies in the countries to which the "aid" is offered.

Advanced medicines must be made available to the patients who really need them, the vast majority of whom are from poor countries. But the management of HIV is complex. As even those who defend antiretroviral therapy point out, the severe toxicity of these pharmaceutical agents must be seriously considered when prescribing their use, despite their notable effects so far.

It is important to note, again, that antiretroviral medicines are not a cure for AIDS and that agreement regarding their use is not unanimous. There are still many questions related to the utilization of this kind of therapy—questions that science has yet to resolve. The problems related to these pharmaceutical agents, just over twenty of which have so far been approved in the United States, include high toxicity, loss of effectiveness as the organism develops resistance after a certain amount of time, and the difficulty for patients to stick to the treatment adequately.

An alternative proposal to confront the AIDS pandemic with any probability of success should include the following basic points:

- Defend national employment and production to promote independent economic development, guaranteeing food security and adequate nutrition for the population. A population with severe malnutrition is easy prey for the illnesses that characterize AIDS.
- Stop and reverse privatizations, particularly those that have eliminated public services and health systems, so the state can fulfill its responsibility to provide services and treat those affected.
- Allow the production of generic medicines, eliminating patent monopolies conceded by the WTO to pharmaceutical transnationals under the guise of respecting intellectual property.
- Expand prevention and treatment of drug addiction as an integral part of AIDS prevention and treatment.
- Guarantee the necessary scientific debate on the causes, prevention, and treatment of AIDS.
- Do not limit research to the commercial interests of a handful of companies that invest more money into publicizing a few profitable products than into basic research to develop the medicines that are really needed.
- Finally, as an integral part of confronting the AIDS pandemic, resist the discrimination and stigmas attached to people and communities affected by the disease. Such stigmas fuel, reinforce, and reproduce existing inequalities related to class, race, gender, and sexuality.

Prevention programs must be based on scientific knowledge about the AIDS epidemic, not on prejudices about sexuality or people's behavior. It is inappropriate for the United States to establish the standards governing the whole world, as it seeks to do in its abstinence programs. Each country, culture, and society has a right to maintain its own standards, rules, norms, taboos, and lifestyles.

DEFEATING THE NEOLIBERAL MODEL TO DEFEAT AIDS

After twenty years during which the relationship among poverty, economic models, and AIDS has been virtually ignored, empirical studies are finally beginning to emerge that not only demonstrate that the incidence of AIDS increases with economic impoverishment but also assert that to reduce the syndrome's prevalence it is essential to expand and strengthen public health systems. Paul Farmer (2001) stated in his report to a U.S. Senate Commission that the fight against AIDS is the fight against poverty. And given that poverty in the contemporary world is of neoliberal origin, it will be impossible to defeat AIDS without defeating the neoliberal model.

NOTE

1. This article was originally published in Spanish (Useche and Cabezas 2004). For a list of full citations, see http://www.deslinde.org.co/Dsl35/dls35_desigualdad_social_sida.htm.

2

In Her Name

The Gender Order of Global Poverty Management

Ananya Roy

❀

Our minds must be as ready to move as capital is, to trace its paths and to imagine alternative destinations (Chandra Talpade Mohanty 2003, 251)

In the mid-1990s, the development project launched at Bretton Woods marked its fiftieth anniversary. That Cold War initiative, formalized in institutions such as the World Bank and the International Monetary Fund (IMF), had proceeded through various phases of development theories and practices. In the 1950s, modernization theories espoused large-scale industrialization and promised trickle-down growth. In the 1970s, there was experimentation with a different approach: development as the satisfaction of basic needs. In the 1980s, these concerns gave way to a free market ideology, a "neoliberalism" that revived the liberalism of Adam Smith and its myth of a perfectly functioning market. But at the point where development institutions were to celebrate their half-century mark, critics gathered in loud protest, insisting that fifty years were enough. Although international development has always been a deeply contested project, by the 1990s this contestation had crystallized in the form of transnational social movements, often simplistically described as the "antiglobalization" protests. The gathering in the streets and beating at the doors of development institutions had quite a bit to do with the neoliberal disaster of the 1980s. That recipe of market fundamentalism involved among other things wholesale privatization, the dismantling of the welfare state, structural adjustment conditionalities, and cheap labor export processing strategies. The antiglobalization social movements organized against the global regime of free trade and regional free trade agreements called for debt relief for heavily indebted countries and insisted on the accountability of development institutions for the impacts of their projects. In the World Social Forum, organized as an alternative to the powerful World Economic Forum, the movement participants argued that "another world is possible." Here then was not simply antiglobalization but an alternative image of globalization, the imagining of a different world order.

A few years after turning 50, the World Bank itself began to endorse parts of this alternative vision. Under the presidency of James Wolfensohn, the investment banker-turned-developmentalist, the Bank adopted a paradigm of "Sustainable Human Development" (Gore 2000). After years of a neoliberal Washington consensus, Wolfensohn called for a "post-Washington consensus," central to which was a poverty and civil society agenda (Bergeron 2003a). Although both the IMF and the newly formed WTO remained stubbornly focused on free market ideologies, the United Nations followed the lead of the World Bank. In 1999 its member-countries ratified the Millennium Development Goals, listing an ambitious set of goals, including a halving of world poverty by 2015. Suddenly and magically there was a kinder and gentler regime of international development, one concerned less with economic growth and more with the alleviation of poverty. It is possible to interpret this new moment as a radical paradigm shift or, alternatively, as a return to an earlier moment in the history of the World Bank—to the McNamara presidency of the 1970s and the attempt to combine redistribution with economic growth. It is also of course necessary to see Sustainable Human Development as an institutional fix for the troubles of brutal and bloody neoliberalism. Wolfensohn was acutely aware of the protests that were taking place each time the World Bank held a major meeting, and he often sought to present the Bank as being one step ahead of the protestors (Elyachar 2002). At the same time, his presidency was marked by a set of highly public autocritiques: the revelations and confessions of insiders like Joseph Stiglitz (2002).

Here, then, is a global order of poverty management. However, this is also a gender order. To a considerable extent, the new poverty agenda hinges on the "Third World woman." From health and population programs to environmental management initiatives, she has emerged as the key agent or, rather, in feminist scholar Cecile Jackson's (1998) phrase, an "instrument" of development. If, as Chandra Talpade Mohanty (1991) once argued, the Western eyes of development constructed the Third World woman primarily as the victim, now she is becoming an icon of indefatigable efficiency and altruism. She is, as Katharine Rankin (2001) notes, a "rational economic woman." I have termed this instrumentality the *feminization of policy*, arguing that it comprises three ingredients: development policy concerned with the fact of women's participation though not necessarily with the terms on which women participate; the coding of women's work as an extension of household and social reproduction responsibilities; and an unshakeable faith in the morality (read: economic success) of women-oriented policies (Roy 2002). I use the phrase *feminization of policy* quite deliberately, to complement the more common phrase *feminization of work,* which has been used to signal the gender order of global labor regimes (Standing 1999). Here too is a "Global Woman," a title that Ehrenreich and Hochschild (2002) bestow on maids, nannies, and sex workers—the laboring bodies through which the globalization of services is constituted. Whereas much of the feminist analysis of the flexible subject of transnational labor has been focused on the circuits of global production capital—the garment factories, the maquiladoras, or the high-end informational capitalism that requires the commodification of social reproduction—my work examines a different circuitry, that of development capital. This capital, which flows through development institutions such as the World Bank, the United Nations, and the U.S. Agency for International Development (USAID), is of course closely tied to production capital and finance capital. But it has its own distinctive logic, including a gendered logic, the logic of development "in her name." It creates a Global Woman that is a counterpart to the Global Woman of labor regimes.

In the circuitry of development capital, the interest in poor women is not wholly new. For several decades, there have been efforts to keep alive Women in Development (WID) initiatives. In the 1990s, various UN summits, such as the Cairo Conference on Population and the Beijing Conference on Women, created arenas for the agendas and activism of thousands of nongovernmental organizations (NGOs), advocacy groups, and activists affiliated with the field. Indeed, as Rankin (2001) argues, the current mainstream development interest in women would not have been possible without the decades of organizing and institution-building by the WID movement. But there is a very specific way in which the WID field has been refracted to create a focus on poor women. Poor women are conceptualized as the "final frontier" in the World Bank's project of including those hitherto excluded from the benefits of development (Bergeron 2003b). Their inclusion is made possible by what is perceived to be their inherent talents and abilities as entrepreneurs (Rankin 2001), an entrepreneurship that manifests itself primarily in the small-scale and informal sectors of the economy—what Elyachar (2002) calls "microinformality." Poor women would thus be empowered by access to markets and, as empowered women, would be seen as good and altruistic agents of development, investing the profits of microinformality in their families and communities. In other words, they would activate not only economic capital but also social capital. The new global order of poverty management is thus an instance of what Spivak (1999, 361) calls the "gendered postcolonial," a "complicitous relationship between UN-style universalist feminism and postcolonial capitalism."

In this chapter, I will take a somewhat unusual approach to the analysis of the gender/global order of poverty management. There has been considerable work evaluating the impacts of poverty alleviation policies on women. I will not attempt to address these ground-level dynamics of poverty, partly because some of my previous research has been concerned with such questions at the scale of the city (Roy 2003). Instead, I will focus on how an authoritative poverty agenda is established at the global scale of development aid and policy. Rather than studying specific sites in the global periphery, I locate my analysis at the core nodes from which the periphery is imagined, produced, and managed. I am inspired by the growing body of work on development and governmentality (Watts 2003), a discussion that applies Foucault's important insights into regimes of power and knowledge to the study of the apparatus of development (Brigg 2001; Escobar 1995; Ferguson 1994; Goldman 2001).[1] Although it is important to assess *what* development does to poor subjects, these studies seek to understand *how* development constructs its subjects, *how* some ideas come to be seen as best practices, and *how* structures of power are perpetuated through such systems of knowledge. Timothy Mitchell (2002) appropriately titles his important work in this genre *rule of experts*. In the following sections, I indicate how, in the context of a new global order of poverty management, there is a rule of experts centered in Washington D.C., how that rule draws upon ideas that originated in the global South, and how this tension has the potential to be transformed into a radical battle of ideas.

ORIGINS STORY

In 1976, Muhammad Yunus, a professor of economics, launched a simple scheme, the Grameen Bank, to provide tiny enterprise and housing loans to the landless poor of Bangladesh. Defying commercial banks that refused to lend to the poor, Yunus devised a system of peer collateral whereby lending groups would be collectively responsible for loan repayment. Since then, the Grameen Bank has emerged as the emblem of grassroots development. As of April 2005, it had 4.3 million poor borrowers, 95 percent of whom were women, and a loan recovery rate of about 98 percent (Grameen Bank 2007). As the legend of the Grameen Bank has spread, there have been efforts to borrow its methodologies. In an intriguing reversal of development practices, "First World" leaders such as Bill Clinton have advocated an adoption of this "Third World" model, transferring the Grameen Bank idea from the riverine delta of Bangladesh to the Good Faith Fund in the Mississippi delta of Arkansas. Today, the Grameen Bank model is being touted as a solution for everything from inner-city poverty in the United States to the reconstruction of Afghanistan (*New York Times,* November 12, 2002). And the United Nations declared 2005 the year of microcredit. As devised by the Grameen Bank, microcredit is undeniably the linchpin of the new global order of poverty management. The concept of microlending to establish microenterprises features prominently in the discourses of development institutions, although it should be noted that the proportions of development budgets actually allocated to microcredit, and indeed to poverty alleviation, remain small.

In his autobiographical account of the Grameen Bank, *Banker to the Poor,* Yunus (1999) locates the origins of alternative development in the disjuncture between the elegant economic theories of his classroom and the reality of poverty just outside the university. The solution for him was not top-down development but, rather, giving credit to the poor, whom he saw as entrepreneurs. Rural, poor women figure prominently in this account. In every written text, interview, and speech, Yunus tells the origins story as a story of the women in the village of Jobra just outside the university at which he taught economics in the late 1970s. He describes watching these women weave stubborn strands of bamboo to make stools and baskets, icons of hope in these dilapidated villages of poverty, small brown hands making beautiful, luminiscent objects. These objects, and these women, were bound in a system of exploitative moneylending, a system that Yunus set out to end. The liberation of rural, poor women came through the transformative power of money:

> The day finally comes when she asks for a first loan, usually about 25 dollars. How does she feel? Terrified. She cannot sleep at night.... When she finally receives the 25 dollars she is trembling. The money burns her fingers. Tears roll down her face. She has never seen so much money in her life.... All her life she has been told that she is no good, that she brings only misery to her family ... that she should have been killed at birth.... But today, for the first time in her life, an institution has trusted her with a great sum of money. She promises that she will never let down the institution or herself. She will struggle to make sure that every penny is paid back. (Yunus 1999, 64–65)

The success of the Grameen Bank lies in the intricate apparatus that it has created to ensure that borrowers repay, a system that has earned the bank considerable criticism (Goetz and Sengupta 1996; Rahman 1999). The relationship between "woman" and "borrower" is managed through the rigorous discipline of lending groups, weekly meetings, and complete subservience to bank staff. The images of women at these meetings—saluting, being ordered and orderly, chanting the Grameen Bank slogan, "Discipline, Unity, Courage"—are now well known. Grameen borrowers make a pledge to the "sixteen decisions"—a set of values, ranging from the refusal to give or take dowry to the use of pit latrines, that seeks to reform Bangladeshi rural society. In other words, the Grameen Bank borrower is a self-disciplined subject, one imbued with the techniques necessary for responsible self-government. In the functioning of the Grameen Bank, it is possible to see what Foucault (2000) conceptualizes as the triangle of sovereignty, discipline, and governmentality. In this case, however, power is perhaps better understood as a triple helix than as a triangle: an interlocking of the sovereignty of a powerful NGO like the Grameen Bank, the discipline of debt, and the governmentality of good (read: feminized) conduct and virtue. Thus, the story of the globalization of the Grameen Bank idea cannot be related in the simple narrative of the neoliberal corruption of a populist, alternative development. Rather, it has to be told as the reconstruction of an ensemble of ideas in which, from the very beginning, poverty alleviation valorized an entrepreneurial subjectivity (Brigg 2001); in which, from the very beginning, the empowerment of women was tied to debt and discipline.

FINANCIALIZATION/FEMINIZATION

The arrival of microcredit to Washington D.C. can be marked by the formation, in 1995, of an unusual development institution: the Consultative Group to Assist the Poorest (CGAP), housed in the World Bank.[2] On the one hand, the founding of CGAP indicates a formal commitment to the poverty agenda; on the other, it indicates the centralization of the rule of experts in Washington D.C. CGAP not only expresses World Bank interests but also establishes and manages the poverty agenda of most of the European donors.

Under the auspices of CGAP, microcredit itself has been transformed—first into microfinance and most recently into financial services. The renaming indicates the financialization of the poverty agenda, one in which the alleviation of poverty is inextricably linked to the powers of finance capital. As Elizabeth Littlefield, director of CGAP and former investment banker at JP Morgan, put it at the launch of the UN Year of Microcredit (2005), the "picturesque, magical methodology" of microcredit is over; this is now about making markets (UN webcast, November 18, 2004). The active construction of financial markets requires quite a bit of work, though. It means transforming nongovernmental organizations into what are now known as microfinance intermediaries (MFIs), refashioning NGO clients as finance consumers, and creating a minimalist framework of microfinance without the social development dimensions of the Grameen Bank model. Such forms of development also require a distinctive type of knowledge, one that entails the metrics of financial calculations, indicators of financial success, and the expertise of bankers. These financial markets also work in and through an expanded field of actors. Whereas microcredit was the domain of NGOs working with donor institutions and nation-states, microfinance operates through alliances among donor institutions, MFIs, national commercial banks, and international corporations such as Citigroup, Visa, and Hewlett Packard. In short, microcredit is like a microprocessor that runs the interlocked circuitries of development capital and finance capital. It is therefore appropriate that the logo of the UN Year of Microcredit (2005) is not the placemaking motif of the Grameen Bank (a rural house that indicates Grameen's commitment to asset-building for the rural poor) but, instead, a global logo that can be interpreted as an expanding capitalist nucleus: capital plus plus.[3]

It is important to note that this financialization happens in the active vocabulary of democratization. Thus Nancy Barry, head of Women's World Banking, makes the case for financial services by arguing that "poor people are a lot like us, they want services, they want low costs" (UN webcast, November 18, 2004).

In various interviews that I conducted between 2003 and 2005 in Washington D.C. and New York, a range of experts from CGAP policymakers to USAID staff to Citigroup executives made the case for financial democracy. In addition to recognizing the importance of creating access to financial services for the poor, they noted that the rituals, solidarity groups, and social programs associated with the Grameen Bank are disciplinary, that they patronize the poor, and that they impose high transaction costs, especially on women. It is thus that the free subject of neoliberalism is produced. It is thus that the democratized subject of populism is produced. In this sense, the new global order of poverty management is the order of neoliberal populism, whereby the concept of work has been replaced by entrepreneurialism. As analyzed by Elyachar (2002), the poor are seen as agents in the "people's economy," freed from the oppressions of the Fordist economy, free to pursue enterprises, free to rely upon themselves. In the writings of microfinance experts such as Elisabeth Rhyne, current senior vice-president of Accion International and former director of USAID's microenterprise division, such freedom takes on even deeper normative dimensions. Invoking Amartya Sen's framework of development as freedom, Rhyne (2001, 183) argues that access to finance is the ultimate means of engendering freedom, economic capacity, and social choice. On the one hand, the financialized model of microcredit can be seen as a mutation of the original Grameen Bank model, a commercialization of a grassroots idea. But on the other hand—and this is its seduction—it can be interpreted as an effort toward democratization.

However, the financialization of development has its risks. The Grameen Bank relies on particular techniques of discipline, many of which involve the immediacy of a village-based solidarity group. What replaces this face-to-face system in the minimalist and increasingly global model of microfinance? As it turns out, financialized development is supported by an elaborate set of management technologies that create transparent financial markets by creating transparent subjects. This includes risk-scoring techniques that form the basis of character-based lending—that is, the ability to predict repayment rates based on consumer characteristics (Christen and Drake 2003, 17). Risk-management techniques are applied not only to individual consumers but also to NGOs, as in rating systems like PlaNet Finance. The scoring of risk regulates the flows of development and finance capital. For example, the Microfinance Information eXchange (MIX)—a project funded by CGAP, Citigroup, Deutsche Bank, and the Open Society Institute—is an online virtual marketplace that connects various financial funds to NGOs around the world.[4] In other words, the new global order of poverty management is a calculable space, one with its own logic prisons, to use a phrase from William Mitchell (2003, 201): zones of exclusion where "bad" subjects or "misrecognized" subjects can be quarantined. In the original model, risk was managed through a gendered argument about women as "good" subjects of development, making their loan repayments and using money wisely in terms of both the microenterprises and the well-being of their households. Quite simply, the "bad" subjects were men, a subject-category whose risks did not need to be calculated or managed. In a financial world of expanding capital, where male borrowers are inevitably the new frontier of microlending, the gender logic of risk management begins to fall apart. The emphasis now is on creating "transparent" subjects.

In the world of financialized development, it is of course not enough to manage risky subjects. It is also necessary to construct new consumers. Thus, one of the endeavors of the UN Year of Microcredit (2005) has been the Serial Drama and Mass Media Project, which uses Latin American telenovellas to reach the poor and convince them of the benefits of microfinance and financial services. In addition, significant energy is being put into the use of information technology to bridge geographic distance and construct markets in remote regions. Here is the utopia of the new global order of poverty management: A very poor woman in a remote rural region of Guatemala or Ghana goes to a point-of-sales kiosk—this could be a phone booth or a local store selling global commodities such as Coca-Cola. She swipes a smart card issued by VISA on a handheld device produced by Hewlett Packard. The smart card encapsulates her credit history, authorizing or deauthorizing a loan, and doing away with the need for loan officers or NGO workers. Her identity is verified by biometric identification: a fingerprint or an optical scan. The swipe of the VISA smart card links her instantaneously to the credit bureau of the country. The transaction is also registered at the MIX market across the street from the World Bank in Washington D.C., updating the information on the MFI with whom she is doing business. What is produced is not just a market but a transparent space consisting of transparent subjects. This is also a geography that connects the hyperglobalized rural realm with the technofinancial power of development institutions in Washington D.C., lined up on Pennsylvania Avenue.

In this new paradigm of market construction and risk management, it is suddenly possible to expand microcredit well beyond poor women. Though men were earlier considered "bad" subjects, now all can be reached and managed by the new technologies of transparency. Indeed, the financialization of development can be partly interpreted as the demise of the feminization of policy. The gendered argument about women as "good" subjects of development seems to be slipping away. With the growing emphasis on the financial sustainability of NGOs and on the minimalism of service provision, concerns about household patterns of spending and consumption, the role of mothers, and the realm of social reproduction seem to be fading. And yet, the Third World woman persists, as a haunting. The language of financialized development is about information technology and portfolios and equity funds, but the Third World woman is there in the accompanying images. Thus, "Capital Plus"—the 2004 report of the Development Finance Forum—has her on its cover, and the CGAP Annual Report 2003 puts an image of her in every section. On the first page of the report, she is the indigenous peasant woman, photographed with both "primitive" abacus and "modern" calculator, a figure that transcends primitivism to adopt modern, calculative technologies. She is a fetish, a magical object. This is "in her name." Prodem, a Bolivian NGO that is now a financial fund, points out in its explanations of its smart card that its consumers, mainly poor rural women, had no personal identity cards and could not read or write. But now they have identities: "We have succeeded in bankizing people in rural areas" (BBC News Online, June 13, 2001). This is the production of what Stone (1991, 193), following Judith Butler (1990), calls the "technosocial subject," a culturally intelligible body that can be read, managed, and "made free." The technosocial subject is a transparent subject. Though not necessarily a feminine subject, it is nevertheless a feminized subject, one whose poverty is represented primarily in the form of the poor woman. Indeed, it can be argued that such transparency takes place through a logic of "saming/othering" whereby the poor are increasingly feminized, an "Other" that can be integrated into the order of sameness that is promised by capitalism.[5]

RADICAL POSSIBILITIES

The new order of poverty management is indeed a global order, what Weber (2002) calls "global development architecture." Weber interprets this order as the facilitation of financial-sector liberalization and of the global trade in financial services, an order that is closely in keeping with the mandates of the WTO. The success of the order, according to this argument, lies in its ability to manage crisis, as in the use of microfinance and other poverty alleviation policies as a political safety net. I have argued that this global order is also a gender order. As Spivak (1999, 386) notes, "in this phase of capitalism/feminism, it is capitalist women saving the female subaltern." Spivak figures the "financializing female diasporic" (1999, 377) as the body that mediates the interlocked circuitries of development and finance capital, of corporate capital and the capitalism of benevolence.

However, let me suggest a few other geopolitical and ontological possibilities. My argument about the gender/global order of poverty management deploys a Foucauldian analysis of the apparatus of development. That framework of power has been carefully explicated in the work of many scholars, and it provides important insights into the production of governable subjects and governable spaces. And yet, it is an analysis that is curiously disembodied. Too often, its subjects lack racialized, gendered, or classed bodies. They are also instrumentalized subjects, usually understood at the point at which the "conduct of conduct" has been fully implemented. But the global order of poverty management has distinctive gendered and racialized contours. This project of rule, precisely because of such embodiments, is messy and incomplete.

The global order of poverty management is in fact various regional orders of poverty management, an example of what Ong (1999) calls "zones of graduated sovereignty." As a new Washington consensus is constructed around the mandate of financialized development, so in Bangladesh some of the world's largest NGOs such as the Grameen Bank and BRAC construct a counterhegemonic alternative.[6] The "Bangladesh consensus," as I have come to call it, insists on an ethicopolitical commitment to ending poverty. Proud of their financial sustainability, these institutions nevertheless eschew financial indicators of poverty management, focusing instead on long-term and intergenerational indicators of health, education, and asset ownership. Whereas Washington D.C. narrows the field of action to the "economically active" poor, arguing that the poorest cannot be reached by financialized development, Bangladeshi institutions, including the World Bank in Bangladesh, experiment with new policies targeting the absolutely destitute. In the last few years, the Bangladesh consensus has directly challenged the Washington consensus. The Grameen Bank not only has set up its own Washington D.C. institution, the Grameen Foundation, but also has allied with powerful lobbying groups such as Results to push through legislation in the U.S. Congress that calls for an end to the "mission drift" of USAID and a return to a poverty focus and poverty targeting.[7]

The Bangladesh consensus makes itself felt at the heart of power in another way. Experts from the global South, usually from South Asia, work in the neoliberal institutions of CGAP and Deutsche Bank and the World Bank. In my interviews with them, I have been struck by the fact that some of them recognize the value of the Grameen perspective, frame the marginalization of Bangladeshi ideas as racist, and put forward a diagnosis of poverty that is often unabashedly Marxist—in the language of bonded labor, modes of production, and exploitation. These scattered embodiments, brown bodies, puncture the rule of experts. In the most disciplined form, such subjects implement the Washington consensus and its neoliberal mandates. But in more disruptive forms, they are racialized, catalyzing a battle of ideas within the regime of truth and creating a space for the periphery at the core of power. It is not easy to make sense of such complexly contradictory subjects; they are simultaneously complicit and subversive. But these contradictory subjects in the apparatus of development indicate what Mitchell (2003, 20) calls the "messy actualities of rule."

In this sense, the Bangladesh consensus is counterhegemonic, creating a critical discourse on the ethicopolitics of poverty and racializing the embodied expert subject. At the same time, as a counterhegemony it maintains elements of the master narrative. The Bangladesh consensus has its own technology fetish, manifested in the gendered trope of the "telephone lady," the Grameen borrower who runs a cellphone business. And not unlike the Washington consensus, the Bangladesh consensus is ultimately concerned with debt, data, and discipline. In a 1998 speech (and this is the one statement by him that still persists in CGAP documents), Yunus says: "Credit without strict discipline is nothing but charity. Charity does not help overcome poverty. Poverty is a disease that has a paralyzing effect on mind and body. A meaningful poverty alleviation program is one that helps people gather will and strength to make cracks in the wall around them" (CGAP 2001, 4). It is not surprising, then, that Yunus is credited with having advised Clinton, who has long been a fan of the Grameen Bank, on how to reform the U.S. welfare system.

The gender/global order of poverty management requires not just the disciplined subject but also, in fact, a chain of discipline, one that extends from the relationship between indebted country and donor country to the disciplining of NGO staff all the way down to borrowers. More important, it requires a self-discipline by which critical thought is suspended, and what is in actuality a command is entered into as if it were a contract (Moore 2001), what is a high-interest loan is received as if it were aid, and what is a lending institution is respected as if it were a donor. Here, once again, is Spivak (1994, 51): "Donor. Who deserves that appellation? Who gives or can give? The gift is a limit that permits and annuls all recognizable human giving? But here, far from that limit, the name of giving is scientifically appropriated for coercive living, solicited by comprador capital and a compromised state, used as staging props for a nation seeking alms.... This monstrosity—a bonded donation—mortgages the future of the country." The gender/global order of poverty management is ultimately a system of debt as development.

However, this seemingly coherent system has its inherent contradictions. As a concluding note, let me point to one emergent feature of the global landscape of development. Increasingly, Washington D.C. has to contend not only with the subjectivity of poverty but also with the subjectivity of terror. Microfinance is being deployed toward national security goals, hailed by Madeline Albright (*San Francisco Chronicle,* May 27, 2004) as a micropolicy with macrobenefits, and applied by USAID to act, as one policy administrator said in an interview, as "a safety valve in moderate Muslim countries." Inevitably, this is a circuitry intensely located in and through the Middle East. It is here that a post-9/11 Washington D.C. seeks to take on its most difficult subject: the Muslim. Alongside the icon of the disciplined and responsible Third World woman other embodied subjects have now emerged. There is of course the veiled Muslim woman, to be liberated by imperial war. Just war, in her name. But there is also the stubborn, young, angry Muslim man who must be wooed, disciplined, and tamed. On Pennsylvania Avenue, at USAID, a few steps from the White House, policymakers now brainstorm about how to use microfinance to stop suicide bombings, how to translate the technology of discipline perfected on married, rural, poor women to one that will work on the men of the Arab street. It is an idea befitting a development apparatus centered in Washington D.C., now governed by Paul Wolfowitz and his imperial Project for the New American Century.

In Morocco, Jordan, and, to some extent, Egypt, the Washington consensus has been successful in constructing microfinance markets and governable subjects. But there are sites in the Middle East—Lebanon, the Palestinian territories, Iraq—that confound. Here, organizations like Hezbollah act as de facto states, sovereign powers with their own technologies of religious discipline and welfare governmentality. And here, just as Washington D.C. constructs transparent subjects through technofinancial dataspace and panopticon software, it also constructs transparent subjects through the vision machine of the heat-seeking missile. Here, then, are the limits of order, the racialized margins at which Empire reveals itself.

NOTES

1. Foucault's concept of "governmentality" sheds light on the "conduct of conduct"—that is, on *how* different forms of power govern, manage, and control. Foucault is concerned not only with power as domination but also with the internalization of power as in forms of self-discipline.

2. CGAP recently changed its name to the Consultative Group to Assist the Poor, an indication of its argument that while financial services are important for the poor, the "poorest of the poor" cannot necessarily be served by financialized development.

3. Capital plus, plus refers to an ever-expanding system of capitalism.

4. The MIX market uses cutting-edge technologies to do its work, including the ironically titled "Panopticon," an information visualization tool for financial markets. The term *panopticon* refers to a prison designed by the nineteenth-century liberal theorist Jeremy Bentham. It was a design that perfected techniques of surveillance. For Foucault, the panopticon is the ultimate marker of modern institutional power and its capacity for discipline and surveillance.

5. I am grateful to the reviewers and editors of this volume for their perceptive comments on this issue.

6. Formerly known as the "Bangladesh Rural Action Committee" (BRAC), the organization has since become emphatic about no longer using the term "BRAC" as an acronym however.

7. HR 192, passed in 2003, amends the Microenterprise for Self-Reliance Act of 2000 and mandates that 50 percent of USAID microenterprise money has to be targeted toward the very poor, defined either as those living on or less than $1 a day or those living in the bottom 50 percent below the national poverty line. It also requires USAID to develop and certify poverty measurement methods.

3

Under the Western Eyes of Fashion

Marie Claire's Construction of Global Feminism

Jennifer Lynn Stoever

❁

A smiling blonde woman with soft, feathered hair and lips of shell-pink places her hand gingerly on a globe, ready to impart her cosmopolitan wisdom to the flock of small African children eagerly gathered at her feet. A white heterosexual couple, swathed in flowing magenta and crème caftans, embrace passionately on a wooden Indonesian boat, while the dark, sun-wrinkled indigenous crew labors and looks on. A red-haired woman, whose feet are trussed in delicate black stiletto sandals and whose long locks have been meticulously ironed into submission, leans languorously on a rickshaw, waiting for a lift. No, these are not images from turn-of-the-century travel journals produced by the British Empire, nor are they Club Med advertisements from the 1980s. Although certainly reminiscent of such imperialist imagery, these particular representations are culled from the glossy pages of recent issues of *Marie Claire* (2002–2005), an American fashion magazine whose spine proudly proclaims its intention to speak to and "For Women of the World."

What is remarkable about such Orientalist discourse is not its appearance in the pages of a mainstream periodical devoted to fashion, beauty, and female

40

body maintenance but, rather, its seeming incongruity with *Marie Claire*'s self-proclaimed devotion to a global, multicultural vision and a "feminist" outlook. Since the North American version of the international brand first rolled off the presses in November 1994, *Marie Claire* has devoted at least one article per month to female-oriented international human rights issues from baby rape in South Africa (February 2003) to female torture in Iraq (June 2003/April 2004). However, by appropriating the idiom of progressive activism and linking it with exoticized and fantasy-oriented fashion spreads that depict First World women globetrotting in the Third, *Marie Claire* actually reinscribes the oppressive colonialist mentality under the guise of modern feminism. The liberated Western woman is then defined in opposition to representations of constrained, commodified, and impoverished Third World victims. In "Under Western Eyes: Feminist Scholarship and Colonial Discourses" (1991), Chandra Talpade Mohanty describes a similar dichotomizing in Western academic feminist work. It is crucial to extend her theorizations to an exploration of the realm of pop culture consumerism and to ask why these images continue to proliferate, circulate, and turn a profit in a mass cultural context, all hiding under the banner of feminist activism.[1]

This chapter explores the linkages constructed among *Marie Claire*, feminism, and notions of global activism. Although the magazine's slogan attempts to conflate the savvy American cosmopolite with global "multicultural" female communities in a sweeping gesture of equality, the content of *Marie Claire* continues to (re)construct and reify the First/Third World dichotomy and to increase the hierarchical distance between First World "self" and the Third World "other" for its American consumers. Inserting itself directly between these two groups, the magazine works to mediate the processes of globalization for its middle- to upper-class female readership, shaping and limiting the possible relationships between impoverished producers and wealthy consumers under late capitalism. Although *Marie Claire* constructs itself as a transparent window upon "You and Your World" outside the United States, it actually presents limiting representations of Third World women that oscillate between the poles of hypervisibility on the opening "social issues" pages and invisibility in the rest of the magazine, which predominantly features white European and American fashion models in fantasy photo shoots. On the rare occasions that Third World women are allowed to cross the boundaries and appear within the latter portion of *Marie Claire*, they are represented as foils that enhance the aura of affluence, mobility, and individuality that surrounds the images of the First World woman (see Figure 3.1).

In our increasingly visual culture, representations of social groups take on a heightened significance. Visual language is a key to communication, power, and political recognition. How we attempt to represent "the reality" of ourselves and "Others" is the primary means by which we think, feel, and comprehend it (Dyer 1997, 44). For precisely this reason, the dichotomous representations that appear on the pages of *Marie Claire* have far-reaching economic and social consequences beyond the realm of U.S. popular culture, as they reproduce the increasing inequities of the global economic system by simultaneously downplaying the need for

Figure 3.1. "Far and Away Pieces" from the December 2002 issue of *Marie Claire*. Photo © Matt Albiani.

continued feminist resistance within the United States and obscuring the objective connections that bind these disparate groups of women. The First World woman's privileged ability to view the women of the Third World solely as poverty-stricken "projects" for Western feminism—and then to pleasurably consume this image in its commodified forms—is facilitated here rather than resisted. Itself a high-performing luxury commodity for the multinational Hearst Corporation, *Marie Claire* does not in fact contest globalization by executing overhyped forays into social activism; rather, the magazine represents a significant and symptomatic part of the Western imperial machine.[2]

"TALK TO US!": ABOUT *MARIE CLAIRE* AND ITS READERSHIP

The *Marie Claire* franchise is an especially interesting case study, owing to its convoluted history and the fact that the U.S. edition is a relative latecomer to its international markets. It was founded by Jean Prouvost as a weekly publication in France in 1937 and, according to its official website (2005), was "the first magazine aimed at women encouraging them to consider their own autonomy, charm, and personal development." The German invasion in 1942 halted production, which was not resumed until 1954, when *Marie Claire* returned as a monthly. International expansion began in 1982—during the era of Reaganomics and the rise of our current global economic configuration—and today there are twenty-five affiliated international editions, each either licensed or in joint venture. In addition to the United States, various incarnations of *Marie Claire* are read in Britain, Australia, Japan, South Africa, Russia, Poland, China, Germany, Italy, Spain, Turkey, Hong Kong, Taiwan, and elsewhere. The magazine, therefore, is global both in scope and in economic configuration. The U.S. version began publishing a little over ten years ago, when Glenda Bailey, editor-in-chief of *Marie Claire* U.K. (slogan: "The Only Glossy with Brains"), spearheaded the effort to bring its blend of fashion and international coverage to the American marketplace.

Today, 60 percent of its American readership lies in the prime marketing niche between the ages of 18 and 34, with a median age of 30.3.[3] The average household income (HHI) of a *Marie Claire* reader is $71,819, a figure slightly higher than that for readers of *Cosmopolitan, Glamour, Vogue, Allure,* and *Elle,* and substantially higher than both the median HHI of the United States, which was recorded at $41,994 in the 2000 census, and the median yearly earnings of employed women in the United States, a dramatically lower $27,194 (which is still a full $10,000 below the average male income of $37,057). In addition, more than 72 percent of *Marie Claire*'s readers are employed outside the home—a figure that is consistent with the 2000 census, which places 70.1 percent of females between the ages of 25 and 54 in the labor force. However, the type of labor they engage in is far from average: 33 percent are college graduates (a figure much higher than the 22 percent of females with a bachelor's degree nationwide), and 30 percent have professional/managerial positions (a figure very close to the national number of 33 percent, which includes men).

Combining such high levels of salary, employment, and education with the fact that "half of our readers are single or married with no children," *Marie Claire* assures advertisers that its readers are affluent, middle- to upper-class women with "a lot of disposable income just waiting to be spent!" As the "primary subjects and objects of consumerism" within Western capitalism, *Marie Claire*'s readership chiefly represents the middle class women, who, Maria Mies argues, are "constantly mobilized to follow all the fashion and fads" in order to perform important (yet often undervalued) "consumption work" that keeps the gears of the capitalist system grinding away at a rapid pace and profits flowing toward the First World (1998, 207). *Marie Claire* furthers this project by using targeted editorial content to hail these women as a readership and then sell their time and attention to the highest advertising bidder. Feminist efforts to obtain freedom, autonomy, and equality within exploitative structures of power and economics are rerouted back into the marketplace; in the pages of *Marie Claire,* purchasing power defines female independence, and individuality comes not through struggle but, rather, through the economic ability to buy desired self-defining goods at the expense of the women who produce them. By normalizing this level of income and affluence as the default model of successful American citizenship and womanhood, the manipulation of this group as (en)forced consumers goes unrecognized, as does their potential for revolutionary change.

"What You Can Do": *Marie Claire* and Activism

Interestingly, *Marie Claire* takes on female-oriented activist projects but deftly avoids the overtly politicized language of what editor-in-chief Lesley Jane Seymour calls "old-style feminism" (*New York Times*, April 24, 2002). Although such a stance used to be considered ambivalent at best and antifeminist at worst, *Marie Claire* has been rewarded with consistently rising sales and a reputation as a leading outlet for feminist discourse among readers and feminists alike.[4] In 2004 alone, organizations like Amnesty International, Save the Children.org, Casa Amiga, the Breast Cancer Research Foundation, and the Step Up Women's Network (among others) found representation in 4 percent of the magazine's editorial content devoted to "world issues." (This number was actually down from a reported 7 percent in 2002.) Opposing the conventional wisdom of the industry, which maintains that controversy doesn't jibe with lipstick and clothing shills, the ad pages accompanying these "feminist" stories now fetch top-dollar, as the majority of readers polled place this section consistently among the most read. Products advertised here vary widely, from the luxury items whose depictions typically litter *Marie Claire*'s pages—Roberto Cavalli dresses, Gottlieb and Sons diamonds—to companies attempting their own socially conscious marketing, such as Ford, whose ads urge readers to buy its 2004 Breast Cancer Awareness Pink Scarf.

With relatively few exceptions, *Marie Claire* constructs a vision of "global activism" that is dependent upon capitalism and harmonious with current U.S. configurations of the international free market. The editors tell the readers "What You Can Do" to encourage them to "shop the magazine for fashion, beauty *and* meaning" (emphasis mine), placing the sensational experiences of Third World women up for sale and positing activism as a commodity transaction. Through the recurrent "charity offer" feature following *Marie Claire*'s investigative reports, readers are encouraged to "Help Victims of Domestic Violence" (November 2004, 142) by buying a specially priced freshwater pearl necklace ("only $39.95" with seven dollars per sale benefiting the National Domestic Violence Hotline) or to "Stop Violence Against Women Around the World" (April 2004, 26) by purchasing a "handmade beaded necklace" ($16.95 with "approximately 30 percent" going to "help Afghan women create independent lives"). As with many of the self-improvement articles *Marie Claire* runs, the means to salvation fall directly onto the shoulders of the private consumer, who then bears the burden of responsibility for the larger—and largely invisible—power structures at fault. This epitomizes the growing links among money, consumption, and democratic participation that Mohanty (2003) dubs "capitalist citizenship," in which collective civic responsibility and notions of freedom and justice are "privatized and crafted into commodities to be exchanged via the market" (184). More than simply charity, the bracelets and baubles purchased by *Marie Claire* readers are visible markers of the privileges of monetary citizenship and the perceived power of the private Western consumer in the global free market—a scenario that exemplifies the dangerous slippage between public activism and personal indulgence and positions the market as the solution to the problems of the Third World rather than as their cause. Marie Claire's charity offers allow First World women to consider themselves social activists simply by performing their everyday consumer activities. Activism is a fashion accessory to be purchased through the same economic channels that continue to devastate and impoverish the Third World. The daily living circumstances of both groups of women remain largely unchanged.

Part of what makes this form of activism so easy—and self-reflection so difficult—is the fact that *Marie Claire* facilitates the disconnect between the daily lives of First and Third World women by rarely implicating the economic, cultural, and military imperialism of the United States in any of its activist-oriented articles. In a glamorous glossy world where a pair of Calvin Klein shoes is described as a "steal" for $100, it is little surprise that poverty does not often find its way into *Marie Claire.* Aside from occasional puff pieces, such as one that made light of women who are "more strapped than ever" by paying a writer to live off of free samples for a week, poverty is rarely mentioned except in the context of the Third World (Marages 2005). And in these cases, poverty is generally described as a default expectation for life outside of the United States, existing without cause and exacerbating the problems that *Marie Claire* readers are being rallied to solve. Poverty causes the suicides of dowryless brides in India (May 2004) and forces women and children (and pets!) to move in with their incarcerated husbands in Manila (October 2004). Although *Marie Claire* readers are encouraged to send money, write letters, or purchase special T-shirts to help solve these problems, the poverty itself is never addressed directly; it is used only to set the stage for the more treatable issues. The struggle of poor women around the world is rarely connected to larger global economic processes and never linked to the politics and consumptive practices of the First World. Dashing off a check to the Revolutionary Association of the Women of Afghanistan or purchasing a basket handwoven by Pakastani housewives becomes a form of consumer tithing that allows American middle-class women to ease their guilt by "acting globally" without having to do the more messy and painful work of "thinking locally" about their role in the world economy.

For example, the article "Hanging by a Thread" in the February 2004 issue describes the struggles of Third World women to continue traditional crafting practices in the face of poverty and economic inequity. *Marie Claire* informs readers that "70 percent of the world's poor are women, living on less than $1 a day." However, the piece attributes this fact to anything but the outsourcing of U.S. corporations, NAFTA, the International Monetary Fund, or the World Bank: Rather, *Marie Claire* points the finger at such factors as the traditions of purdah in India or the increased number of Guatemalan men using looms to compete with female handweavers (Gianturco et al. 2004). So, what type of activism does *Marie Claire* suggest to help support these women? Readers are supplied with e-mail addresses allowing them to buy Turkish dolls and Panamanian molas that will enable Third World women to survive another day in the damaged and damaging world economy. Similar to what Suzanne Bergeron (2003a) argues is the goal of the World Bank's intensified focus on women in "Challenging the World Bank's Narrative of Inclusion," further integration into the world market is once again posited as a solution to women's subordination and poverty, not as its cause.

Thus, *Marie Claire*'s readers, constructed as the default models of feminist empowerment by favorable comparison, can easily perform mail-order missionary work that channels funds to help modernize and liberate their Third World sisters who—outside of the larger political and economic context—are depicted as drowning under the weight of their oppressive and archaic cultural traditions. Mohanty describes this process in "Under Western Eyes" as the utilitarian construction of the stereotypical "Third World difference" by the West, which serves to heighten "the (implicit) self-representation of Western women as educated, modern, as having control over their bodies and sexualities and the freedom to make their own decisions"(1991, 22). Such a construction not only continues to support the world systems that dominate and oppress the Third World but also creates a binary geopolitics that falsely posits the Third World as somehow separable and completely distinct from the First. The activist model in *Marie Claire* potentially blinds Western women to their own struggles in those same structures: both the racist, classist, sexist, and heteronormative power dynamics in their own societies and the economic inequities faced by the members of "the third world in the first" (Friere 1985) who labor in sweatshops, fields, kitchens, and construction sites across the United States and other industrialized nations.

Tellingly, aside from the campaigns against domestic violence waged yearly since 2001, the overwhelming majority of activist-oriented articles in *Marie Claire* have focused on the oppression of women on foreign soil, depicting American women as free, enlightened, "postfeminist" subjects and positioning global women as the victimized objects they must save, largely from their own cultures, traditions, and familial relationships. Paralleling what Mohanty describes in "Under Western Eyes," Third World women are systematically described as universal victims of male violence and desperately under male control. Feminist activism is represented as an absolute necessity in places like Afghanistan, where heavily veiled "women have endured decades of oppression and abuse" (Stop Violence, 2004, 26) in search of "Western-style freedoms and rights"(Sevcik 2004, 60); but the mission seems largely accomplished in the United States, where readers are free to worry about "the 7 sneaky reasons [they're] still stressed" (Cover 2004). Such dichotomous representations in the Western media, Mohanty argues, have flattened the veil, a complex and often contradictory religious and cultural symbol, into the universal marker of sexual segregation and control of women (2003, 33). The ubiquitous photos of veiled women in *Marie Claire,* coupled with the magazine's neoliberal discourse of rights and freedoms, is frighteningly similar to the "feminism" recently used by U.S. President George W. Bush to justify the wars in Afghanistan and Iraq to the American people. It was not coincidental that "as U.S. leaders were selling the nation on war against the Taliban, there were a lot of pictures of shrouded Afghan women in the news" (Flanders 2001, 36). The suffering of these women under the oppressive patriarchy of their fundamentalist government is made hypervisible in order to justify U.S. imperialist practices. The women themselves are silenced.[5]

"EXOTIC ACCESSORIES": VISUAL REPRESENTATIONS OF THE THIRD WORLD IN *MARIE CLAIRE*

Whereas the wealthy, educated American reader constructed by *Marie Claire* is free to slide in and out of identification with the Other and is frequently encouraged to discover and explore her multiple roles, selves, and identities, the Third World woman appears almost exclusively in the discretely bounded space of the "activist" articles. Whereas she is overrepresented in the human rights section, she is largely invisible in the last half of each magazine, the fantasy photo spreads. In the issues reviewed for this chapter, there are few exceptions to this rule. On the rare occasions when Third World women are present in the dreamlike travel shoots, they are predominately utilized as exotic extras in the colorful "foreign" backdrop, there as the markers of cultural difference from the white models at center stage. They are usually desexualized and placed in service roles that depict them as socially inferior to the white models and highlight their economic dependence on Western tourism. For example, in the July 2004 issue a plump, elderly Celia Cruz look-alike in her "native costume" hawks flowers to a blonde visitor to Cuba (Brosch 2004, 107). And in a March 2005 spread titled "Passage to India," a gathering of Indian women and children dressed alike in multicolored saris shower a white woman with rose petals as they ready her for marriage to her white male travel partner. Never for a moment does the primary focus leave the bride and groom. In fact, the editor blurs the faces of the Indian women to bring the white couple into sharper focus, portraying the former as insignificant, barely visible carbon copies whose primary purpose is to serve as local color for (white) tourist vacations.

This power is further highlighted by *Marie Claire*'s use of Sudanese Alek Wek as the sole representative "Third World" model in their fashion pages. Although Wek has been plucked from the backdrop and granted the focus of center stage, she still suffers from a limited range of representation designed to emphasize her "Third World difference" from *Marie Claire*'s stable of (white) Western models. Wek, who fled her small village in war-torn Sudan at the age of 14, is in many ways a *Marie Claire* "success story." She was granted asylum in Great Britain and discovered as a model while shopping at a London market in 1995. From there it was a quick rise to the runways of companies such as Fendi, Ralph Lauren, John Paul Gaultier, and Halston. The fashion world covets the tall, close-cropped, dark-skinned Wek for her perceived difference from the usual runway faces. In *Marie Claire*, she is exclusively featured as an exotic(ized) model in their haute couture fashion issues, representing "Global Glamour" in a March 2004 photo spread by Joshua Jordan that has her posing in "pieces from every corner of the globe," such as Indian prints, African beads and bangles, and British-inflected safari gear. The brief copy calls attention to her as a "global woman," Sudanese-born but now

Brooklyn-based. Wek appears again cloaked in a similar guise in a March 2005 shoot (also by Jordan) titled "Wild at Heart," this time clearly marked as African. "Wild at Heart" simultaneously references a highly sexualized and violent romance film of the same title by David Lynch, on the one hand, and alludes to Africa as the "Heart of Darkness," a venerable and racist Western stereotype, on the other. Wek is repetitively posed in photos that pair "safari jackets" with a succession of animal prints: tiger, leopard, snakeskin, even zebra. Strikingly, the two shoots are almost identical. The camera's obsessive emphasis on Wek's skin tone fulfills the magazine's desire for exotic difference; behind her there is no island paradise or foreign backdrop, just a stark grey photography studio that calls all attention to her physical form. Unlike *Marie Claire*'s typical white models, Wek is not allowed to travel in her photo sequences, nor does she get to experiment with a self other than the limited "global" one that the magazine has already constructed for her. According to the racialized terms of representation established by *Marie Claire*, Wek does not need to be posed next to an Indian temple to be "exotic" or "Third World." Although there is a sense of identity play and slippage with the white models—they are portrayed as South American doñas one second and as suburban housewives the next—Wek always retains her essentialized Africanness. Such dramatic differences in representation emphasize the privilege of the white models (and readers) "to be various, to literally incorporate into themselves features of other people" (Dyer 1997, 49), whereas Wek's identity remains fixed in place and marked with the cultural baggage that the West layers upon the Third World. No matter how far Wek travels beyond the human-interest pages of *Marie Claire*—both literally and figuratively—she remains bound by the same restrictive representation as the other Third World women in the magazine.

For the most part, international locations are a fixture in the glossy high-fashion photo layouts that comprise the final third of each magazine, but they serve primarily as an "exotic" stage for Western (and predominately white) models who are draped in Western interpretations of "multicultural" commodities. These fantasy travel sequences also work to efface Third World women, as the white models are literally placed in their stead and readers are invited to imagine themselves as glamorous "women of the world" through the magic of photographic pastiche (see Figure 3.2). However, these whitened-up representations tellingly lack the violence and the poverty so prominently foregrounded in the opening pages of the magazine. A quintessential example of this practice is found in a March 2003 spread that depicts the "romance" of spring fashion through a fantasy (white) couple's getaway in neocolonial Africa.[6]

The key image of this shoot features the fashionable blonde superwoman graciously taking time away from her safari to enlighten the young African children who gather excitedly at her feet (see Figure 3.3). Her liberated status is clearly articulated by the "Good Morning, *Ms.* Anderson" breezily scrawled across the chalkboard (emphasis mine). She stands poised with the world literally at her manicured fingertips, pointing out Europe on the globe to the attentive children whose hands reach for the sky; undoubtedly they are filled with questions about

Figure 3.2. "Haute Hippie: What to Show off Your Personal Flair? Try Mixing and Matching Ethnic" from the April 2002 issue of *Marie Claire*. Photo © Ben Watts.

Figure 3.3. "Good Morning Ms. Anderson" from the "Wild at Heart" photo spread in the March 2003 issue of *Marie Claire*. Photo © Matt Albiani.

the center of all important knowledge in the "modern" world. Although the model is dressed simply, especially compared to the ruffled bodice featured on the preceding page, the price tag on her schoolmarm chic comes to a grand total of $1,206—more than enough to alleviate the obvious poverty of the classroom, which is evidenced by its outdated and yellowed educational materials. Images like these are a fixture of *Marie Claire* and work to construct and consolidate the authority of the First World woman, especially as she is depicted as rising to economic equality in the United States.

Interestingly, *Marie Claire* has a tendency to place the white models in these photo shoots with Third World men, although these representations are always hierarchical and largely devoid of sexual tension (see Figure 3.4). The male "models" are never shown meeting the woman's stare or gazing at her body, and they are clearly restricted to positions of servility; Third World men may drive the beautiful white woman around on a safari, steer her exotic ship, lead her desert camel caravan, help her onto her elephant, carry her flowers, and pliantly submit to her souvenir photo, but never can they embody sexually compatible equals. Essentialized in their native dress, they simultaneously create an air of exotic adventure and pose a "primitive" contrast to the chic, stylish, and ultramodern *Marie Claire* cosmopolite. Often the female models are significantly taller than the men who trail after them. Such layouts are reminiscent of early anthropological photos and colonial travel shots from the British Empire, intended to illustrate racial superiority and extreme cultural difference.

Figure 3.4. Ms. Anderson goes on safari in the "Wild at Heart" photo spread in the March 2003 issue of *Marie Claire*. Photo © Matt Albiani.

In addition to the visual disparities of representation, the copy of the activist-oriented pieces also works to reify the divisions between First and Third World women through graphic language and horrendous depictions of violence. Thick and provocative depictions of brutality are a staple of all international women's rights pieces in *Marie Claire*. In the span of a single year, the magazine's readers are treated to dozens of horrific accounts of baby rape, infant genocide, genital surgeries, rape, executions, forced prostitution, starvation, torture, domestic abuse, murder, and sex slavery, all taking place in Third World locations. Especially because it is embedded in a site traditionally designated for fantasy, travel, and desire, the visceral style of writing functions to normalize and reinforce a dichotomous relationship between the First and Third Worlds. Even as the graphic portrayals of physical and verbal abuses have some potential to disturb the fantasy world of commodity on display in *Marie Claire*'s glossy pages, such possibilities are always being absorbed and redirected.

For example, in the November 2002 special issue on world peace, it is astonishing how well the horrors of war mesh almost seamlessly with the rest of the magazine, connecting activism and fashion in subtle and dangerous ways. After using a lengthy piece entitled "War Is Hell on Women and Children" to create a provocative and problematic tear in its fabric, *Marie Claire*'s editors work to repair it, assuaging and diffusing energies through commodity and imperialist fantasy sequences. India, for instance, appears as a particularly violent place in the war reportage, especially near the border of Pakistan, where "more than 30,000 have died [and] thousands more, including children, have been tortured (Goodwin 2002, 200). In the latter part of the issue a fashion layout dubbed "Haute Culture" recovers India as a boundless resource of cultural stimulation for Western fashionistas. As designer Matthew Williamson remarks: "I love India; I go there to get inspired by the people, the colors, and the diversity." Underneath Williamson's quote, a languid white model lounges on a pewter settee, posing as a modern-day ranee in a rhinestone-encrusted Indochic ensemble. Upon further examination, several articles of clothing worn by the people featured in the "War Is Hell" exposé are appropriated as haute couture throughout the rest of the issue. Although declaring its steadfast allegiance to feminist activism, *Marie Claire* effectively conceals the connections between neoliberal neocolonialism (see Chatterjee in this volume) and poverty and repression in the Third World, substituting the pleasures of commodity feminism for analysis.

"POLITICS AND PRADA": *MARIE CLAIRE* AND THE SCHIZOPHRENIC SUBJECT

By rights, this form of imperialism should be old news, especially for feminist theory. Critics such as bell hooks (1984), Gloria Anzaldúa and Cherríe Moraga (1983), and Mohanty (1991) have described the process by which U.S. mainstream reform feminists have co-opted and diluted the political potency of Third World feminism and feminisms of color, masquerading as radicals without examining their own privilege and the "atomistic and competitive individualism of liberalism" (hooks 1984, 7). Activism in *Marie Claire* is in fact inextricable from a relentless focus on the individual and her entitlement to freedom and choice. Whether deciding which of twelve black skirts would best express the reader's new fall look or considering the pros and cons of a body-altering operation, the publication addresses its female readers as atomistic individuals striving to construct and refine their personal identities through commodity purchase. The ultimate feminist project of this magazine is not truly the Third World but rather the reader, who must strive to exhibit the particular brand of complexity and multiplicity deemed desirable by the editors and advertisers, a type of capitalist schizophrenia ripe for niche marketing. As *Manifesta* co-author Jennifer Baumgardner remarks, "a willing reader can handle reading about women in Afghanistan and still have the quick tips for firming up before the bathing suit season" (*New York Times,* April 24, 2002). Readers are not invited to criticize the magazine for requiring that they sculpt their bodies (this has been normalized); instead, they must interrogate themselves for not being "willing" or able to absorb both messages.

Attempting to strike that desirable, contradictory, and impossible balance between what *Manifesta* describes as "politics and Prada'"(Baumgardner and Richards 2000, 124), *Marie Claire's* shiny pages construct the consumer world of American femininity not as a guilty paradise where women step down into objectification but, rather, as a pleasurable world of individual freedom and choice, where women step up to both global power and consciousness. However, the bridge *Marie Claire* draws between activism and consumerism is most often the representation of the physical body of the Third World woman, whose material pleasures, pains, and cultural artifacts provide a stark counterpoint to the lavish lifestyle of the upper-middle-class (white) Western female reader hailed within its pages.

So this is the point in the chapter where I am supposed to make the necessary concession that, yes, *Marie Claire* tackles some very important issues and certainly any activism is better than none. Although I do not begrudge even one of the millions of dollars the magazine has brought to deserving organizations, I am troubled by the fact that *Marie Claire* allows its readers to feel a common emotional attachment to the representations of Third World women that does not extend beyond what Mies (1998) calls "paternalistic rhetoric and charity" (232) into the more threatening questioning of the nature of the economic, political, and racial divides between them.

In addition, both classes of women are being used by capitalism—although from decidedly different positionalities—but naturalizing the role of American women on top of the capitalist system decidedly obscures this concrete link. *Marie Claire's* very existence demands that it aestheticize and naturalize the hierarchical relations between the First and Third Worlds and obscures the fact that our current standard of living derives in part from the control of international markets and the incredibly cheap labor demanded and exploited by multinational companies both at home and abroad. Even as it trumpets itself as a new force in the fight for worldwide female equality, the magazine continues to fetishize racial and cultural difference and to reinscribe and expand liberal middle-class consumer desires. A careful look at texts such as *Marie Claire* reveals the critical limitations of neoliberal and neofeminist discourse, especially the lack of a coherent theoretical critique of capitalist structures that could provide a solid backbone for organized and liberatory feminist activism. Essentially *Marie Claire* encourages women to experience and revel in their pleasures, but never to interrogate them. It encourages women to consider themselves feminists and activists without noticing how closely their fantasies resemble colonial exploitation.

NOTES

1. Following Chandra Talpade Mohanty's important criticism in "Under Western Eyes," I realize the limitations and the racism inherent in the term *Third World Woman;* however, I continue to use it self-consciously throughout this chapter to underscore the homogenizing colonial structures referenced, replicated, and systematized by *Marie Claire.*

2. I thank the participants of the U.K. and Ireland Women's Studies Association Annual Conference held in Dublin, Ireland, on July 10, 2004, for their insightful commentary on these issues, especially Marguerite Waller, Priscilla Peña Ovalle, Cara Cardinale Fidler, and reina alejandra prado. Peña Ovalle was a special inspiration, giving tireless attention to many drafts. My adviser Carla Kaplan, my mentor Sarah Banet-Weiser, and my colleague Bridget Hoida Mulholland also gave thoughtful and incisive feedback on various incarnations of the chapter.

3. Unless otherwise cited, all quotes and figures in this section were obtained from *Marie Claire*'s corporate website through Hearst Magazines, the media conglomerate that publishes it. The sources of the marketing analysis are cited in detail there, with the majority of the figures supplied by MRI or ABC. Notably, this information is not linked to the magazine's public homepage, www.magazines.ivillage.com/marieclaire.

4. Since 1995, *Marie Claire*'s circulation has grown steadily, a rare feat in an industry that has reported flagging sales overall in the same period. In 2001, *Marie Claire* gained 3 percent while its primary competitors, *Glamour, Jane,* and *Vogue,* lost 11 percent, 19 percent, and 11 percent respectively. In 2002, its readership numbered 947,662, more than double its debut figures. And in 2004, it maintained a steady 946,971 with a surprisingly heavy number of newsstand sales (57 percent), more so than any other fashion magazine besides *In Style.* (For additional information, see http://www.marieclairemk.com /r4/home.cgi.)

5. In the rare instances when women's rights issues are addressed in a U.S. context, the treatment differs in both degree and kind, usually appearing in sidebars rather than in full-length articles or embedded in larger, more graphic depictions of abuse in other countries. Even these are fairly new practices, having been added when Lesley Jane Seymour assumed the editor-in-chief role in 2001.

6. As both Cynthia Enloe (1989) and Caren Kaplan (1999) note, the number of such images of "imperialist nostalgia" has increased in recent years. As Kaplan argues, "many of the primary tropes of European colonization can be found in each ad that glorifies 'travel': nostalgic placement of a white, female subject in the highly generalized site of the 'colony,' displacing indigenous residents and erasing political conflict" (140). I contend that *Marie Claire*'s imagery functions in a similar manner.

II

Impacts of Neoliberal Policy and Ideology: Case Studies

4

Tea's Fortunes and Famines

Global Capital, Women Workers, and Survival in Indian Plantation Country

Piya Chatterjee

❋

Unilever's mission is to add vitality to life. We meet the everyday need for nutrition, hygiene and personal care with brands that help people feel good, look good, and get more out of life. (Unilever 2004a)

Chandramoni [of Ramjhora Tea Estate] says that her two sons have died. She herself and her only surviving daughter suffered from the same illness—cough, fever and diarrhoea.... Her sons became very thin and emaciated before they died. As there was no food in the house, she often gave them water to fill their stomachs. She said, "My sons were very good and quiet. They never cried or fussed even when they were hungry." (West Bengal Advisor 2004, 13)

In early November 2003, a group of women workers at New Dooars Tea Estate in the Dooars plantation belt of North Bengal, India, tell me about fellow workers dying of hunger in the neighboring plantation, Kathalguri. They describe conditions of horrifying deprivation: of children with distended bellies; women, eyes hollow with a madness that only continuous hunger can bring; men lurching around begging for some rice before collapsing to die. They also tell me of their attempts at providing relief from their own meager stock of staple cereals—sending a few sacks of rice collected from households in their plantation where, mercifully, there is still paid work.

By looking at those who live there, anyone who has visited the labor hutments of these tea hinterlands of northeastern India will know that malnutrition, hunger, and disease are a daily part of life. It was so a century ago. It was so ten years ago when I lived in plantation country[1]—and now it has reached a certain "crisis" threshold whereby the mainstream Indian media and the state have registered these famine-like conditions. Hunger and starvation are daily realities for those who have lost work in the plantations, abandoned by managers and their owner-bosses.

As it was a century ago, the story of those who die in the shadow of capital is inextricably connected to the story of the commodity's circulation: in the spaces and places where capital can sell its brands of vitality and good health.

Yet, bodies become transparent without sustenance. Capital works with impunity. A grotesque dance between death and profit, famine and fortune, is performed on center stage. Here in this historical landscape of labor, which has built some of the greatest fortunes of the British Empire, another brutal chapter in the narratives of global capital is being written. The economic crisis of the Indian tea industry, one of the largest foreign exchange earners for the Indian exchequer, begins first in these moments of annihilation: where the very bodies that make capital possible disappear into the shadows of language itself.

How does one come to a feminist analysis of "globalization" and of capital when faced with the immediacy of such horror? How does one measure the violence of such a system, its genocidal effects?

In this chapter, I examine the work of capital within the current period of global expansion as one way to illuminate the strategic actions taken by transnational corporations and states that have imperiled the lives of tea workers. Indeed, tea's importance in the history of global trade cannot be underestimated. For five centuries, this commodity charted the fortunes of the first, and most powerful, imperial conglomerate in the world: the English East India Company (EIC). The thirst for Chinese tea led to a trade that, in the eighteenth century, constituted one-third of the EIC's profits.

Taxes were raised, famously, leading to one of the most important tea parties in the world in Boston, signaling the beginning of the end of British rule in North America. English demand for the commodity led to the opium-tea trade in a brilliant and ruthless attempt by the British to curtail the Chinese control of the tea supply market. The sale of Indian opium into southern China led to such mass-scale addiction that the Chinese imperial state decided to act against the British-controlled opium market. It was a challenge that resulted in two opium Wars (in 1839 and 1856) and a defeat of the Chinese imperial state. The resulting annexation of Hong Kong, and unequal treaties that allowed for greater expansion of European-controlled trade in East Asia, signaled the end of Chinese dynastic rule.

The desire for one commodity—and the fortunes enabled by its trade—remained an intriguing and important leitmotif in these multiple narratives of global and regional imperial expansion, encounter, and conquest.

In the 1850s, as another strategy to counter the Chinese hold on a trade that had led to a "silver sink" for British merchants, colonial administrators began to settle plantations in what they deemed "wastelands," across northeastern and southern India, as well as in Ceylon (now Sri Lanka). Because of the local villagers' refusal to work in the new plantation regime, workers for the northeastern plantations were brought in from tribal and lower-caste communities from the Chotanagpur Plateau and the Nepal Himalayas. An elaborate ethnoracial hierarchy of labor emerged. By the end of the nineteenth century, women from these communities started to outnumber men in the most arduous aspect of tea production, the actual plucking of tea leaves.

Out of these feminized and racialized labor practices emerged a fetishism of labor practice—nimble fingers for nimble plucking—that imbues the marketing and consumption of the commodity itself. The cost of these fetishisms is a bodied one, both in the field and in the material wage value given to deeply gendered, and sexualized, work.[2] It is, then, no surprise that women, who are primary wage earners in the postcolonial plantation, bear the brunt of the latest crisis in the most immediate and brutal ways.

"FROM GARDEN TO TEA POT": CENTRALIZING CAPITAL, COMMANDING THE SUPPLY CHAIN

Capital Struggles

India produces 30 percent of the world's supply of tea, making it one of the largest producers of black tea in the world. This export market, in turn, makes tea one of the largest foreign exchange earners for the Indian exchequer. Not surprisingly, the Indian state has historically protected the business of tea. In the postcolonial context, plantation production has been corralled within three tiers of capital ownership: (1) companies whose stocks are based in the global North, originally known as Sterling Companies; (2) large Indian-based companies, with ownership that might be divided between local and foreign capital ownership; and (3) small Indian family-based companies with indigenous trader-capitalist ownership, known as "*bania* capital."

The current crisis within the domestic and export Indian tea market, which leads to the abandonment of tea plantations, began in 1999 with a sharp decline in tea leaf prices at the auctions where the branding and pricing for the retail markets is determined. By 2002, the standard explanation for this price collapse was a problem of oversupply attributed to an expansion of plantations in the northeast, a decrease in the demand for low-quality tea, the breakdown of the Soviet Union (a steady source of market demand), and the domination of the "high-quality" tea market by estate-owning multinational corporations such as Indian-based Tata Tea and Dutch-based Unilever (Asian Foodworker 2003).

It was because of this plunge in auction prices, Rai (2002) notes, that small tea producers, mostly belonging to the third tier of capital, have been unable to survive. Known as *bania* capitalists, many of these owners (*maliks*) have short-term investment goals and have inherited small older estates where rates of return have not been high relative to the large multiple plantation-owning companies, which function very well within economies of scale (*New York Times,* January 20, 2002).[3]

Some of these *bania* capitalists have also played the volatility of the market for their own short-term, high-profit returns. For example, Dhaulajhura T.E. was selling its tea at 30 rials (Rs.) per kilo, well below the average price at the auctions during the crisis. However, outside of this official market price, the same tea was sold at Rs.60 per kilo, garnering a total return of Rs.90 per kilo for the company. "Black market" operations of this sort allow owners to claim huge losses in the books, though they actually profit hugely from such sales. Some have used a narrative of "official losses" to close down the plantation.[4] It is worth noting that the demise of plantations, along with the "backstage" work of *bania* capitalists, signals an important battle between unequal "factions of capital"[5] in what we shall see is a Darwinian struggle waged within the terms set by international capital as it strengthens its base in the global North.

The Behemoth Behind the Scenes

If *bania* capitalists can, on occasion, manipulate local auction prices to their benefit, it is perhaps easier to understand another explanation about the price decline. Although not denying other causal factors, close observers of the auction process point to a central contradiction in the market collapse: "[The] retail price of domestic tea was never threatened and continued on its steady climb upwards through the crisis at more than double the auction prices" (Nandy 2005, 1). "Branded tea," in other words, did very well, and "incidentally [*sic*] all major tea brand owners are owners of tea gardens: Hindustan Lever [the Indian subsidiary of Unilever] and Tata Tea not only control the leading brands, they also have substantial holdings in the tea plantations" (Mandal 2002).

Unilever appears, and disappears, in these narratives of tea capital and price collapse. It is the "white elephant" in the tea parlor—an extraordinarily powerful MNC that keeps a very low profile despite its tremendous transnational reach.

The result of an early-twentieth-century merger between English and Dutch companies, Unilever is one of the largest personal care and food conglomerates in the world. It controls 62 percent of the Australian tea market, 30 percent of the British market, 49 percent of the U.S. market, and 95 percent of packet tea sales in India. It owns Lipton, the world's leading brand of tea, and it is a major player in the global nonalcohol beverage market. In 1984, Unilever paid $618 million for Brooke Bond, thereby corralling a 35 percent stake in the global black tea trade

(Unilever 2004b). Equally significant, Unilever has been aggressively acquiring shares in companies with plantation holdings in India, beginning with Rossell and Jokai (Unilever 1999). By December 2001, Unilever had bought 95.88 percent of Rosell, despite never having received final approval from the Government of India (GOI) (Nandy 2005, 4).

What connections are there between Unilever's acquisition strategies and auction prices? In the middle of the 1980s, the GOI decided to set a minimum export price for Indian tea in an attempt to control the price manipulations of heavyweights such as Hindustan Lever. Unilever immediately retaliated by withdrawing from the Indian auctions and the market collapsed. The GOI almost immediately conceded and slashed the minimum price supports. In the late 1990s, the GOI began to back down on its own foreign direct investment (FDI) rules as the five-year market crisis progressed. Unilever, as noted earlier, precipitated this latest crisis as these FDI debates were raging. In short, in the now familiar script of neoliberal capitalist expansion, the nation-state is further constrained by the power of a megalith multinational corporation.

Controlling the Supply Chain

Unilever can exercise this level of power because of its command over several important links in the supply chain. Its domination in the global retail trade is enabled, for example, by its ownership of Carrit Moran, the second-largest tea brokerage house in India. When the price collapse occurred, Unilever could easily have jump-started a recovery process, but it did not (Nandy 2005, 2). In 2003, when the Indian state attempted to reform the auction procedures in the northeast, small buyers and brokers (representing *bania* capital) went on strike. After ten days, brokers from Unilever and Tata Tea reentered the floor and opened up trading. Both of these companies demonstrated to the state, and to local *bania* capitalists, their preeminence in the pricing arena—and their capacity to overrule the Indian state's own attempts to regulate pricing mechanisms.

What seems clear from these onstage developments (keeping in mind the offstage machinations of the state and other capital actors) is that a process by which international capital "recolonizes" internal postcolonial and national capital formations has been set in motion. The fact that this is happening with tea—a stalwart, high-profit commodity for British imperial trade—is not insignificant. Further, it is a process by which the "centralization of capital," in the global North, is made possible. Unilever flexes its muscle against the Indian state because, as its acquisition strategy suggests, it wants to penetrate further down the supply chain: that is, to control not only the brokerage houses of the auction but also the source and site of the commodity itself—plantation production.

Despite its own powerful law, the Foreign Exchange Regulation Act (FERA), passed in 1973 (Dhar 1988; Nandy 2005, 4), the Indian government now allows "foreign direct investment" in tea. No longer must ownership be at least 26 percent Indian; 100 percent foreign ownership is now allowed. Veteran trade unionist

Vaskar Nandy has noted that Unilever's pressure on the Indian state regarding direct foreign investment occurred at around the same time that the Indian tea auctions collapsed. Surely such timing is not pure coincidence.

In this phase of global capital expansion, Unilever continues to follow a highly successful policy of conducting mergers and alliances—jettisoning low-profit brands, controlling the supply chain, and deftly using its corporate subsidiaries to do this work. In short, a company charts higher profitability by (1) controlling the source of raw materials and (2) centralizing capital through various mergers, acquisitions, and alliances.[6] For example, in 2003, Unilever (with sales totaling 48 billion euros) joined with Pepsico (with sales totaling 27 billion euros) to expand the marketing and distribution of Lipton in the 23 billion euro Ready-to-Drink (RTD) market. Lipton, as noted earlier, is one of Unilever's largest food brands, with sales well in excess of 2.8 billion euros (Unilever 2003). Pepsico, at 27 billion euros, is one of the largest food and beverage companies in the world. Having disposed of its "low-profit" brands, Unilever is now focusing on expanding Lipton's reach through alliances with leaders in the RTD market (Food and Drink Europe 2003).

Cartesian Conquests

In a brilliantly telling statement, Peter Cescau, a top executive at Unilever, rationalized the merger: "We have a strong presence in the developing and emerging markets, yet there is plenty of '*white space*' to move into. These markets are the next in our placement rollout, and we see Pepsi as the best partner to help us achieve this. This new venture makes a truly significant step in the expansion of the brand, bringing it within the reach of millions of new consumers" (emphasis mine) (Food and Drink Europe 2003). Through this somewhat enigmatic metaphor, a certain kind of ideological constitution takes place of a space that is "white": clear, Cartesian, flat, empty of human subjectivity—open to a "new" phase of consumer-capitalist entry.

This is a constitution both metaphoric and material: Multimillion-dollar mergers enable such a "space" to be imaginatively constituted. It is a space that will soon be peopled by consuming subjects, whose value is marked by their desire, willingness, and ability to buy and consume tea (and other goods). Yet such a discourse of "space" spins on the brilliant elision of other subjects—those whose bodies and labor are the pivot upon which global markets of consumption are made possible. Absent, but ever present, then, in the metaphor of "white space" is the other story of capital—peopled by dark and often female bodies, whose invisibility in such matters is the price paid for the consuming desires of profit and fortune.[7]

KILLING LABOR AND RENAMING DEATH

"Does he mean that deaths were not starvation-related, or does he wish to rename death?"[8]

The struggles between factions of international, national, and local capital work themselves out, finally, on laboring bodies. When the Indian state capitulates to Unilever, it allows for an economy of scale with which smaller plantations cannot compete.

Vaskar Nandy argues that, even more important than centralizing capital, what is "involved in maximizing profits" is finally about the "restructuring of capital-labor relations in favor of capital" (2005, 6). How might this work? When plantations are abandoned, at-risk plantations use these cases as a reason to push down wages; to increase the piece-rate amount, which is part of the daily wage structure; and to flout basic labor laws. Since it is not clear when and how plantations become truly vulnerable structurally (or when the books are being "cooked"), the threat of closure is enough to coerce workers to labor under even more punitive conditions of work.

Wages and ration entitlements, for example, are not paid in time. Many workers told me that threats of closure are common during daily plucking rounds, and are used to raise *ticca* (the piece rate) or to justify the nonpayment of wages for weeks.[9] The possibility of closure is the Damocles Sword hanging over the heads of tens of thousands of plantation workers who don't have alternative employment and who see, in their own neighborhoods, the devastation wrought as a result of plantation abandonment.

For the big players, such as Unilever or Tata Tea, the closure of small plantations is an added benefit: They might be able to increase their holdings in the future, and the demise of small plantations hardly causes a ripple in the larger battles of boardroom capital. Yet, these decisions, made in boardrooms and auction bazaars, fundamentally shift capital-labor relations. For labor, these battles of capital have stunning Darwinian effects.

Munnu Kujoor, a plantation worker whom I have known for many years, was born in Kathalguri T.E., a plantation which has been among the hardest hit by the closures. When I met her over ten years ago, she still worked as a plucker in her natal plantation, though she had married into the neighboring plantation where her husband was a full-time worker, an electrician. About five years ago, she exchanged her job with that of a woman from her in-laws' plantation who was marrying "into" Kathalguri. When this exchange in the labor roster took place, it spared Munnu Kujoor a long four-mile walk to and from her field of daily labor; it also saved her wage earnings in the long run. It is, of course, another story for the woman who married "out." Munnu, who lives in the Factory Line at New Dooars, is intimately aware of the starvation deaths at Kathalguri.

She and a few other women at New Dooars take me to Etha Bhata Line in Kathalguri where some of the worst cases of starvation deaths were reported—and where state-sponsored relief has not reached. They tell me that this set of Labor Lines (village clusters) is among the hardest hit because it is one of the most disenfranchised in the plantation: The people dwelling there are primarily *adivasi* ("original inhabitants") and are tribal in their ethnic identifications. Historically, they are descendants of "tribal" communities, *adivasis,* from the Chotanagpur

Plateau. These communities of labor are least able, because of a racialized labor hierarchy, to "broker" themselves into overseer and union positions. Munnu also takes us to the hutments of her natal village and shows me a row of three houses where entire families have died because they did not have enough food to eat. "All dead, *didi* [sister]. All dead."

North Bengal accounts for 30 percent of India's annual tea production, with the "champagne of teas" being produced in Darjeeling. The Dooars plantation belt, where Munnu Kujoor lives and works, caters to a less discerning palate. Both the Dooars and the Darjeeling hills have been badly hit by this crisis. As many as twenty-two plantations have closed, and a minimum of 21,000 workers have been laid off work, affecting more than 95,000 people altogether.[10] A survey report on hunger in the plantations, commissioned by the Supreme Court of India (for an all-India case against the Government of India filed by the Right to Food Network), was conducted at the end of 2003. It showed that following these closures, the number of deaths registered in plantation hospitals increased by 241 percent (Asian Foodworker 2003).

The right to food and work is enshrined in the Indian constitution. Within international human rights discourses, such a right "enshrined" in statist preambles is further elaborated in universalist language. If the right to exist is threatened because livelihood is curtailed, then surely—as in any zone of institutionalized violence such as war—the most basic human right is violated. Starvation, as in other cases of famine, is institutionally enabled and structurally manufactured: Its effects are analogous to what happens in war and genocide. Human rights violations can be further categorized by the lack of health care and medicine, schooling, and shelter—as well as the impunity with which tea capitalists have been allowed, within the state administration, to get away with this despite labor legislation. The effects of human rights violations upon tea labor have reached catastrophic proportions.

But let us focus, briefly, on hunger, and on the issue of how wages and entitlements (in working plantations) are deeply tied to food. In short, workers' vulnerabilities are already structured into the wage regime. The calculus of food ration entitlements is also worked through a patriarchal logic. For example, a female worker—and the majority of fieldworkers are women—and her two minor dependents are entitled to a maximum of 2 kilos of rice and 3.7 kilos of wheat per week. Her dependent husband will not receive any rations. But if a husband is a worker, the wife is considered a dependent and will receive an allotment (Final Report 2004, 4). In this nuclear family equation, the food entitlement is about 200 grams a day—a paltry amount for the hardest kind of physical labor.

The current daily rated wage is Rs.45.90 (Rs.45 = U.S.$1). When one holiday per week is factored in, the actual wage is reduced to Rs.39.78. And after state-regulated employer deductions are taken for social security (provident funds) and electricity (for gardens with electricity), the actual wage is further reduced to Rs.30 a day. Daily wages are linked to food consumption in other coercive ways. Daily rated work means no work, no pay—and adjustments to subsidized food allotments. For example, the subsidized cost for ration is 40np/kilo per week for six days of work. Just one day of absence will require the worker to pay five times the rate at which s/he would have paid if s/he had worked six days.

This amount of cash in hand cannot cover any significant cereal or non-cereal diet. Indeed, nutritional sufficiency is rare among tea garden workers, even when plantations are functioning. Protein deficiency is common in single-wage households, run primarily by women workers; the family cannot afford meat or fish even once a week. Given these statistics on wage rates, it is easy to see how nutritional deficiency and serious malnutrition can quickly shift to starvation. Doctors who deposed for the March 2004 People's Tribunal on the Tea Crisis spoke of a worker "wailing for rice on the hospital verandah for days on end hoping that the hospital would provide a 'diet,' who eventually died at home from eating roots and leaves not fit for human consumption" (Final Report 2004, 5). The small garden hospital was itself gutted of resources. Its staff, also without wages, had nothing to give.

According to official statistics, 800 people died of starvation in these tea belts in the period from 2002 to 2003. However, many close observers of the situation, including myself, have noted that the public health infrastructure is sufficiently poor that plantation hospital registers cannot be relied on for accurate demographics on deaths. Indeed, other estimates suggest that over 3,000 people have died from starvation during the same period. Furthermore, although the causes of death for some clearly identifiable diseases (such as TB) are recorded, deaths due to circumstances such as "low caloric intake and the inability to buy medication on account of poverty" are not (Final Report 2004, 11). Significantly, these circumstances "give rise to many diseases and clinical conditions [as well as] to death. The death registers would then record the diseases or clinical conditions. The real causes would then have vanished. *Starvation is prior to clinical description and beyond it unless accompanied by social and economic descriptions*" (Final Report 2004, 11; emphasis mine). Although it is beyond the scope of this chapter to pursue the important epistemological and political implications of these debates about "clinical evidence," it is important to note that the framing of "evidence" can, and does, elide the multiple causal factors leading to death—including starvation (EPW Commentary 2003).

The political implications of both the lack of an accurate census and the lack of "clinical evidence" have been quite clear. In West Bengal, the latter has allowed most ruling members of the Left Front government to deny that these deaths were caused by starvation. For almost three decades, within the federal structure of the Indian state, West Bengal has been governed by the Communist Party of India (Marxist), or CPI(M). Because the starvation deaths are viewed as a state and regional issue, the central government remains a close observer but stays out of the debates, only to register that there is a crisis and that there "have been no starvation deaths" due to plantation closures.[11] However, within the larger Left Front political context, other communist and socialist leaders have been vocal about the state's responsibility to intervene. Local trade unions connected to other party outfits such as the Revolutionary Socialist Party (RSP) have publicly alleged that the state government is responsible for the starvation deaths of tea laborers and have "blamed the government for 'sitting tight' on desperate pleas of the union and others concerned to look into the plight of tea labourers in the region and initiate corrective measures." The general secretary of the RSP trade union (UTUC) alleged that the chief minister's "stunning silence for the past five months has saddened us" (*Deccan Herald*, 2003). And a leader of CITU, the powerful CPI(M)–led tea union, agreed that there was a rise in mortality but was unwilling to call it "starvation"—preferring instead to formulate the cause as "malnutrition and lack of medical care" (Final Report 2004, 8).

This local response is perfectly understandable because this leader, the chief minister of West Bengal, was making the same assertion to the Supreme Court Commission investigating the issue for the Right to Food and Work Network. Official denials have permeated the health bureaucracy, with top government officials failing to offer the correct numbers and so forth. However, because of increased media attention and visits by political workers and activists from South Bengal, the center of political power, the Jalpaiguri and Darjeeling District administration's relief efforts have come under scrutiny. In particular, the Supreme Court Commission has conducted surveys and interviewed district officials about the tea crisis, and documents (such as those cited in this chapter) are being used to compel the government to intervene with state-sponsored relief through its local and village-level organizations, known as *panchayats*. However, as we shall see, corruption permeates every aspect of governance—and in conditions of extreme deprivation, local *panchayat* leaders are manipulating the dispersion of food rations and entitlements.

Why would a popular elected government, running on a populist mandate, offer such egregious statements of denial? Certainly, it is deeply embarrassing for a leftist government to be held accountable for the human costs of a working-class crisis. But what, indeed, is the implication regarding CPI(M) rule? Might there be a "special" relationship between tea capitalist interests and the state government? There is no question that for a left-wing government, an official recognition of these deaths might lead to deeper questions about the entire business of tea. Although it is beyond the scope of this chapter to track the terms of complicity and alliance between regional state and tea capital, it is important to note that the "protection of tea" has always had a structural place in the history of Bengal.

In fact, observers of trade union politics for the past two decades have noted the deep collusion between union bosses and managers to ensure that there is no viable union-run social movement against the plantations regime. Over many years of fieldwork and in discussions with numerous union officials, activists, and ordinary workers, I have learned that a deep cynicism exists about working-class politics. "Those days are gone," I am told by one woman who remembered earlier years of "red flag" formations. "Now, everyone is in the *sahib's* pockets."

Politics and governance in these hinterlands are conditioned by their distance—geographically, historically, and culturally—from the centers of power in

Kolkata and Siliguri. This is an isolation deeply rooted in the settlement politics and logics of British administration. Ruled separately from the rest of Bengal, the plantation regime was its own Raj. In the popular Bengali imagination, these are landscapes of deep jungles, tigers, and tribes—best left alone. The fact that these peoples and landscapes have produced some of the greatest fortunes of colonial and postcolonial Bengal is also left alone.

Indeed, it is striking that senior Left Front leaders, often upper-caste Bengali *bhadralogs* (gentlemen), will not venture past Siliguri, the regional capital. The current chief minister (CM) gave a speech in Siliguri recently in which he again denied the starvation deaths. When I told some of the plantation women about this speech, they were outraged. "If the CM-*sahib* would like to know of our conditions," they say bitterly, "then why doesn't he step out of Siliguri into a *cha bagan* [tea plantation]? Next time he comes, we will invite him here and garland him with necklace of slippers.[12] How dare he mock our suffering. How dare he."

Because of these distances, local-level politics continues in its old feudal routines. "Big men" (and they are almost always men) become union leaders and can rule their plantation for a lifetime. As long as they help keep workers quiescent for the labor regime, and bring in the votes during elections, managers and local party bosses are satisfied. Any political organizing to the contrary will be violently subjugated—either by local hoodlums belonging to various parties or by state administrators, who, along with tea planters, want to ensure that "law and order" will be maintained.

In October 2003, when I returned to visit the Central Dooars, a plantation close to where I conduct research and organize, experienced a violent conflagration. Workers in this plantation had attacked a local CPI(M)-supported trade union leader, Tarakeshwar Lohar, and burned nineteen people alive. This grisly news hit the mainstream newspapers and, combined with the starvation deaths, painted a grim political picture of tea plantation politics for Kolkata readers. Lohar was known to be a powerful local strongman. Ten years ago, the story goes, when challenged by two other union leaders, he ordered their decapitation and hung their severed heads on the gateposts of the plantation. Neither the manager nor the district police moved against Lohar—though everyone knew he was responsible.

Local political power is based on a feudal patronage system that allows relatively high-status men to gain prominence in plantation country. This patronage system is vetted by political parties and their unions, and, not surprisingly, the ruling government's CPI(M) both backs and creates these strongmen as union leaders and bosses in the plantation. The complicity of the state in Lohar's local rule was very clear: He was a small but powerful local satrap in the CPI(M) machinery in North Bengal. When asked about the event, the CM allegedly responded, "Oh, he is a *dushto chele,* a naughty boy." Such are the terms of paternal rule.

Political violence is a constant, and though outside the daily purview of the state it is aided and abetted, when necessary, by that very state apparatus. Violence, both statist and nonstatist, is increasing. It is a violence made possible by a distance marked by tribal, gendered bodies—beyond the realms of *bhadrata* (civilization and civility), too *jungli* (primitive) to bear concerted attention. If such bodies die, their value has already been marked by the logic of invisibility. Annihilation is a reasonable outcome. The effects are genocidal.

REFUSING DEATH: WOMEN'S COMMUNITY-BASED AND COALITIONAL ACTIVISM

Coalitional Visions and the Politics of Location

The plantation women who first alerted me to the killing effects of these tea crises on their neighbors and kinfolk are from the Factory Line, in New Dooars T.E., where I first did fieldwork over a decade ago. Our reflections on the current crisis, and our dreams for political and health literacy programs run by women, emerged through "coalitional" conversations. Coalition, following the meditations of Bernice Johnson Reagon,[13] does not elide difference and power; it encounters hierarchy, holds subjects of privilege accountable, and then moves into the difficulties of doing social justice work, building on the ground (Combahee River Collective 2004; Reagon 1983, 356–369). In that light, "my" participation has remained open to the possibilities of coalitional work that becomes actualized in social practice: in the places of paradox, contradiction, tension, and co-implication that are the stuff of social action (Mohanty 1994, 145–166).

Thus, when I rhetorically claim these as "our" vision, I do so with an acute understanding of those structural parameters of power—their limits and their possibilities. Indeed, such differences of power were not, and cannot, be elided in the terms of plantation politics. This is a historical terrain that permits no such masking of power and inequality: I/You are from the Big House; or I/You are not.

It is through the skein of these contradictions that I continue to work through the problematic of textual representation without allowing its possible angst to paralyze *both* participation in and reflection on coalitional and collaborative work about social justice.

THE TERMS OF ENUNCIATION AND WOMEN'S HUMAN RIGHTS

In March 2004, members of Dooars Jagron, the community-based organization we created, participated in a commission of inquiry on the starvation deaths organized by Swaadikar (another North Bengal–based nongovernmental organization), Vaskar Nandy, and the Indian People's Tribunal on Human Rights and the Environment (a civil rights group based in India's financial capital, Mumbai). Led by a distinguished high court judge of the Mumbai Courts, Justice Suresh, this tribunal traveled into plantation country to meet directly with workers in abandoned plantations. The main purpose of the tribunal was to inquire into the reasons for the crisis as well as to find out what the state was doing in terms of relief aid.

We met them at the Etha Bhata Line of Kathalguri T.E., where we had started some of our organizing work. At least thirty-five women and ten men were present during the *lok adalat* (people's court), and they spoke eloquently about their daily deprivations and struggles for survival. Throughout most of the hearing, local leaders, all of whom were men, got up and spoke—rarely giving the women, sitting on the ground, permission to speak. Finally, however, some of us insisted that the women be given a chance to speak, and they started offering their own testimonials of survival. The gendered conditions of public speech are striking. Sarita Pradhan and Poonam Rai, two extraordinary Nepali women (who are on the Dooars Jagron Board) spoke about doing daily contract labor on road construction—breaking rocks with chisels and falling sick because of the dust. Others spoke, with some fear, about how ration entitlements (from the government) were not reaching their distant Line.

In another plantation, Dekhlapara, which we visited with the tribunal, women seemed openly frightened and did not want to speak. The tribunal, all men except for one Mumbai lawyer, sat on chairs nearly surrounded by a semicircle of local village men (*panchayat*, village and local council members, leaders). Women ringed the verandah of the abandoned hospital. Many of them were widows.

Rita and I went to speak to one woman who told us that she was eking out a living with daily work she could scrounge up here and there. She said she was frightened to speak because some of the local men who were deposing had stolen the food to which she and the others were entitled, and had also threatened them if they spoke. She said, "I am a widow. My *marad* [man] died from starvation. I have two children. I have to feed them. If they come at night to beat me up, who will protect me?"

When members of the tribunal asked women to speak, we let them know that the women were frightened of repercussions. When the tribunal assured them they would be protected, a few spoke. Rita and I argued with some of the members of the tribunal: "Who will protect them? Will you?" We knew, in the absence of any viable will of the state (from which food relief was being stolen), that state regulation—let alone "protection"—was a dream.

One old woman howled. We had met her before but could not understand her (we were told she was mad). Rita tried to translate this "incomprehensible" speech for the tribunal. One journalist immediately pulled out a camera to take shots of this old woman: her rocking body on the stool, her keening.

I wanted to smash his camera. Rita pulled me back, murmuring, "Didi, forget it. It won't be a good thing." What politics of value was at play in this desire to capture human suffering? What politics of value allowed for such sexed and racialized abjection to be made "spectacular," and for whose consumption? For whose pity? Where will that camera be if any of these women's lives are jeopardized by their testimony?

I remain deeply uneasy about the ethical slippery slope we were on with respect to the conditions of speech at that moment. How can we claim a human rights agenda if we do not protect people from possible violence, especially when they have the courage to speak? Personally, many members of the tribunal—veteran administrators—were sympathetic to the dilemma. Yet, the paradox remained. It is extraordinarily important that such detailed accounting takes place—so that statistics can be fleshed out by names, and by powerful text. The tribunal's presence created a register of accountability, which is rare in the history of these hinterlands. Its report (2004) becomes evidence in the larger material and discursive games of the state—and the state might respond. It, too, is porous. We have yet to track the report's effects.

Language

Beyond theories, abstractions, statistics, and metaphors—perhaps beyond language itself—might there be a space within which we are able to comprehend what it means to experience such daily trauma and loss? How *do* we enunciate a possible ethics of the human (of "human rights") in the face of such daily structural violence? How *do* we make sense of a devaluation of humanness that renders your heart speechless? Can we articulate such loss without imagining, and expressing, both pain and rage? Can we speak to any of this, first, without mourning?

It is in the shadows posed by these questions, then, that I want to end this exploration of capital and violence—by invoking for you the distant places some inhabit.

But I want to remember someone in particular, in that distant place. I want to remember the old woman of Dekhlapara plantation. I want to remember her with you, to you. I want to remember her body, her white hair in a messy bun, her bare scrap of sari: the curve of her old back. I want to remember her trying to speak to Rita and me—a little light in her eyes—as she tries in vain to articulate something that is beyond our grasp.

Rita touches her shoulder, kindly, and helps her sit on the stairs. We offer her some water. We speak to other women. When the tribunal asks for "women's talk," many of the young women refuse.

But she understands what the *sahibs* and *memsahibs* want.

She gets up. She walks to the wooden stool. She leans forward and back in a rocking motion.

She speaks, her voice getting louder and louder. No one can understand her, but everyone is silent. In that act, as she positions herself in front of power; in that public space of attention, she becomes something "else." Mother Courage, perhaps.

In her keening, through her apparent incomprehensibility, she becomes the living wound of a mourning and a rage that escape, finally, the realms of all language.

NOTES

1. I began fieldwork for a Ph.D. in anthropology in this area of North Bengal in 1991. I lived for one year in the plantation circle I speak of in this chapter. I revisited in 1998 when discussions about organizing were raised and have continued to visit and stay in the area, every year, since 2000. In my earlier work, *A Time for Tea: Women, Labor and Post/Colonial Politics on an Indian Plantation*, I describe in detail the contradictions of my location as an upper-class, upper-caste woman subject in this space—and the ways it laced every aspect of ethnographic epistemology and its politics on women's labor.

2. I have elaborated on what I call the "feminization of labor/commodity" by tracking these forms of fetishization in *A Time for Tea*.

3. Management and labor practices have also been highly personalized, often ad hoc, and feudal in these smaller plantations. Higher costs for labor are also given as a reason for noncompetitiveness. In one case, the labor bill for a small plantation in Assam doubled in four years, from 49¢ for eight hours of work in 1998 to 87¢. The owners claim that the margins of profit are not sustainable for their businesses. For further discussion, see Rai (2002).

4. This information was provided by Vaskar Nandy, whom I interviewed in Jalpaiguri on August 25, 2004. A veteran trade unionist and communist activist in Northeastern India, Vaskar provided many of the key insights about tea capital and Unilever that are offered in this chapter. Any errors of interpretation and analysis are, of course, mine. I am deeply indebted to him for his generosity in sharing these insights, and for remaining one of my most brilliant teachers on tea and politics in the past decade. It is an education that has shaped my understanding of Indian history and politics in the most profound ways.

5. Ibid.

6. Ibid.

7. What is suggested here is a deeper exploration of the philosophical imaginings of the Enlightenment (and, even earlier, Euclidean geometry) in which "space" becomes deeply inscribed by a new geometry—indeed, a new cartography—of the "globe." I am interested in exploring this spatiotemporal vision/politics, and its racialized suggestions, within neoimperial tropes such as "white space" in a new book project titled *Sipping Desires: Race, Commodity and Capital.*

8. In a human rights report, the reply given to an Indian Tea Planter Association official who, when asked to participate in a tribunal on the starvation crises, responded by saying that starvation was a "misnomer" when describing these deaths (Final Report 2004, 9).

9. Plucking wages are divided into (1) *haziri,* the daily wage for showing up to work; and (2) *ticca,* the piece rate calculated at 50 naya paise per kilo. The piece rate is staggered seasonally, but to get your *haziri* you must pluck a minimum number of kilos. During peak season, the piece rate is used as an incentive for more leaf production. Arbitrary increases in the *ticca* rates flout labor laws. But it is important to note that such disregard of labor laws is common.

10. Plantations create an enclave economy within rural areas. States regulate any and all industrial development work in plantation enclaves, as was particularly true during the colonial-settler period. State regulation ensures compliance from local peasants (who often have to redirect their own crop markets to supplying the plantation) and the absence of economic competition. Over the last hundred years, this has meant a quite explicit underdevelopment of the region. As a result, there are no large-scale alternative employment sectors. If plantations fail, people try to migrate; but in depressed and overpopulated economies, this means seasonal work at very low wages—or simply no employment at all.

11. See "Calling Attention to a Matter of Urgent Public Importance: The Plight of Tea Garden Workers Due to Sickness and Closure of a Large Number of Tea Gardens Leading to Starvation Deaths," response by Minister of Law and Justice and Minister of Commerce and Industry Arun Jaitley, as reported in the *Rajya Sabha: Synopsis of Debates,* Friday, December 19, 2003.

12. In many Indian (and, more generally, Asian) contexts, the feet—and anything associated with feet—are considered polluted and dirty. For a Hindu Bengali, obeisance to an elder is expressed

by touching his or her feet—the *pranam*. Conversely, it is considered deeply disrespectful to kick or hit a person with your shoes. Women will take off their slippers to slap people when angry—and as a public way to humiliate a person who has wronged them. It is not clear to me how gendered this is in practice, or whether it is a common act of subversion. But to garland the chief minister of West Bengal with a "necklace of slippers" is clearly the ultimate humiliation and disrespect—as well as subversion of status and power.

13. I am indebted to Bernice Johnson Reagon and other U.S. women of color theorists who have argued for a "politics of location" to be worked through an understanding of "interlocking oppressions"—particularly around ethnoracial privilege/dominance and class. However, I am most interested in Reagon's formulation of "coalition politics" as a way to think about social justice work. In this connection, see also the Combahee River Collective (2004).

5

Macroeconomics and Microentrepreneurs

Comparing Two Island Nations' Responses to Neoliberalism and Its Impact on Women's Lives

Marina Karides

Across the globe women historically have relied on themselves to create a means of earning an income through food, textile, and craft production, domestic service, or street vending and more. Yet scholars and practitioners of economic development throughout the 1960s and 1970s rejected women's various enterprises, identifying them as economically unviable. Governments and international development institutions such as the World Bank, the International Labour Organization (ILO), and the UN Development Program (UNDP) now argue that women's independent income earning activities offer the most promise for employment creation, poverty alleviation, and economic growth (Dignard and Havet 1995; Grosh and Somolekae 1996; Johnson and Kidder 1999; Mosley and Hulme 1998; Portes 1997; Rakowski 1994).

With the promotion of microenterprise development, governments and development agencies suggest they have a definitive solution for women's poverty and unemployment in the global South. Providing women with loans and training in vocational and business skills, microenterprise development has been specifically indicated for small island economies that cater to tourism and are considered vulnerable to shifts in the global economy (ILO 1998a).

The assumption is that with credit assistance and skills training, poor and low-income women can create employment and alleviate their conditions of poverty. At the same time, these institutions promote neoliberalism—a program of policies that reduces or eliminates the state's role in the redistribution of economic gains and adheres to strict market principles. For instance, although many microenterprise development programs distribute credit, they do so at market rates. Without subsidization, low-income borrowers with limited capital are subject to extremely high interest rates. Another obstacle to the success and survival of fledging microenterprises is that in a free trade environment these businesses must compete with multinationals that produce the same goods.

Yet this latest panacea for women's poverty and unemployment in island economies is prescribed by international agencies, regardless of the particularities of a national context. What kinds of national policies interfere with, or support, women's microenterprise development? Certainly cutbacks in, or the expansion of, social policies are relevant to women's poverty and unemployment, but macroeconomic policies, such as the removal of national trade barriers, also impact poor and low-income women's survival. Indeed, how a nation addresses or responds to neoliberalism may greatly affect not only the likelihood that women's microenterprises will create the necessary income to meet basic needs but also the opportunities open to women who pursue business expansion.

I compare state policies vis-à-vis neoliberalism and women microentrepreneurs in two island nations: the Republic of Trinidad and Tobago, located in the Caribbean Sea, and the Republic of Cyprus, located in the Mediterranean Sea. Both former British colonies, these nations are considered relatively successful examples of postcolonial development as measured by macroeconomic indicators such as high growth-rate levels and GDP per capita. At the ground level, however, these two semiperipheral nations differ greatly: In Cyprus income inequality, rates of poverty (almost nonexistent), and unemployment (2–3 percent) are distinctly low, even when compared to European nations, whereas in Trinidad and Tobago, a nation with a successful energy sector, these rates remain particularly high—20 percent of the population is unemployed, and 35 percent fall below the poverty line.

The Republic of Cyprus is a national entity, recognized by the United Nations. The majority of the population consists of Greek Cypriots (77 percent), although Turkish Cypriots (18 percent) continue to live there. Starting in the mid-1950s, British colonizers fomented division between Turkish Cypriots and Greek Cypriots in order to thwart Cyprus's independence movement. Britain's attempts to maintain control of the island eventuated in Greece's interference in Cypriot politics with the intention of annexing the island nation. Turkey eventually invaded in 1974, after which the United States became involved in the division of the island into separate political and economic entities. Lefkosia remains a divided city. The formal division of the island led to the displacement of both Greek Cypriots and Turkish Cypriots. Turkish Cypriots living in the southern region fled, or were forced to relocate to the northern part of the island controlled by Turkey, and Greek Cypriots who resided in the North had properties confiscated and were forced to flee to the South where they are recognized as refugees. Despite the refusal of Greek Cypriots to reunite the island before the nation's entrance into the European Union in 2004, both Turkish Cypriots and Greek Cypriots maintain their national identity as Cypriots rather than as Greeks or Turks.

Like the Republic of Cyprus, the Republic of Trinidad and Tobago gained its independence from England in the early 1960s, but with distinctly less resistance from the British. The People's National Movement, the African Trinidadian-dominated political party that controlled national politics until the 1990s, led the drive toward independence. Indian Trinidadians, who, like African Trinidadians, make up approximately 40 percent of the population, live in the southern rural areas of Trinidad and were, until recently, less engaged in national political affairs. Beginning with World War II, when U.S. military bases dominated the island, Trinidad and Tobago became increasingly linked with the United States rather than with its former colonizer.

Both nations currently deploy microenterprise development for decreasing women's unemployment rates. In Cyprus, microenterprises dominate—95 percent of businesses there consist of five persons or fewer, and microenterprises were one of the primary strategies for national development after the Turkish invasion (Nearchou 1999). Trinidad also has a legacy of microenterprises, but these have existed primarily in the informal sector and only recently have been supported as a development strategy. The Trinidadian and Tobagonian state more directly pursues the reduction of gender inequality. For example, various forums at national and local levels exist to increase awareness of gender equity. The government has enacted legislative reforms in family, marriage, and domestic violence laws. Education and retraining programs have been created for older or rural women in order to increase women's representation in male-dominated employment sectors (Women's Affairs Division 1995). Unlike Cyprus, Trinidad maintains a Ministry of Gender. It is a global leader in women's political representation and in strategic thinking about how to give official value to women's unpaid work. Yet women microentrepreneurs and low-income women generally are far more economically and socially secure in Cyprus than in Trinidad and Tobago.

The comparison I develop indicates the importance of national macroeconomic policies for women living in the global South. Resistance to neoliberal reforms permits the development of nascent entrepreneurs by protecting them from the infringements of foreign capital investment and competition with foreign-made products. This study also suggests that microenterprise programs premised on assisting women to manage their dual roles as breadwinners and caretakers can burden women with household duties, reducing their opportunities for economic advancement. Unless governments maintain broad social policies that serve to assist women and families to meet basic needs, supporting poor and low-income women one microenterprise at a time cannot overcome the hardships of economic survival. In the next section, I provide a critical review of microenterprise development as a gendered development strategy. I then compare the stances of Trinidad and Tobago and Cyprus toward neoliberal reforms that were implemented in the 1980s and some of the national policies that impact women microentrepreneurs. I conclude by elaborating why, despite persisting traditional gender roles in Cyprus, women microentrepreneurs fare better in Cyprus than in Trinidad and Tobago.

NEOLIBERALISM AND MICROENTERPRISE DEVELOPMENT

As a platform for economic development, neoliberalism's arrival coincided with the apparent failure of modernization policies. Although most postcolonial nations accepted and implemented modernization development strategies recommended by the United States, by the early 1980s it had become clear that the rapid economic advancement of the postcolonial nations predicted by U.S. policymakers was doubtful. Mexico was the first nation to conclude, in 1982, that it was unable to repay the loans that were so quickly granted less than a decade earlier (Kiely 1998; McMichael 1996). The optimism of the previous decade about the economic advancement of the global South quickly subsided when much of the postcolonial world followed suit (Kiely 1998). Modernization scholars were forced to reconsider their prescriptions for Third World development. How could this lack of economic success be explained?

Blaming state involvement in the economy and redistributive economics for the international economic crisis, the IMF and the World Bank responded to the Third World debt crisis through strict market liberalism—nation-states no longer "developed." Rather, they positioned themselves in the global economy (Kenworthy 1995; Kiely 1998; McMichael 1996). Indebted nations have been forced to rescind their involvement with the economy and to starkly reduce social spending. In other words, government-controlled enterprises, such as utilities, were sold off to private companies (usually to capital from wealthy nations), and governments were required to cut costs by limiting services in health and education as well as programs for those socially and economically marginalized.

From the neoliberal perspective, good government is determined by the ability of a state to promote development through market forces (Kiely 1998). International financial institutions degrade any considerations that do not accept the interests of capital as primary (Klak 1998). In the early days of neoliberal reforms, all governments' attempts at poverty alleviation and the reduction of social inequality were considered contrary to economic growth. The increases in poverty and inequality that neoliberal policies produced forced the IMF and the World Bank to modify their stance against direct social assistance, yet these institutions continue to herald market-based solutions as the best approach for alleviating poverty and inequality.

Construed as part of the neoliberal project, the advancement of microenterprise development appears as a market-based solution to the so-called blunders of postcolonial nations. States were accused of inhibiting entrepreneurship by imposing regulations on industry, such as health and safety codes and minimum-wage requirements (Portes and Benton 1984; Rakowski 1994; Weiss 1987). Neoliberalists attribute the explosion in numbers of unemployed, underemployed, and informal workers in the global South to "ineffective" states (Gugler 1982; Lipton 1977; Portes and Benton 1984; Smith 1996; Weiss 1987). Thus, by promoting microenterprise development, government officials feel that they can offer some assistance to poor and low-income people but still remain in compliance with the neoliberal reforms they are obliged to implement.

Microenterprise development also harbors the support of poverty advocates and feminists. Some feminist proponents argue that women are advantaged by self-employed informal work because it offers them autonomy to manage household duties and to earn an income. The development of microenterprises is viewed as a means of lifting women out of poverty and giving them control over their own income, making them less dependent on men and the state (Rodriguez 1995; Scully 1997). In addition, self-employment is flexible, can be started with women's home skills, and can provide a path for upward mobility to women with limited education. Finally, microenterprise programs may offer poor women a source of capital other than usurious moneylenders (Everett 1989). Some research suggests that the current focus on developing women's microenterprise is promoted as evidence that governments and international development agencies are advancing women's social and economic independence (Isserles 1999).

Despite the popular appeal and vast expansion of microenterprise programs in postcolonial nations, there is limited assessment of the societal, economic, and national conditions that may increase or decrease the likelihood of small-scale economic activity to reduce unemployment or stimulate economic growth. In their support, many women-centered nongovernmental organizations overlook the suitability of microenterprises for their particular contexts given national social policies and macroeconomic policies.

My critique of microenterprise development is that it developed as a knee-jerk response to the failures of modernization rather than as a coherent development program based in any theoretical tradition. There is very limited theoretical explanation as to why small and microbusinesses, which were previously accused of hindering economic development because they defied large-scale industrial development, have become a vital part of national economic growth and poverty alleviation in the global South. Its uncanny appeal to feminists, populists, and many Marxists, as well as to advocates of neoliberalism, suggests that microenterprise development is serving not as a viable development strategy but, rather, as a quick fix or bandaid for a program of modernization that has mired the majority of persons in the global South in poverty (Escobar 1995). Certainly, microenterprise development's emphasis on self-dependence appeals to American sensibilities of individualism; however, as this chapter suggests, success in economic independence or self-employment is dependent on the larger economic context and on supportive social policies.

METHODOLOGY

To investigate how government development strategies impact women microentrepreneurs in the Republic of Cyprus and the Republic of Trinidad and Tobago I made research trips to each nation to conduct interviews with microenterprise professionals, government workers, and microentrepreneurs. The interviews took place primarily in urban areas and totaled more than forty in each nation. In addition, I collected documents and statistics produced by the various government agencies and organizations from which my interview participants were drawn. I used grounded theory for analysis and sorted through developed categories, integrating them, abandoning them, allowing data and written sources to interact, and maintaining flexibility and reflexivity throughout (Glaser and Strauss 1967).

In both countries the majority of microentrepreneurs consists of the traditionally economically active population—namely, persons over the age of 18 and preretirement. Although in both nations elderly persons are evident in street trade, taxi service, and room letting, in neither nation is there much evidence of children working in booths and selling items, as occurs in some countries. Cyprus, more than Trinidad and Tobago, relies on tourism, and many of the microenterprises in downtown Nicosia target tourists. Numerous microbusinesses, each the size of a typical bedroom, line the city streets, selling cups, trays, and tablecloths with insignia of the nation. Tavernas, small restaurant cafes that are family owned and run, are also numerous throughout the island. In addition, each major city in Cyprus—Lefkosia, Larnaka, Limassol, and Pafos—holds regular markets where villagers come to sell their farm products and homemade goods.

By contrast, in downtown Port of Spain a few businesses target tourism, but most businesses sell products for everyday consumption. Unlike Cyprus, urban streets in Trinidad are lined with street vendors selling products such as shoes, clothing, fruits, and vegetables. Most households in Trinidad and Tobago are engaged in some informal microenterprise such as selling food items from home, mechanical work, taxi service, room rentals, hairdressing, and textile production. Unlike formal enterprises, informal enterprises are undocumented, or "off the books." They are not taxed or regulated by the state. For some, informal enterprises provide an additional source of income, but for many women they serve as the primary source of income.

In both nations men and women participate in microenterprises. However, more women seem to be engaged in street or market trade, whereas men dominate transportation services, which are more lucrative.

A Small Nation in a Big Sea

As one of Trinidad's main programs for addressing unemployment and poverty, microenterprise development is supported by international agencies such as the UN Development Program, the World Bank, and various government ministries (ILO 1991; Republic of Trinidad and Tobago 1996). By encouraging women to create their own means of employment, microenterprises also are considered a primary solution to Trinidad's gendered labor market, in which women work more than men for lower wages and are officially excluded from some types of formal employment (Women's Affairs Division 1995; Yelvington 1993).

A lender to the IMF until 1984, the Republic of Trinidad and Tobago turned to the institution in 1988 to reschedule its large debt to international commercial banks (World Bank 1995). Based on the expansion of the nation's energy sector in the mid-1970s, national leaders, assuming future economic gains, borrowed heavily to develop infrastructure and to establish a good credit rating internationally during its time of prosperity. However, with the downturn of the petroleum prices in the early 1980s, the country's debt had reached U.S. $891 million by 1986. The nation's choice to turn to the IMF did not go uncontested. Economic and development specialists and grassroots organizations drew the public's attention to the intensification of poverty and unemployment that structural adjustment would trigger and held forums to garner support for an alternative solution to Trinidad's economic crisis.

As discussed earlier, the IMF and World Bank charged that the economic crises of Trinidad and other nations resulted from government's mismanagement of the economy. Yet the same international agencies had encouraged political leaders to borrow heavily from commercial banks supporting the indebtedness of postcolonial nations. When the debt crisis of the 1980s overwhelmed the global economy, these agencies responded with global economic restructuring, introducing an international division of labor and deregulating capital flows in and out of countries. The force behind neoliberal reforms was "structural adjustment." Indebted nations like Trinidad and Tobago had to subscribe to structural adjustment policies (SAPs) in order to reschedule their national debts.

The neoliberal reforms of economic development strategies demanded a reduction in government expenditure. Trinidad was thus required to dismantle much of its state-centered economy by privatizing state-owned enterprises and reducing state expenditure on social programs and employment. Between 1985 and 1989 the government reduced its labor force by almost 30,000 workers (Theodore 1993). And between 1986 and 1992 social expenditures declined by 47 percent, decreasing the quality and availability of health and education services to the general public (Theodore 1993). Government subsidies on basic food items to assist the very poor were reduced or discontinued, and a value-added tax (VAT), a 15 percent tax on every item formally sold in the country, raised the cost of basic living items, economically straining low-income residents.

Women are particularly hard hit during periods of structural adjustment, owing to increases in women's unpaid work at such times (WorkingWomen 1993). The highest incidence of poverty is seen in urban households headed by African Trinidadian women (Bourne 1993; Women's Affairs Division 1995; World Bank 1995). The rise in prices of basic goods and the decrease in earnings and access to social services increase women's responsibilities as household managers and caretakers. For instance, women must spend more time shopping and searching for the lowest-cost goods, or refurbishing items to extend their use rather than purchasing new and more efficient items. They must also prepare more items at home rather than purchasing them.

In addition, although both men and women have lost jobs due to retrenchment, in Trinidad women's employment losses are considerably higher (Women's Affairs Division 1995). Women suffering from gender discrimination in Trinidad's labor market are relegated to low-level government jobs, which are quickly retrenched as the government attempts to reduce expenditures. Indeed, gender discrimination in Trinidad's labor market is evidenced by wage difference and women's high unemployment rates (Women's Affairs Division 1995; World Bank 1995). Women earn half as much as men in the formal labor force and have an unemployment rate 30 percent higher than men (World Bank 1995). In addition, although women average higher educational levels, they receive lower economic returns on education than do men in the same racial group (Coppin and Olsen 1992). Although 20 percent of women workers are estimated to be unemployed, another 20 percent are estimated to be involved in informal self-employment (CSO 1999).

With limited alternatives, women have addressed the economic hardships of unemployment, underemployment, and discrimination in the formal labor market by engaging in informal independent income earning projects, which are labor intensive and require minimum capital (Women's Affairs Division 1995). Engaging in food preparation, providing domestic services, or street and market vending, Trinidadian women in the informal sector suffer from low earnings, lack formal employment benefits, and risk fines or arrests for street vending. African Trinidadian women are documented as having greater participation in self-employment than other racial/ethnic groups (CSO 1999). By promoting microenterprise development the Trinidadian government prescribes for women's unemployment the same tactic women have been utilizing for years.

Trinidadian women's microenterprises are supported by governmental and nongovernmental organizations as a way of generating employment and assisting women to manage childcare and other household duties (WorkingWomen 1993). Advocates of women's microenterprises as a means to overcome the difficulties created by structural adjustment suggest that the low earnings of informally self-employed women in Trinidad could be raised through training in marketing strategies and long-term business planning.

Some Trinidadian women activists waged critiques of microenterprise as an employment strategy. They questioned the economy's ability to sustain the increasing number of women's microenterprises (Reddock 1993) and argued that self-employment does not offer the kind of security that is provided by the government jobs women had held before retrenchment. Self-employed workers assume full responsibility for benefits such as maternity, sick leave, and pension, leading to a decrease in workers' rights and the casualization of labor. Although microenterprise development is maintained as a national development policy, it does not appear to be changing the living conditions of many microentrepreneurs, who continue to work without health benefits, sick leave, or social security.

SMALL IS BEAUTIFUL

The Republic of Cyprus, a postcolonial nation that gained independence from England in 1960, provides an opportunity for understanding the conditions and policies that can facilitate successful microenterprise expansion. The economic revival of the Republic of Cyprus since the 1974 Turkish invasion is largely attributed to the success of microenterprises. Currently, 95 percent of Cypriot businesses are small or microbusinesses and employ 60 percent of the population (Nearchou 1999).

The majority of these microenterprises are family owned and located in urban areas, providing services and retail venues for Cyprus's burgeoning tourist economy. The Cypriot "economic miracle" most often is attributed to the entrepreneurial spirit of Greek Cypriots, particularly the third of the population who were displaced from their homes and jobs and needed to create new lives in the less-developed southern half of the island. My research in Cyprus demonstrates that government macroeconomic policy and the widespread availability of social assistance are largely responsible for the success of microenterprises, the survival of the Northern Cypriot refugees, and the entire revival of the economy after the invasion. It was the Cypriot government's active involvement in the economy throughout the 1970s and 1980s that catapulted the nation to a level of development comparable to its northern European neighbors.

Macropolicies for Microentrepreneurs

How should a nation manage its involvement in the global economy if it is interested in assisting microentrepreneurs? Contrary to the advice given to the nation by U.S. officials in meetings held after the invasion, Cyprus did not open its economy, nor did it peg its currency to the U.S. dollar. Rather, it set up a protectionist economy with a strong emphasis on import substitution, helping the population establish its own productive industries. The political leadership, postinvasion, decided that resources for national redevelopment should be directed toward developing local businesses rather than pursuing foreign investment. Supporting local industry also was considered the best strategy for creating enough employment for the Greek Cypriot refugees.

Cypriot government leaders recognized that in order for microbusinesses to succeed they required protection. Between 1968 and 1978, Cyprus held an extremely protective trade policy, including high tariffs on most imports, sometimes up to 100 percent on goods similar to those produced nationally. It also banned imports on some primary products, such as olive oil, that were produced in Cyprus (Nicolaou 2003). These policies were extended through the 1980s, as the rest of the postcolonial world joined the neoliberal bandwagon.

Eventually, Cyprus was forced to retract many of its trade policies. The reductions of tariffs were initiated first in 1988, when the nation pursued inclusion in the European Economic Community. Tariffs were further reduced in 1994, and eventually all tariffs were eliminated in order for Cyprus to qualify for membership in the World Trade Organization (WTO) when it was formed. The new trade environment has been particularly hard on the apparel industry, which had the most difficulty competing with transnationally produced goods. Although it is too early to tell, it may be that the earlier protection the Cypriot government provided for its other local businesses and microentrepreneurs will give them the grounds to survive as the nation subscribes to global market legislation.

Policies That Assist Microentrepreneurs

Along with armoring microbusinesses from decades of free trade, the Republic of Cyprus deploys various forms of social assistance that encourage the survival of microentrepreneurs and enable families to meet basic needs. A clear indication of support is the availability of social insurance to the self-employed person. A government report states, "Self-employed persons are treated in the same way as employed persons in cases of accidents or hospitalization, and pensions and the state contribute equally to self-employed and employed persons at a rate of 4 percent" of yearly income earnings (Department of Social Insurance 2001). Although self-employed persons are not entitled to unemployment insurance, maternity allowance is granted to both employed and self-employed persons. Maternity grants are a financial transfer from the state to women when they give birth.

Another indication of government support of microentrepreneurs is the allotment of vending locations at nominal prices in central locations. The absence of illegal street vending in all of Cyprus is quite remarkable given its ubiquitous presence in cities around the globe. Nicosia, the nation's capital, maintains several outdoor markets with nominal fees for renting a small area. The city provides more formal, indoor venues that are only a bit more costly. As stated earlier, Cyprus's other main cities—Lefkosia, Larnaka, Limassol, and Pafos—also hold regular markets on specific days. An affordable location from which to sell goods is one of the primary needs of microentrepreneurs, and it is embedded in Cyprus's urban development policy.

Although microenterprise development does not figure prominently as a national development strategy, it is emphasized by the Ministry of Commerce, Industry, and Tourism as a strategy to increase women's labor market participation.

In addition, the recently organized Women's Cooperative Bank was officially sanctioned by the state to address gender inequities in microbusinesses. The Women's Cooperative Bank is a public banking institution controlled and invested in by women. Although both men and women can approach the bank for microlending assistance, women are given preferred treatment—a policy that, after much effort on the part of women organizers, gained government approval.

The leader of the Women's Cooperative Bank argues that gaining government support to charter a bank organized around the principle of assisting women's microenterprises relied largely on the efforts of elite women such as herself, who could speak directly with, and influence, government officials. In addition, preparation for entrance into the European Union (EU) required the nation to address gender equity and, ironically, small-business development, in which Cyprus leads most European nations. It seems that support for microenterprise development in the Republic of Cyprus was brought forward by a network of elite women and policy prescriptions from the EU, rather than by grassroots feminists and women's advocates.

In the Republic of Cyprus, women run only 12 percent of the businesses—a figure that is particularly low when compared with the EU, where women control 27 percent of businesses overall (Women's Co-op Bank Cyprus 2003). However, if one considers that 95 percent of Cyprus's enterprises consist of fewer than five employees and are family run, then a considerable number of women who, together with their spouses, manage family businesses are overlooked as microentrepreneurs.

In 2001 the Ministry of Commerce, Industry, and Tourism implemented a program to finance unemployed women in order to support women's entrepreneurship. Women starting businesses in trade, services, or tourist activities would be provided 50 percent of startup costs. The other focus of the program to enhance women's entrepreneurship was to provide a business incubation period to enable women's businesses "to develop their business in a well-protected environment" (Nicolaou 2003). This incubation period provides nascent entrepreneurs with various grants for equipment or technological upgrade as well as access to government-subsidized loans and training and consultation services.

Finally, advocates for Cypriot women microentrepreneurs call for a series of policies that recognize the dual demands of business development and household care and management. They explain that "the reconciliation of entrepreneurial activity and family life is a major impediment that needs to be addressed" (B.P.W. Cyprus 2000). Therefore, along with the standard recommendations of policies for increasing women's access to credit and training in skills and business development, there is a provision for childcare and family-friendly business hours, because the "gendered division of labor is an impediment to women's entrepreneurial success." These advocates also recommend that "men (already when boys) need to be taught that housework and child rearing must be dealt with as [a] shared responsibility of the two spouses and that parental leave should be implemented and fathers encouraged to take it" (B.P.W. Cyprus 2000).

Although microenterprise development is being promoted in Trinidad and elsewhere as a strategy for women to manage their dual roles as workers and caretakers, in the Republic of Cyprus efforts are being made to create policies that permit women the time and energy necessary for enterprise development. Generally, the social programs available to the Cypriot population, including family assistance policies, permit a higher quality of life than in many postcolonial nations.

CONCLUSION

Women's economic independence as a solution to poverty and unemployment is certainly an effort to be applauded, supported, and expanded. Yet this effort must address and influence national government policies so that they, in turn, can combat the worst effects of neoliberalism. Despite the plethora of arguments about the diminishing role of the state in the context of globalization, a comparison of the conditions for women microentrepreneurs in the Republic of Cyprus and the Republic of Trinidad and Tobago suggests that, in small island nations, policies that resist capitulation to neoliberalism and provide strong social programs are particularly beneficial to low-income women who often bear the brunt of the ills of globalization.

Greek Cypriot women continue to suffer from traditional gender ideology. With many of these women's economic activities embedded within family units, their labor and business skills are overlooked and unrecognized. Advocates of women's microenterprise development clearly identify the uneven distribution of household work as an impediment to enterprise development. Although Greek Cypriot women enjoy the relative economic comfort and access to social services that may reduce household labor, their entrepreneurial advancement is limited by gender ideologies that maintain carework and housework as their primary responsibility.

Although the Republic of Trinidad and Tobago has enacted a national program toward achieving gender equality, much of the support for women's microenterprises is framed as a strategy for women to co-manage a business and a household. This may be a response to the structure of Caribbean households in which women tend to be the heads of households. Microenterprise development appeals to policymakers as a method for promoting gender equity, yet it can overburden women with economic and household responsibilities, limiting their success as entrepreneurs.

Assisting women microentrepreneurs requires more than increasing women's access to loans and training in business skills. Indeed, the survival and expansion of women's microenterprises depends on the provision of ample social services that recognize the self-employed as workers who deserve access to the same benefits as formally employed workers. Yet in a neoliberal policy environment, nations like Trinidad and Tobago are forced to implement microenterprise development in lieu of providing other forms of social assistance.

A comparison of the socioeconomic conditions of Cyprus with those of the Republic of Trinidad and Tobago reveals a clear distinction in income inequality, poverty, and unemployment. Although these appear almost trivial in Cyprus, they are major concerns in Trinidad and Tobago. Greek Cypriot women microentrepreneurs clearly benefited from their government's decision to resist neoliberal reforms throughout the 1980s. In contrast, because of its indebtedness (incurred as a result of the implementation of U.S. policy recommendations), the government of Trinidad and Tobago had limited options in its response to global economic restructuring. It was forced to cut social expenditures and to open its economy to external competition. Protectionist policies with a high level of social services are quite possibly the best strategy for ensuring the survival of small island economies in the world system and for creating conditions under which even the most discriminated-against members of the population can live decently.

NOTE

I thank the interview participants for their time and information, which greatly contributed to the development of this book. I also gratefully recognize the fellowship awarded by the American Association of University Women, the Stasinos Research Grant awarded by the Inter-American University Consortium on Cyprus, and the Creative and Scholarly Research grant awarded by the Division of Sponsored Research at Florida Atlantic University.

6

Politicians, Think Tanks, and the Global Promotion of the "Wisconsin Model" of Welfare Reform

Ellen Reese

❀

In conferences and his relationships with the media, the governor [Tommy Thompson] showcases that Wisconsin and Milwaukee County benefited from W-2. We, who are up close, have seen the exacerbation of poverty and homelessness throughout Milwaukee County due to W-2. (Interview, homeless shelter worker, August 2002)

Since first taking office in 1987, Wisconsin's former governor Tommy Thompson implemented a series of bold welfare reform initiatives, including the first time-limited welfare program in the nation. His latest initiative, Wisconsin Works (W-2), replaced the state's Aid to Families with Dependent Children program in 1997 following the passage of the 1996 federal welfare reform act. W-2, which serves poor families, most of which are headed by women, upholds market principles through an elaborate system of regulations that are designed to ensure that "for those who can work, only work should pay" (Wisconsin Department of Workforce Development 1999, quoted in Smith-Nightengale and Mikelson 2000, 2).

In exchange for benefits, adult recipients of W-2 are expected to engage in at least forty hours of "welfare-to-work activities," although actual work hours are usually less (Dodenhoff 2004). Depending on their skill level and readiness for employment, clients are assigned to one of four rungs of W-2's employment ladder and given particular job assignments, job preparation and training activities, and support services by case workers, known as "Financial and Employment Planners" (Moore and Selkowe 1999, 9, 27). To further reinforce the idea that W-2 is a work-based program, disabled parents are served through a separate program (Institute for Wisconsin's Future 1998a, 2–4). Following the implementation of Pay for Performance and W-2, the state's welfare caseload declined dramatically, by 87 percent between 1993 and 1998 (Wiseman 1999, 19).

In this chapter, I explore how and why politicians and corporate-sponsored think tanks aggressively promoted the "Wisconsin" model of welfare reform, both nationally and in other Western industrialized nations, during the period from 1994 to 2005. Advocates of this model claimed that the state's sharp caseload decline demonstrated the effectiveness of tough rules and regulations for putting welfare mothers to work. Yet, this caseload decline was partly due to the state's booming economy in the late 1990s, which made it easier to find work. When economic conditions worsened, between 2000 and 2004, caseloads rose by 46 percent (Wisconsin Department of Workforce Development 2005, 11). W-2's promoters also provided a distorted image of the program's impacts on poor families, glossing over the hardships that it created and the structural barriers that kept low-income mothers in poverty. Combining insights from interviews with social service providers and welfare mothers and from surveys of current and former recipients of W-2, I examine the consequences of this program for poor families in Milwaukee, where most of the state's W-2 participants reside.[1] Far from being a model antipoverty program, W-2 failed to reduce poverty among, and caused tremendous hardships for, poor female-headed families.

THE NATIONAL AND GLOBAL PROMOTION OF W-2

The promotion of W-2 as a model program for the nation and other Western industrialized nations was part of a broader backlash against welfare that served multiple elite interests. Politicians' attacks on welfare mothers and the call for "get tough" welfare rules appealed to white voters' resentments against taxes and racist, classist, and patriarchal stereotypes of the poor that portrayed them as lacking "family values," lazy, and in need of greater discipline. Attacking welfare helped politicians to compete for white votes and took pressure off of them to address the structural barriers that kept mothers in poverty, such as racial discrimination, the shortage of living-wage jobs, and lack of affordable childcare for low-income workers. At the same time, restricting poor mothers' access to welfare and requiring them to work served business interests; it minimized their tax burdens and helped to ensure a ready supply of low-wage workers, who were increasingly in demand with the rise of neoliberalism and economic globalization. Business groups promoted welfare reform through their lobbyists as well as through conservative think tanks, mainly funded by wealthy donors and corporate contributions (Reese 2005; Stefancic and Delgado 1996).

Conservative think tanks were intimately involved in both the design and the promotion of Wisconsin's work-based welfare reforms. In the mid-1990s, the Thompson administration relied on researchers from the Hudson Institute, a conservative think tank, to design W-2 and then to evaluate its performance. Not surprisingly, the Hudson Institute's evaluations of the program, circulated among policymakers and the press, emphasized W-2's capacity to reduce welfare dependency (Hudson Institute 2002; Wilayto 1997). As the U.S. Congress geared up for the passage and reauthorization of the 1996 federal welfare reform act, various conservative think tanks, including the Heritage Foundation, the Heartland Institute, the Manhattan Institute, and the Wisconsin Policy Research Institute, promoted Wisconsin's welfare initiatives as model programs for the nation (Manhattan Institute 2002; Rector 1997; Stefancic and Delgado 1996, 86).

Thompson himself also played an active role in shaping welfare policy debates. As one observer described, "Thompson was a relentless campaigner for his welfare reform agenda. This was manifest in each of his statewide election contests, his legislative negotiations, his national policymaking roles, and his extensive interaction with the media. His message was so consistent that a *Chicago Tribune Magazine* cover story dubbed him 'Governor Get-a-Job'" (Hein 2002). Thompson's leadership on welfare issues contributed to his popularity among voters and politicians. After serving as the state's governor for three successive terms, Thompson was appointed by President George W. Bush as secretary of the Department of Health and Human Services in 2001. In this post, Thompson advocated more stringent work requirements for welfare mothers.

Advocates of W-2 also promoted the program as a model for other Western industrialized nations, many of which were seeking ways to reduce their rising welfare caseloads. Calls for work-based reforms, actively promoted through the international circulation of policymakers and corporate-sponsored think tanks' "policy experts," shaped the agendas of even center-to-left political parties. The rise of neoliberal doctrines, behavioral models of poverty, and other trends, whose importance varied across nations, combined to increase political support for these reforms (Handler 2004; Huber and Stephens 2001; Mendes 2003; Peck 2001; Swank 2001). As summarized by Joel F. Handler, such trends included "the decline of European economies in the late 1970s and 1980s, the aging population, changes in manufacturing, international[ization of] finance, globalization, growing deficits, and budgetary restraints" (2004, 12). In many countries, antiwelfare rhetoric and work-based reforms targeted programs serving the most stigmatized sectors of the poor, such as minority youth, immigrants, and single mothers (Bashevkin 2000; Handler 2004).

In 1997, the Hudson Institute promoted the virtues of the Wisconsin model of welfare reform through an international conference attended by experts from England, Germany, Holland, and Denmark who were interested in reforming welfare in their own countries (Flaherty, *Wisconsin State Journal,* November 21, 1997). "Germany, Austria, New Zealand.... Everyone is looking at Wisconsin to see how it is developing its [welfare] program. Wisconsin is famous around the world for it," claimed a manager at the New Zealand Employment Service attending another welfare conference held in Wisconsin in 1997, who was preparing for the overhaul of welfare in his own country (Sharma-Jensen, *Milwaukee Journal Sentinel,* May 7, 1997). Roland Koch, president of the upper house of the German parliament and governor of Hesse, led a delegation to Wisconsin, in part to learn more about W-2. Koch's welfare reform proposals, though rejected by the German parliament in favor of more moderate reforms, mimicked key features of W-2 (Hein 2002; Mayers, *Washington State Journal,* October 24, 1996). Under Tony Blair's leadership, British Labor Party officials carefully studied W-2, inviting several Wisconsin professors to their country to discuss it and later sending a group to Wisconsin to examine it (Carleton, *Capital Times,* March 14, 1998; Dresang, *Milwaukee Journal Sentinel,* March 19, 1998). Drawing on the advice of Wisconsin's welfare officials and experts, the Blair government enacted a number of work-based welfare reforms in the late 1990s (Mayers, *Wisconsin State Journal,* May 7, 1999). Dutch policymakers and advisers also visited Wisconsin, bringing back ideas that helped to shape the design of community-service job programs (Hein 2002). A Dutch reformer later spoke at a conference in Australia about the influence of the Wisconsin model within Europe (Hein 2002). Tommy Thompson was also invited to Australia as a featured speaker for the libertarian Center for Independent Studies. These speeches added fuel to mounting attacks on Australia's welfare state, leading to the adoption of work requirements for welfare recipients there in 2000 (*Cairns Post,* December 15, 2000; Mendes 2003, 42).

THE IMPACTS OF W-2 IN MILWAUKEE

Promoters of W-2 presented the program as a magic bullet for reducing welfare caseloads and putting poor people to work, glossing over the problems that it created. The negative consequences of W-2 were particularly evident in Milwaukee County, where the vast majority of its participants live.[2] Seventy-one percent of the county's W-2 participants are African American and, due to a high level of racial segregation, they are concentrated in the central city area where jobs, especially stable and living-wage jobs, are scarce. In the late 1990s, there were nearly five times as many job seekers as job openings in the central city, and severe transportation barriers prevented inner-city workers from obtaining jobs in the outlying suburban counties (Milwaukee Women and Poverty Public Education Initiative 2001, 6–7; Wisconsin Department of Workforce Development 1999, 1–4). The year that W-2 was implemented, the black unemployment rate for metropolitan

Milwaukee was nearly 17 percent, the highest rate among metropolitan areas in the Northeast and Midwest (Milwaukee Women and Poverty Public Education Initiative 2001, 5–6). Moreover, as service jobs replaced higher-paying manufacturing jobs, nearly 40 percent of the county's parents in 2000 were part of the "working poor" (Milwaukee Women and Poverty Public Education Initiative 2001, 2, 6). Job shortages, transportation barriers, racial discrimination, lack of affordable childcare, and low wages were formidable barriers for moving low-income mothers out of poverty—barriers not fully addressed by W-2.

Welfare Privatization

In 1997, public welfare departments in Milwaukee, along with those in eight other Wisconsin counties, lost their right to administer W-2 because they failed to reduce their caseloads quickly enough to meet the state's tough performance standards. Since then, Milwaukee's W-2 program has been administered through a market-based service delivery system in which private agencies compete to receive the state's welfare contracts. Initially, five private agencies were awarded W-2 contracts: three nonprofit agencies, United Migrant Opportunities, Opportunities Industrialization Center, and Employment Solutions (a division of Goodwill Industries), and two for-profit agencies, Maximus, Inc., and YW Works (an affiliate of YWCA) (Huston, *Milwaukee Journal Sentinel,* March 24, 1998; Smith-Nightengale and Mikelson 2000, 4). Between 1997 and 2001, W-2 agencies garnered nearly $78 million worth of unrestricted profits (Wisconsin Department of Workforce Development 2005, 16). Maximus gained additional profits by placing W-2 participants in jobs through its own temporary agency, Max Staff. Max Staff garnered fees for employing welfare recipients, and Maximus was paid for the placements (Interview, 9to5 staff, June 2001).

Milwaukee's welfare contractors had strong financial incentives to reduce the caseload. As one welfare advocate explained, "The measure of job performance for the agencies was moving people off. The lower the number of people getting benefits, the more the agency could gain in terms of bonuses and incentives." Given these incentives, it is not surprising that W-2 agencies used all sorts of diversionary tactics and policies to deny benefits to welfare applicants and recipients. For example, applicants for aid were encouraged to ask their relatives, friends, and churches for help and to return in thirty days. Other recipients were turned away because they were classified as "job ready" (ready to work), regardless of whether they had received any job offers (Institute for Wisconsin's Future 1998a).

By 2005, three of the county's five W-2 agencies had become involved in highly publicized scandals, leading to the discontinuation of several agencies' contracts. In 2000, Goodwill's Employment Solutions and Maximus came under heavy fire for improperly billing the state for nearly a million dollars. Auditors questioned hundreds of thousands of dollars' worth of other expenses, including expenses incurred while welfare contracts were being sought in other states (Schultze, *Milwaukee Journal Sentinel,* October 14, 2000; Schultze, *Milwaukee*

Journal Sentinel, June 8, 2001). Maximus weathered the storm, agreeing to a financial settlement with the state, but Goodwill's Employment Solutions, seeking to avoid negative publicity, gave up their W-2 contract (Schultze, *Milwaukee Journal Sentinel,* 2001). In 2005, Opportunities Industrialization Center closed its offices in response to a criminal investigation of its operations and criticisms by state auditors. State officials claimed the agency misused at least $2.4 million, including $500,000 for an illegal kickback scheme involving a state senator (Schultze, *Milwaukee Journal Sentinel,* February 26, 2005; Wisconsin Department of Workforce Development 2005, 12).

Milwaukee's Workfare State

> W-2 was portrayed initially as a program that would result in people moving out of poverty.... Let's just say what it actually is, which is a program that puts people to work and stops public assistance, and it doesn't matter what the work is. (Interview, 9to5 staff, June 2001)

Like other welfare reform programs around the nation, W-2 emphasized the importance of work, rather than education and training, for reducing poverty. A 1998 survey of 670 welfare-to-work (WTW) participants in Milwaukee found that most respondents were doing nothing but their job assignments and received no training or education. Most of these job assignments were in menial, low-wage jobs, such as food service, cleaning, or packing and sorting jobs (Institute for Wisconsin's Future 1998b, 11). Although Milwaukee's welfare department claimed these assignments provided on-the-job training, it was often minimal. As one participant explained, "At regular jobs, I have done factory work, packing, and cashiering. Through welfare, I have done the same type of work. Even though they call it training, I am already experienced in this work" (ACORN's W-2 Workers' Organizing Committee member, 1997). Describing other job assignments of W-2 participants, a welfare advocate said, "One of the things they used to have them do was count hangers in order to get a grant.... They're not giving them any skills" (Interview, 9to5 staff, June 2001). In 1999, only 16 percent of Milwaukee's W-2 participants were enrolled in Jobs Skills training programs (Milwaukee Women and Poverty Public Education Initiative 2001, 8). Later studies suggest that actual work participation among the state's W-2 participants declined over time, whereas participation in other activities increased. Nevertheless, only 7 percent of the state's W-2 participants received Job Skills training in the first six months of 2004 (Dodenhoff 2004; Wisconsin Department of Workforce Development 2005, 28).

The emphasis on work rather than on education and training made it difficult for W-2 participants to gain the credentials and skills that employers required for better-paying jobs. Participants in subsidized employment were allowed to spend only ten to twelve hours of their required forty hours of work activity per week in education and training, and the type of education and training allowed was tightly restricted. It was "usually restricted to a two-month preparation course for the high school equivalency test, English as a Second Language (ESL) courses, soft skills training in job preparedness, or on-the-job training" (Moore and Selkowe 1999, 1–2). Survey research found that more than 90 percent of Hmong welfare mothers in Milwaukee read little or no English, 60 percent have no formal education, and more than half sought job training; nevertheless, only 10 percent were receiving any skills training or English-language instruction. Two-thirds of these mothers were assigned to jobs requiring little training, such as cleaning, sorting, or packing jobs (Moore and Selkowe 1999, ii, 11).

Many welfare mothers enrolled in higher education and extended training programs were forced to quit them. In 1994, there were about 7,000 welfare recipients enrolled at the Milwaukee Area Technical College, but only 274 by 1997 (Institute for Wisconsin's Future 1998a, 4). Testimonies from former and current welfare mothers reveal their frustrations with the rules against long-term education and training. As one explained, "A lot of people are not able to attain their dreams and goals because they've had to cut everything short to get a minimum-wage job at Wendy's or McDonald's. Working in those places, no one is going to be able to become independent and support a family" (Testimony of W-2 participant for the Workers' Rights Board Hearing on W-2 in Milwaukee, Wisconsin, December 1997). Welfare advocates recalled examples of welfare recipients in associate degree programs, sometimes close to graduating, who were pulled out and put into minimum-wage jobs (Interview, 9to5 staff, June 2001). Even teen parents receiving W-2 complained about being pressured to find work rather than stay in high school (Huston, *Milwaukee Journal Sentinel,* March 28, 1998).

Work requirements were often rigidly enforced with little regard to their impacts on mothers or their children. As two former welfare mothers testified,

> I will have to move to a [homeless] shelter because my benefits were cut off mainly because I [have a] very high risk pregnancy (losing my baby possibly) and they still want me to work! I couldn't do it.
>
> A child gets sick and you cannot go to your W-2 work.... You will be sanctioned because it wasn't "good cause." (quoted in Milwaukee Women and Poverty Public Education Initiative 1998)

Studies suggest that 88 percent of former recipients in Wisconsin who exited welfare in 1995 and 1997 found work and were employed during the next three years, but only 42 percent were employed continuously over this period. Most former recipients were working full-time or close to full-time, but they were concentrated in low-wage jobs, mainly in service or retail trade. In Milwaukee, nearly one-third worked for temporary agencies (Smith-Nightengale and Mikelson 2000, 28–32). Only about one-fifth of former participants exiting W-2 between 1999 and 2002 lived above the poverty level a year after they left welfare. Although former recipients' incomes increased over time, most of those who exited W-2 in 1999 earned below-poverty wages in 2003. Many also cycled back into the W-2 system. About 52 percent of all W-2 recipients in subsidized placements in 2004 were returnees (Wisconsin Department of Workforce Development 2005, 5). Such outcomes are not surprising given that the W-2 system did little to restructure the low-wage labor market.

Difficulties in Obtaining Social Services

> Temporary job ended. Had to take cans in and clean up people's yards and buses. Have not received subsidized child care yet. Didn't receive [Food] Stamps for June or July or August. (former welfare mothers, quoted in Milwaukee Women and Poverty Public Education Initiative 1998)

According to W-2's "light touch" philosophy, case workers should not offer too much help to welfare applicants and clients because it would encourage dependency. As a result, case workers did not provide information about welfare services, such as Food Stamps or childcare, unless they were directly asked about them. Many recipients did not know their rights or hesitated to request services because of the stigmas associated with disabilities, substance abuse, domestic abuse, and poverty. As a result, W-2 participants and applicants often did not obtain services for which they were entitled (Interview, Community Advocates, June 2001).

Clients also found it difficult to communicate with case workers or got the bureaucratic "runaround" because of inadequate training for case workers and understaffing. As one advocate recalled, "The very first time I started to work on behalf of a client, I personally had to make probably about 30 phone calls before I got a return phone call" (Interview, HOSEA, June 2001). Surveys of former welfare mothers reported similar problems (Milwaukee Women and Poverty Public Education Initiative 1998). Despite laws requiring welfare agencies to provide language assistance to those with limited English proficiency, 70 percent of Hmong W-2 participants surveyed in Milwaukee indicated that they were unable to communicate verbally with case workers. Nearly 90 percent received written materials in English, even though (as noted above) more than 90 percent read little or no English (Moore and Selkowe 1999, 12–13, 19).

W-2 participants were even denied the supportive services, such as childcare, that were necessary for completing their work assignments. Despite an increase in subsidized childcare in Milwaukee, these programs were serving only about one-quarter of families eligible for them at the end of 1999 (Milwaukee Women and Poverty Public Education Initiative 2000, 2). As one welfare advocate explained, "They'll be assured that their W-2 placement will be there and their childcare will be set up and then come the first day of work there is no childcare. Then they can't get to work obviously, and it begins a cycle" (Interview, 9to5 staff, June 2001).

Survey responses from former welfare mothers also reported problems with obtaining childcare assistance. One pointed out that "trying to get a job is hard without child care with six kids and one on the way" (quoted in Milwaukee Women and Poverty Public Education Initiative 1998). And a Milwaukee childcare provider claimed that the assistance given to W-2 participants for transportation and childcare expenses was insufficient: "The mothers complain because they have no time or money to get their kids to the center and to work on time" (Testimony of childcare provider for the Workers' Rights Board Hearing on W-2 in Milwaukee, Wisconsin, December 1997). Many W-2 participants were also forced to use substandard childcare facilities because reputable centers were full (Interview, Community Advocates, June 2001).

Welfare departments' failure to provide adequate, affordable childcare for WTW participants took a considerable toll on the children involved. The consequences were sometimes fatal. For example, a 13-year-old child with cerebral palsy, Deandre Reeves, accidentally scalded himself to death in a bath tub after his mother, a WTW participant without access to affordable childcare, left him in the care of her teenage son. The teenager was downstairs making lunch when Deandre, unable to call for help, turned on the hot-water faucet. Even though Yvette Reeves, a single mother, was previously exempt from work in order to take care of her disabled son during the summer months, her case worker, following Wisconsin's tough new WTW regulations, required her to work for Pizza Hut (McBride, *Milwaukee Journal Sentinel,* June 16, 1998).

Material Deprivation

Interviews with former W-2 participants provide harrowing descriptions of the material deprivations they experienced after losing cash aid (quoted in Milwaukee Women and Poverty Public Education Initiative 1998). One reported: "My life is very sad. I spent some days without food so that my children have a little." Another explained how she was surviving after being denied welfare: "I sell cans and popsicles sometimes. I beg [for] food in many places. I beg [for] clothing for my children." A third described her personal observations of the impacts of W-2 in this way: "W-2 has broken up families.... People evicted, not eating, a living hell."

Restrictive welfare policies and practices contributed to a rise in the demand for emergency shelter and food. Although the number of working-poor families in Milwaukee County increased, 28,000 fewer children received Food Stamps in 2000 compared to 1993. Meanwhile, the demand for emergency food rose (Milwaukee Women and Poverty Public Education Initiative 2001, 1–2). An investigation by federal U.S. Department of Agriculture officials determined that much of the decline in Food Stamp cases in Milwaukee was due to confusion over eligibility rules and W-2 agencies' failure to inform low-income parents of their right to these services and to process applications in a timely fashion (Norman, *Milwaukee Journal Sentinel,* August 4, 1999; Adam, *Milwaukee Journal Sentinel,* November 23, 1999).

In 1999, 40,000 eviction notices were sent to families in Milwaukee, many of whom were former W-2 recipients who could not pay their rent. Homeless shelters could not keep up with the rising demand for beds. By 2000, despite efforts to increase emergency shelter space, sixty to seventy families were on waiting lists for emergency shelter at any one time (Milwaukee Women and Poverty Public Education Initiative 2000, 1). The demand for emergency shelter was particularly acute among single women, many of whom were forced to give up custody of their children. As a welfare advocate explained, "We had an emergency overflow shelter that was open usually in the winter and only on the bitter-cold nights—it was in a church basement. That shelter has been open now for two years straight" (Interview, Community Advocates, June 2001). Earlier, a shelter worker had told me that other women "had their children taken from them, found in their destitution and poverty (as many have been found), guilty of neglect of their children. They've had their children removed from them to foster care or even to adoption" (Interview, Repairers of the Breach, September 2000). Three former welfare mothers at this shelter shared their own stories about giving up custody of their children:

> My daughter? She's in foster care. I asked them to put her in foster care because I didn't want her to be in this homeless situation with me like this. This ain't right for no child.

> My life has been going up and down and I don't want her going through all of that because she's only three. If her life goes up and down with mine, she won't be stable.

> My daughter is eight. She's in the third grade. Ain't no way I would have my baby out on the streets. It's too rough for me as it is and it would be even worse for her (September 2000).

Within a five-month period between 1998 and 1999, the Red Cross homeless shelter in Milwaukee reported 386 different women seeking shelter, more than half of whom had minor children. Many of these children were living in foster care or with relatives (Milwaukee Women and Poverty Public Education Initiative 1999, 7). Another report estimates that about 5 percent of former welfare recipients in Wisconsin had to give up custody of their children (Gordon 2001, 4; Patriquin 2001, 87).[3]

Material deprivation, including homelessness, resulted from the implementation of various types of restrictive welfare policies and practices. Delays in obtaining benefits or services also caused homelessness. As one service provider recalled, "People, when they would initially sign up for the program, could have up to two months where they wouldn't receive a full check. So, we got a lot of calls from tenants wanting to know how they were going to pay their rent without help out there" (Interview, Community Advocates, June 2001).

Former welfare mothers provided similar stories of delayed assistance: "I have a 24 hour notice to move because I couldn't get child care and W-2 to help me at the time" and "When we needed help, it was too late and I got evicted" (quoted in Milwaukee Women and Poverty Public Education Initiative 1998). In some cases, recipients—many of whom suffer from depression, traumas related to sexual abuse and violence, learning disabilities, and addictions—were sanctioned because they were unable to fulfill stringent program requirements (Milwaukee Women and Poverty Public Education Initiative 1999; Interview, Repairers of the Breach, September 2000).

It is difficult to know how common these various causes of benefit loss or denial were in Milwaukee, but the results of a 1998 survey of 134 former welfare mothers are suggestive. Respondents had open Food Stamp cases and no reported income, and they had not received cash benefits for at least two months for reasons other than employment. According to the respondents' self-reports, 34 percent lost their benefits due to case worker error, 29 percent because of sanctions, and 28 percent because they were deemed "job ready." Nearly one-third, or 29 percent, of these respondents had been threatened with an eviction in the previous two months, and 18 percent reported that at least one person in their family had gone without food for a day. More than one in ten of these former welfare mothers reported that they had a child who lived with someone else or in foster care (Milwaukee Women and Poverty Public Education Initiative 1998, 9–10).

Even families that received benefits experienced tremendous material hardship. As a local childcare provider described: "With a few families I can see that the children are not getting enough food or they are wearing the same clothes every day. One poor baby didn't have a winter jacket, so we bought him one" (Testimony of childcare provider for the Workers' Rights Board Hearing on W-2 in Milwaukee, Wisconsin, December 1997).

The material deprivations caused by W-2 were concentrated among blacks, who made up most of the county's W-2 cases. Within the first year of W-2's implementation, black infant mortality rose 37 percent, compared to an 18 percent increase countywide (Milwaukee Women and Poverty Public Education Initiative 2000, 1). Hmong welfare mothers, most of whom have five children or more, also experienced tremendous hardships under W-2's flat-grant system, which did not take family size into account. A survey of this population found that "fully 80 percent of respondents stated that their lives are worse under W-2, with three out of four saying they have less income and over half saying they have less food." One-third of these respondents claimed that they ran out of food during the past six months (Moore and Selkowe 1999, ii).

THE FUTURE OF W-2

Despite the well-financed, aggressive promotion of the "Wisconsin model" of welfare reform, there has been resistance to it. Within Milwaukee, welfare recipients and their advocates won a number of minor victories that curbed some of the worst abuses of the W-2 program. For example, in response to heavy public criticism and pressure from federal agencies, W-2 agencies increased their outreach to the poor about the services available to them and hired more bilingual staff to better serve Hmong clients. The state also took measures to increase its oversight of W-2 agencies in response to public controversies surrounding agencies' mismanagement of public funds. Tireless advocacy by Legal Aid lawyers also improved the appeals process for W-2 applicants and recipients who were unfairly denied benefits. However, support for W-2 is remarkably persistent within Wisconsin's legislature despite its inability to significantly reduce poverty and the scandals surrounding its implementation by private agencies.

Other Western industrialized countries, where public support for welfare spending is significantly higher than in the United States, have adopted softer versions of the "Wisconsin model." Even in Canada and Great Britain, where support for workfare is higher than in other Western industrialized countries, WTW programs have imposed less severe sanctions, especially on mothers, and provided more training opportunities compared to U.S. welfare programs (Handler 2004; Peck 2001). Furthermore, the international promotion of W-2 is significantly limited to the global North; the implementation of W-2 would have represented a huge improvement in the safety net for many nations in the global South, where welfare is lacking or subject to severe cutbacks through structural adjustment programs. Despite these limits in the diffusion of W-2, the spread of work-based welfare reforms across Western industrialized nations has been remarkably quick.

Political support for WTW requirements and welfare cutbacks reflects a powerful interest in maintaining a ready supply of cheap labor and in minimizing taxes within an increasingly competitive global economy. It also reflects punitive attitudes toward poor racial minorities, immigrants, and female-headed households (Peck 2001; Reese 2005). Unfortunately, given this context, the well-financed promotion of the "Wisconsin model" tends to drown out the voices of those most affected by the W-2 system and their advocates.

NOTES

1. All interviews took place in Milwaukee, Wisconsin, unless otherwise indicated.

2. In 1994, 57 percent of welfare recipients resided in Milwaukee County. By 2004, 80 percent did so (Smith-Nightengale and Mikelson 2000, 26; Wisconsin Department of Workforce Development 2005, 4).

3. Following passage of the 1996 federal welfare reform act, many states used welfare funds to screen sanctioned recipients to determine if their children were at risk of abuse or neglect. According to a national law passed in 1997, if children stay in the foster care system for fifteen out of the past twenty-two months, their mothers will permanently lose custody of them (Mink 2001, 87).

7

Service Provisioning as Political Activity

Struggles for Citizenship in Britain's Declining Welfare State

Tracy Fisher

❋

Most people don't know what it means to be a citizen in this country [England]. We don't have a constitution here ... or a Bill of Rights, or anything. So we're just trying to find somewhere or something to hang our hats on. Black people (in particular), women, and other ethnic minorities [*sic*] know what it's like to be excluded, but not necessarily what it feels like to be a citizen. (Katherine,[1] community worker and activist, London, England)

Katherine, a community worker and activist with whom I spoke in the summer of 2003, has been concerned about issues of inequality, race, class, and gender for nearly twenty years in London.[2] Her statement above reflects what it means to be a citizen at large in Britain, while at the same time echoing the exclusionary tensions that lie at the core of citizenship. This quotation emphasizes that whereas people in Britain generally do not know, or have a tangible sense of, what it really means to be a citizen, black people, other ethnic minorities[3] (e.g., South Asians and Africans), and poor, working-class women have experienced exclusion and know what it feels like *not* to be a citizen. It is precisely citizenship's inherently contradictory ties to equality and inequality, belonging and (un)belonging, that continue to make this concept important at several levels—theoretical, political, social, and cultural.

Citizenship—its inclusionary and exclusionary forces and its universalistic ideals—is located at the heart of competing discourses that range from human rights to the devolution of welfare, labor markets, and social movements. Citizenship sheds light on the relationships between the state and social movements, on the relationships between the state and individuals, on collective organization, and on the ways in which these relationships are fundamentally shaped by gender, race, and class. Debates around what constitutes citizenship are critical because they speak to the limits of an identity politics based on essentialized and exclusivist notions of, for example, gender, race, or culture. One of the key dimensions of citizenship includes the struggles that those excluded have been involved in, and the ways in which people actively participate in processes of citizenship-making.

This chapter examines the ways in which some poor and working-class women of color in Britain experience citizenship, as well as the ways in which they claim rights and entitlements in the context of a welfare state that is being transformed. Transformations specifically connected to the complex impacts of globalization are central in directing my attention to the relationship between citizenship and women's activism as both a scholarly concern and an issue of social justice. Attention to this case raises such questions as: What are the ways in which neoliberal policy is dismantling citizenship rights? How are grassroots organizations responding to the devolution of state welfare in Britain? These questions have emerged from my ongoing ethnographic fieldwork on the transformation of black women's grassroots organizations alongside shifts in Britain's political economy over the past thirty years.

My methodological strategies involved interviews, collection of oral/life narratives, archival and historical research, and participant observation; and I used ethnographic fieldwork to pay close attention to vernacular terms and practices as well as to identify people's own categories of analysis relating to activism, empowerment, and their critiques of power (Gender and Cultural Citizenship Working Group 2003). I argue that in Britain there is a syncretic relationship between grassroots organizations and the state (Fisher 2001). Alongside shifts in Britain's political economy, grassroots organizations have transformed from highly mobilized entities to service providers.[4] Using the case of the Southwark Black Women's Centre, I examine the complex yet valuable role of state-funded grassroots groups as service providers. Such organizations provide services to the community in the face of social and political-economic transformations as well as the gradual erosion of social welfare. More generally, I explore the linkages among neoliberalism, women's community-based activism, and the ways in which people experience citizenship. In so doing, I use service provisioning within a community-based organization as a lens through which to understand people's own sense of citizenship and "the political" in Britain. In my discussion of one long-standing community-based organization in London, I argue for a more nuanced understanding of the ways in which women engage in political activities for themselves and for their geographical, political, or racial-ethnic communities. Ultimately, my aim in this chapter is to unravel the complex relationships between individuals and collectivities and to examine the ways in which these groups both indirectly and directly engage with the state.

NEOLIBERALISM AND WELFARE REFORM

In Britain, globalization in the form of neoliberalism, couched in the language of "welfare reform," has been a political-economic and ideological force in transforming Labour's social policy and the welfare state. New Labour's promise differs from Labour's old traditions by supporting a social policy that focuses on the individual. Rather than addressing structural problems of inequality in the society at large, New Labour's approach tends to individualize forms of poverty (Mullard 2000, 45). This Thatcher-like approach to welfare reform fundamentally reinforces boundaries based on race, ethnicity, class, culture, and gender.

The individualist discourse that accompanies this approach tends to emphasize personal responsibility, obligations, rights, and the individual experience. For example, it is the individual who is responsible for finding and securing employment. The discourse constructs a false dichotomy between "active" (positive) and "passive" (negative) forms of welfare. Active welfare citizens desire to move from "welfare to work" and are constructed against workless, passive welfare citizens/dependents. This approach deemphasizes the range of variables (i.e., race, gender) often articulated through "difference" that are critical in structuring, institutionalizing, and justifying inequalities. It leaves the individual solely responsible for his or her place in society and does not consider the importance of history, the role of the state, or shifting social, political-economic conditions. In actuality, then, this approach to welfare reform is not a break from Thatcherism but, rather, a continuation of neoliberal forms of policy.

REFLECTIONS ON CITIZENSHIP

In recent years, the concept of citizenship has been challenged on several fronts. Most reconceptualizations of citizenship question T. H. Marshall's classic formulation: "Citizenship is a status bestowed on those who are full members of a community. All who possess the status are equal with respect to rights and duties with which the status is endowed" (1950, 28–29). Citizenship references rights and entitlements associated with membership in a collectivity/community. This idealized notion of citizenship—the ideal of equal participation in a democratic community—has never been a reality. There are implicit assumptions about the notion of community—a false universalism, a homogeneity—that privilege assimilation and flatten voices and forms of politics that underscore difference, diversity, and/or dissent. Scholars such as Stuart Hall and David Held (1989) have shed light on the fact that racism and immigration have fueled citizenship debates for years. They describe the tension between citizenship's basic premise, which is rooted in ideals of universality and equality, and the current emphasis on difference and diversity.[5] One of the leading social analysts of citizenship, Ruth Lister (1997a, 1997b), contends that, overall, citizenship is a highly contested and significant concept that is often at the heart of struggles by those excluded from citizenry rights. She and other social analysts of citizenship have convincingly argued that the understanding of citizenship as a static bundle of rights and obligations is both an inclusionary and an exclusionary mechanism—one that is imbued with power and rooted in masculinity (e.g., Lister 1997a, 1997b; Walby 1994; Werbner and Yuval-Davis 1999) and whiteness (Glenn 2002; Hill Collins 1999; Lowe 1996; Paul 1997; Smith 1997).

In everyday life, citizenship intersects with various axes of stratification. Formal, legal-juridical aspects of citizenship often mask, rather than reveal, people's differential access to resources, their structural inequalities, and the positioning of the people in political-economic, social, and cultural realms. Moreover, such a focus often obscures the ways in which people experience citizenship in everyday life. For this reason, feminist scholars of citizenship (e.g., Lister 1997a, 1997b; Walby 1994; Werbner and Yuval-Davis 1999; Yuval-Davis 1997) have made the case that the exclusionary tensions inherent in the notion of citizenship, which result in barring women from full citizenship, must be located within a gendered analysis and grounded in a framework that analyzes other forms of inequality (see also Dietz 1992; Lister 1997a; Young 1989). In other words, in order to understand the ways in which citizenship has shaped and been shaped by, for example, race, gender, and class, we must analyze citizenship in relation to race, gender, and class in the larger social, political-economic context.

As Evelyn Nakano Glenn's (2002) work brilliantly illustrates, the formation of the United States serves as an example to underscore the exclusionary tensions that have barred women, people of color, and the poor from full citizenship. Historically, people in the United States have been differentially racialized and categorized along the spectrum of citizenship. This country has a long history of defining the characteristics of its citizens (and of citizenship) in terms of gender (as men, as masculine), race (as white), and class (as white "nondependent" property owners). Citizenship permitted access to and ownership of land. It also helped reinforce naturalized notions of territory and rationalized clear distinctions between "American" citizens (white propertied men) and "other" noncitizens (people of color, women, the enslaved, and the poor). Thus, citizenship was an interdependent construction that was defined against, and gained meaning through, the oppositional concept, the noncitizen (Glenn 2002, 20). Through colonial and imperial conquest, annihilation, and labor that was imported and exploited, citizenship was simultaneously fixed and malleable in form, status, and practice.

SERVICE PROVISIONING AND BLACK WOMEN'S
COMMUNITY-BASED ACTIVISM

The story of Southwark Black Women's Centre (SBWC) begins in the early 1980s when a small group of women, initially part of an informal community group of concerned African, Caribbean, and black British women and men in London's borough of Southwark, decided to meet independently. Overshadowed by men, the small group of women felt both unheard and dismissed in the community group. The women's definitive decision to break away from the group was made during a period in which many people felt a heightened sense of politicization. The interlocking issues of gender, race, and class, as manifested through inequalities, exploitation, and differential access to resources, were central in the lives of these women. Such concerns served as the basis for collective action, and the result was the formation of a women's grassroots organization known as the Black Women's Action Group. The organization was formally launched in 1983—a time of conservative retrenchment, racial tension, protest, urban uprising, and radical activism. Emerging two years after the British Nationality Act, which restricted Asian citizenship in Britain, from its inception it mobilized women of color across racial and ethnic lines.

The small group of founders—from St. Lucia, Trinidad, Jamaica, and Nigeria—consisted of working-class women. The majority of these women had not attended a university. They were single mothers in their middle to late 20s who lived in council housing on the Aylesbury Estate[6] in south London's borough of Southwark. Most of the charter members, described by many as "just ordinary women in their homes," frequently met in a member's council flat (apartment) located on the Aylesbury. As the group grew in membership and participation, meeting in each other's flats was no longer possible, so they began to utilize space in one of the local schools for meetings. Within a couple of years, seed money from Southwark Council (a local-government entity), combined with public funds known as Urban Aid, enabled the group to lease and renovate an abandoned house.

A small street in an area surrounded by council flats was the home of the SBWC. The area is the home of many "diverse communities," or ethnic populations, each of which is geographically concentrated. Many participants (predominantly women, and of all ages) who came to the organization seeking services were from low-income and unemployed families. Like many other residents in the borough, they received public assistance in the form of child benefits, income support, and low-rent estate housing. In short, many of the people who utilized the SBWC's services were "on the dole," or had "signed on."[7] For this reason, a primary concern of the SBWC was women's access to employment. To this end, the SBWC provided training in personal development skills, interviewing techniques, résumé preparation, and back-to-work skills. With an emphasis on self-help and advocacy, the SBWC was also concerned with such issues as domestic violence, immigration, education, and healthcare. Members of the staff included the coordinator, an advice worker, two administrative workers, two permanent/full-time volunteers, and three adjunct staff counselors who were employed by an outside agency.[8] Service delivery counseling at the SBWC had grown over the years owing to the increasing number of referrals that the organization received from such outside community agencies as the Southwark Police Domestic Violence Unit and the Southwark Council for Community Relations (SCCR).[9]

The SBWC was located in south London's borough of Southwark. Today, 45 percent of Britain's ethnic minorities reside in London; in Southwark more than 40 percent of the 253,800 residents are considered ethnic minorities. Single-headed households comprise more than 40 percent of the total number of households—nearly twice the average in London at large. Forty-two percent of Southwark's residents live in council housing. And 7.8 percent of these residents are unemployed—more than double the average in England overall.

The Aylesbury Estate is adjacent to one of south London's most thriving markets—East Street, where two-bedroom flats sell for over £150,000[10] (Lemos 1999). Approximately half of the 10,000 residents on this estate, one of the largest in Europe, have lived there for over ten years, and most of them are either elderly or families with young children. Education levels here are low (e.g., 37 percent of 16- to 19-year-olds have no high school diploma), unemployment stands at 17 percent, and the crime rate is high. It is within this context that the SBWC provided services to the community for nearly two decades.

Throughout the 1980s, the SBWC, then known as the Black Women's Action Group (BWAG), participated in various community-based activities and established links with other grassroots organizations. BWAG was instrumental in terms of focusing on race and gender, particularly in the areas of housing and employment. As a result, the BWAG pressured Southwark Council to hire black women employees and, at the same time, lobbied the Council to change adoption and foster care practices, which have traditionally neglected black families.

The BWAG addressed occurrences of racial injustice and inequality not just in Britain but throughout the world. For instance, it participated in antiapartheid movements and demonstrations in London. This example and others speak to the BWAG's more radical ideological and political position throughout the 1980s.

During this time, however, Britain's overall political-economic and social context continued to shift to the Right. Consequently, "a flattening of the Left" occurred, an outcome that included the demise of the Greater London Council and marked shifts in community activism. Grassroots organizations transformed. Some gradually disintegrated; others emerged. Many underwent changes in funding, converting them from highly mobilized entities to service providers, resulting in shifts in activism and politics. During this continuous shift to the Right, BWAG transformed from a more radical activist, service provider organization to a group that recognized (1) a dramatically significant decline in social services, (2) a tightening of resources distributed to grassroots organizations concerned with issues of gender and race, and (3) an overall conservative restructuring of state welfare.

This shift was marked in the early 1990s, when the Black Women's Action Group changed its name to the Southwark Black Women's Centre. This occurred not long after the abolition of the Greater London Council, which had redistributed resources to communities and groups that traditionally had been provided with fewer resources despite greater needs (e.g., women and ethnic minorities). Several members commented that the name change echoed the organization's conflict over being associated with militarism, radical feminism, and feminist ideals; thus it was part of the organization's overall self-critique. The name change also reflected the organization's strategic effort to survive within a neoliberal context that was fostering continuous cuts in funds distributed to community-based groups in the public sector.

In the next section I discuss the type of service provisioning activities with which the SBWC was concerned—a topic that provides a good point of entry for analyzing (1) the ways in which people are made to feel as if they are second-class citizens and (2) service provisioning as a form of political activism.

RACISM, SECOND-CLASS CITIZENSHIP, AND SERVICE PROVISIONING

It was a cool damp day in May 1999 when Ruth, a community worker and St. Lucian woman in her 50s, and I arrived to survey the repairs needed in Mrs. Mukherjee's council house in the Lambeth borough of London. Mrs. Mukherjee, a Bengali Hindu woman in her late 30s, who was "on the dole" at this time, welcomed us into her house. As we entered, the front room—overcrowded with furniture—was immediately before us. Ruth commented that there was indeed enough furniture in this house for two homes and/or two families. She told us that "around four" people lived in this space. As we stood momentarily amidst the crowded furniture, I realized that this was a multipurpose room. It was used as a bedroom, and it was also an extension of the kitchen as it included a refrigerator. Subsequently, we noticed that the ceiling was on the verge of collapse and that the doorframe leading into the kitchen was detached. In the kitchen we saw large patches of brown discoloration on the ceiling, a clear indication of water damage. It was then that Mrs. Mukherjee quietly said, "These are [some of] the concerns I've been telling you about. How do they [the Council] expect us to live like this?" As we walked up the stairs leading to the second floor, a bubble-like effect on the walls surrounded us—again, caused by water damage. In the master bedroom of this small two-bedroom house the ceiling was cracked, and under our feet the floorboards were warped and had gaps in between them. From the hallway we peeked into a small bathroom and saw a leaky toilet. At this point Ruth firmly stated, "This house is definitely in need of repair, but you see the Council does this kind of stuff to Black and [South] Asian people here. This is how they treat them!" We went back downstairs to the kitchen to discuss the situation.

Although the local housing authority agreed to relocate Mrs. Mukherjee, they wanted to move her to Rotherhithe—an area of London where she feared that her family would suffer from racist attacks. According to Mrs. Mukherjee, the housing authority told her that because she did not agree with the Council's suggestion to move to Rotherhithe, she forfeited her opportunity to improve her living conditions. As Ruth talked to Mrs. Mukherjee regarding several possible scenarios, one of which was to be placed in the borough of Lewisham (a more racially diverse area), Mrs. Mukherjee became extremely upset, began to cry, and explained that she was tired of "going back and forth" with the housing authority. She stated that she suffered from depression, was on antidepressants, and was very afraid that she could not emotionally withstand several moves.

Ruth's comment regarding the treatment of people of African and Asian descent reflects the racism and discrimination they experience in Britain. Mrs. Mukherjee's comment and condition reflect her fragile emotional state, which was exacerbated by her living conditions and her struggles with the local housing authority. Both comments reflect the racialized and gendered dimensions of marginalization, particularly as it applies to people of the Black and South Asian diaspora in Britain, and, in so doing, provide a platform on which to rethink agency, political activity, politics, and citizenship.

As an advice worker, Ruth provided outreach, advice, and assistance on such issues as housing, immigration, welfare benefits, and domestic violence. She was often the liaison between women seeking help and the local authorities. Like many of her colleagues, she had no previous involvement in black women's organizations before working at the SBWC. According to Ruth, "In 1983 there was nowhere to receive advice in the community.... [W]omen had no help in the community" (Interview by author, September 1998). While reminiscing about her early years in England, she told me: "When I was younger, there was nowhere or [no] one to turn [to] ... to seek help. And that was difficult. I had no one to show me how this country worked" (Interview by author, September 1998). Ruth's statements, about isolation and lack of support networks, speak to the necessity of black women's community-based organizations and the lack of information in the community. Her comments suggest how a lack of knowledge, information, and procedures regarding housing benefits, childcare, and social welfare programs engender a feeling of marginality.

Ruth worked with Mrs. Mukherjee for a few months, helping her as she waged a long-term struggle with the local housing authority to have repairs made on her council house. The housing authority suggested that she move to another borough. The waiting list for council houses in Lewisham was very long, and, in reality, a transfer to a council house in Rotherhithe would have been the quickest solution. Ultimately, Mrs. Mukherjee decided to take up the housing authority's offer to move to Rotherhithe; indeed, she has lived there as of the summer of 2000. Unfortunately, the SBWC did little in the way of follow-up with her after she moved.

Mrs. Mukherjee's case was not unusual. For the women of the SBWC, such outreach visits were part of the organization's overall service provisioning activities. The SBWC and other community-based organizations like it hold local authorities accountable and demand rights, entitlements, and public services for those most excluded—low-income people, ethnic minorities, the unemployed, "the poor," and women.

Mrs. Mukherjee's case serves as just one example of the racialized and gendered dimensions of (un)belonging, in relation not only to the nation-state but also to the welfare state. It is in this arena that community organizations such as the SBWC wage battles with regard to citizenship. Below I provide a different example detailing the extent to which South Asian women of Southwark experienced a sense of isolation and (un)belonging.

The Bangladeshi Group

During Ruth's years at the SBWC she was perhaps best known for her outreach efforts in the South Asian or, more specifically, Bengali Muslim community. Ruth helped many Bengali users of the Centre, who expressed a reluctance to seek help from other local South Asian community organizations. Although they may share certain cultural tendencies with these organizations, differences in class propelled many of them toward the SBWC because, as one Bengali Muslim woman put it, "[Here] they treat us as equal, they do not judge." Bengali Muslim women's reluctance to seek help from South Asian organizations is also due to the tremendous national and religious anti-Muslim bias confronting them. Therefore, not surprisingly, many Bengali Muslim women felt uncomfortable at South Asian women's organizations whose membership is primarily non-Muslim.

The Bangladeshi people who utilized the SBWC lived on the nearby Aylesbury Estate. Over the years, this community viewed the SBWC as an important resource. Women told me that the SBWC was "an important place," "a place where we can get good and kind help," "where we feel comfortable." The group—created for Bangladeshi men, women, families, and children—met once a week for two to three hours. The largest subset of members was made up of married women, mothers, unemployed women, and recent immigrants. Most were practicing Muslims, and many of the women did not speak English fluently.

During my fieldwork I met with some of these women as well as with Nilana, a Bangladeshi volunteer who taught English as a Second Language (ESL) classes to South Asians at the SBWC. I learned that many of the women in the Bangladeshi Group felt very isolated and lonely and wondered whether this, perhaps, affected them the most emotionally. Responding to my inquiry, Nilana explained the following to me:

> Because many of the women who utilize the Group have very little confidence, they are not confident to go to places far from the Aylesbury Estate, where they live. Many of the husbands work while the wives stay at home. Also, because many are poor, receive income support, or are unemployed, they do not have the bus fare to travel around the city. They do not speak English well and have problems with basic services. Without this Centre, they would stay at home all of the time and feel psychologically depressed. Because Katherine and Ruth (in particular) are friendly and welcoming, these women feel comfortable. In the Group they have a sense of community because on the estate they are more

spread out. Because of the Centre, they are gaining confidence and are getting information regarding agencies, advice centers, health centers, and a better life. (Interview by author, May 1999)

A close reading of these comments reveals the significance of the Bangladeshi Group, particularly in the context of empowering communities and citizenship-making. The collective experience of marginalization and alienation, the increased number of Bangladeshis on the nearby estate, and the increased number of Bangladeshis seeking services from the SBWC inspired the creation of the Bangladeshi Group. Similarities in class, the SBWC's proximity to the Aylesbury housing, and the fact that the women did not experience racism at the SBWC were factors that encouraged them to continue using the organization's services. Race, class, and gender—both here and in the larger social, political, and economic context in Britain—shaped the ways in which these women individually and collectively experienced citizenship and (un)belonging.

Nilana's comments also bring to light the difficulties that immigrants encounter upon migrating to a new place. For example, limited English proficiency causes them to feel marginalized and dislocated. They experience a heightened sense of their differential positioning to others, particularly those whose first language is English. And the working poor and unemployed, in particular, have limited options. The members of the Bangladeshi Group were acutely aware of their status as immigrants vis-à-vis the state and the society at large. On the one hand, a lack of resources limited their freedom and mobility in London, and the language barrier created the daily constraints associated with (un)belonging in Britain (e.g., How does one access services?) On the other hand, however, the state-funded SBWC provided the Bangladeshi Group a friendly space in which to meet and to receive emotional support, information about social services, and overall knowledge to empower their lives.

Redefining Citizenship and Political Activism

Important in feminist approaches to citizenship is a redefinition of citizenship and "the political" that encompasses what is traditionally considered to be informal politics. Here the expanded domain of political struggle and experience, along with the ways in which people define themselves and make claims for full rights and entitlements, is most significant, for it is in this arena that women are often the leaders in the struggles of marginalized groups (Lister 1997a, 1997b). This expanded notion of citizenship and the political disrupts traditional definitions and emphasizes oppositional struggles and the various forms of politics used by those most often marginalized.

The ways in which people experience citizenship in everyday life are embedded in the ways in which race, gender, and nation are played out in the larger social, political, and economic context. The SBWC not only addressed issues of social injustice but also educated the communities and individuals who sought services from the Centre. In this process they expanded the realm of politics and agency. According to Katherine, "What we [at the SBWC] do *is* political in a nontraditional way. Many people, however, may not see our work as a form of political activity. We enlighten people about local authorities, policies, the government and things like that. It's a way of politicizing people" (Interview by author, September 1998). Katherine's statement clearly reflects the belief that service provisioning should be understood as a form of political activity. The ability to provide long-term service to the community despite shifts in Britain's political economy is, in part, what distinguished the SBWC from other black women's organizations that folded. This emphasis on service provision has been a powerful vehicle for the politicization of both its members and the people it served. As a form of politicization, the commitment to service provision was the SBWC's main priority. However, as I explain in detail in the next section, the organization's agency was limited. In recognizing this form of political activism as different from mass political mobilization, we gain insight into broader definitions of politics.

NEOLIBERALISM, CIRCUMSCRIBED AGENCY, AND CITIZENSHIP

As a government-funded, community-based organization, the SBWC was inextricably tied to the state. This kind of intimacy sheds light on the ways in which neoliberalism as implemented through privatization effects community-based organizations. Below I suggest some overlapping arenas for reflection on these issues.

The Gradual Erosion of Social/Public Welfare

In the context of neoliberal policies, the role of the state in providing social services is dramatically declining. Neoliberal decentralization policies, which call for reductions in healthcare and social service provisioning, are a reflection of processes in which government policies shift the responsibility of public administration from the state to the local and regional levels. In Britain, numerous government proposals support this move to privatization—in which the state itself shifts from serving as the direct provider of public/social services to being the commissioner of services (Gutch 2005). The SBWC, as a service provisioning organization, fits squarely within such decentralization processes. As a state-funded organization, it provided services primarily to women of low-income, poor, working-class, and ethnic minority communities. In doing so, it served a primary function of the state.

Circumscribed Agency

Although the SBWC's commitment to service provisioning, making communities more politically aware and knowledgeable, was long-standing, the organization helped people *negotiate* the system, not radically transform or contest it. Despite its efforts to hold local authorities accountable, its agency was limited in demanding that the councilors (members of the local authority) take their issues to the next level in government. Controlled political activity is also directly connected to organizations that are geographically accountable to their locality and are solely involved with small-scale, localized struggles. This aspect of restriction is in marked contrast to organizations in the 1970s and 1980s that attempted fully to engage with struggles in the larger national and international context.

Cycles of Dependency, or Working In and Against the State?

Community-based organizations that receive state funding continue to be a controversial issue on several fronts. Some social scientists (e.g., Solomos and Back 1995) have analyzed the role that funding has played in co-opting grassroots struggles by turning activists into service providers; others (e.g., Sudbury 1998, 82–85) argue for a more critical analysis and suggest that organizations that receive state funds are engaged in a dynamic relationship with the state and often are able to challenge local authority. Sudbury (1998, 83) makes the case that when we accept the "idea of a simple causal relationship between funding and political censorship" we have failed to see the political acts of those highly mobilized groups, which are claiming rights to such funds. Both approaches highlight the complexities and contradictions involved in receiving state funding.

Community-based organizations must fulfill several bureaucratic requirements in order to receive funds—a time-consuming process, as several members of the SBWC pointed out. Indeed, administrative bureaucracy takes away valuable time needed to recruit and cultivate new members, a key dimension of community-based activism. Organizations that find themselves dependent on the local authority's resources for support are also in a precarious position with respect to challenging structures within the state that could impact funding.

The Gradual Erosion of Welfare and Citizenship

The SBWC bore the brunt of Britain's gradual move to privatization, especially during the final years of the organization's existence. In 2002, after providing services to the community for nearly twenty years, the SBWC folded. This closure raises numerous questions about state-funded organizations and internal conflicts within community-based groups, but it also has implications for citizenship and citizenship-making. Since the closure of the SBWC, the local authority has neither taken measures to provide the services that the organization offered to the communities nor ensured that services are being provided elsewhere. The "citizens" themselves are of little concern to the state. Indeed, we are left to wonder to what extent the state is reinforcing their marginalization and social exclusion. How will they negotiate their way through the system?

CONCLUSION

The work of service provisioning at the SBWC addressed women's very personal experiences of disenfranchisement and entitlement. In the process, "on the ground" experiences of citizenship, (un)belonging, and inequality were highlighted. As we have seen, one example involved Mrs. Mukherjee, who waged a battle with the local housing authority. It was Ruth at the SBWC who assisted Mrs. Mukherjee and made the case that the condition of Mrs. Mukherjee's house was part of the larger racialized and gendered dimension of discrimination and (un)belonging in the British context. In addition, it was Ruth who assisted, advised, and negotiated on Mrs. Mukherjee's behalf. A second example involved the collective experiences of marginalization, which compelled many Bangladeshi women to use the SBWC as a place of refuge and a source for community-building. In both of these cases, although the women experienced second-class citizen status, they were exposed through the SBWC to other means of becoming active agents in transforming their lives, and in doing so they actively participated as citizens.

By situating the SBWC within the larger political-economic context of Britain we not only gain insight into the subtle shifts brought about by globalization but also, ultimately, become able to grasp the rather complicated set of issues related to political activity, funding, and citizenship—and how these shape and transform community groups.

NOTES

1. Pseudonyms have been used for the names of interviewees in this chapter.

2. I thank Amalia Cabezas, Ellen Reese, Margie Waller, Piya Chatterjee, and Priya Srinivasan for their incisive and critical comments on earlier drafts of this chapter. I also thank the Gender and Cultural Citizenship Working Group for their continued support. None of the above are responsible for the comments or omissions contained herein.

3. In the U.K. the term *ethnic minority* is used descriptively to refer to people of color.

4. In this case, service provision means giving advice, information, and service to individuals while at the same time addressing the underlying issues that may cause such problems. A service provider often acts as an advocate, negotiator, or referral and ensures that the person seeking services understands his or her rights and responsibilities in such areas as immigration, domestic violence, housing, and employment.

5. In the aftermath of 9/11 and the London bombings, "difference"—especially around issues of race—is vectored in Britain's state debates. In Britain there continues to be an onslaught of attacks on British Muslims, Muslim communities, and the religion of Islam. Anti-Muslim prejudice is a current manifestation of racism in Britain.

6. An estate is typically a group or cluster of (often high-rise) government-run public housing structures. Commonly known as council flats, these structures are under the jurisdiction of the borough in which they're located. The Aylesbury Estate is regarded as one of the largest in Europe.

7. These are phrases used in the U.K. to describe someone who is on public assistance.

8. During the final years of the organization, six workers were employed for two specific government initiatives/projects—Southwark Parent and Child Educational Scheme and Sure Start.

9. Today, this entity is known as the Southwark Race and Equalities Council (SREC). The name changed from SCCR to SREC in 2001/2002.

10. £150,000 is approximately equivalent to $300,000.

III

Laboring Under Corporate Globalization: Case Studies

8

Neoliberalism, Globalization, and the International Division of Care

Joya Misra and Sabine N. Merz

❂

Across the globe, nannies watch small children play, caretakers push wheelchairs, and maids scrub floors. These scenes are repeated hundreds of thousands of times every day, across a wide range of countries and regions. And in many of these places, immigrant workers from different regions or countries—carry out much of this carework.

In Morocco, a young Berber woman in a pink uniform cleans the home of her employers, washing the clothing and linens by hand, and carefully hanging, pressing, and folding each item. In Austria, a Hungarian au pair works sixteen-hour days caring for three children under the age of 5, and must tend to her charges when they cry at night. In Saudi Arabia, a Sri Lankan woman washes, dresses, feeds, and cares for an elderly woman, in order to send remittances home to care for her two children and her mother. In New York, a Filipino man cares for a disabled man around the clock, afraid to leave for more than fifteen minutes at a time. In Nepal, a young girl is encouraged to migrate to Kathmandu, where she is promised the opportunity of schooling and good pay, but soon discovers that her employers have enslaved her.

Although their experiences vary in significant ways, these immigrant workers share some commonalities. Much of the work they do remains invisible to the outside world and is regarded as unskilled labor, although it is critical to daily life. Most of these workers are paid fairly little for their work, often well below a living wage. Many are also undocumented workers, so they have little opportunity to increase their wages or otherwise improve their working conditions. And all of these workers are hoping to make their own lives, and the lives of their families, better by taking part in an international system where immigrant workers provide care in wealthier regions and countries.

Carework includes taking care of children, the elderly, the sick, and the disabled, as well as doing domestic work such as cleaning and cooking. Although capitalism has always relied upon the unequal division of reproductive labor, based on gender, class, race/ethnicity, and nationality, the increased mobility of workers has exacerbated the global nature of these processes. There is a growing trend in the transnational identities of domestic workers, nannies and childcare providers, home healthcare workers, nurses, teachers, and other care providers who are part of these global chains of care (Ehrenreich and Hochschild 2002).

Immigrant women have provided care for wealthier families for centuries, but recent decades have witnessed an intensification of the economic, political, technological, cultural, legal, and other connections among states and societies that are associated with such care. Immigration patterns have substantially changed as workers have become more mobile (Sassen 1998a, 2003) and as the demand for carework has heightened, partly owing to middle-class women's increased labor market participation. Women currently account for more than half of all immigration flows, and in certain countries (such as Indonesia, the Philippines, and Sri Lanka) they strongly predominate (Koser and Lutz 1998; Organization for Economic Co-operation and Development 2001; Sassen 2003).[1] There has also been a significant expansion in immigration across countries, to North America, Europe, the industrializing countries in Asia, and oil-rich Middle Eastern countries. Workers come from South and Southeast Asia (particularly Sri Lanka, India, Myanmar, Thailand, the Philippines, and Indonesia) to the Gulf countries as well as to the newly industrialized countries of Asia. Workers emigrate from South and Southeast Asia (particularly the Philippines and Sri Lanka), Eastern Europe (particularly Russia, Ukraine, Romania, Poland, Albania, Bulgaria, and Moldova), Africa (particularly Morocco, Ethiopia, Somalia, and Nigeria), and Latin America and the Caribbean (particularly Ecuador, Dominican Republic, Peru, Guatemala, Colombia, Chile, and Jamaica) to Southern and Western Europe. And workers come from the Caribbean, Central America, and Mexico to the United States and Canada (Ehrenreich and Hochschild 2003, 275–280; see also Anderson 2000; Gamburd 2000; Hondagneu-Sotelo 2001). Indeed, this movement around the globe is increasing at such high rates that it is difficult to document all of the relevant immigration flows—a trend that supports Hondagneu-Sotelo's (2001, xii) argument that much carework has "left the hands of wives and mothers and has entered the global marketplace."

These immigration patterns also touch off new patterns of immigration known as "global care chains," which involve immigrant domestic workers employing other immigrant domestic workers (Hochschild 2001, 2004). In some instances, careworkers with more resources emigrate, leaving poorer women to provide care to family members left behind. Parreñas (2001a) shows how Filipina immigrants working in the United States or Italy employ rural immigrant Filipinas to care for their families at home. Similarly, Polish domestics working in Germany may hire Bulgarian domestics to care for their families in Poland (Lutz 2004). In addition, fathers, grandmothers, and other family members may be left to care for children, aged parents, and others (Escrivá 2005; Gamburd 2000; Hochschild 2004). Or, as Escrivá (2005) points out, Peruvian grandmothers may emigrate to Spain to care for their grandchildren while their daughters do domestic work in Spanish households. The shape of these global care chains are often directly related to the resources of the workers, the poverty of the sending country, and the receptiveness of the receiving country's immigration policies regarding family reunification.

In this chapter, we examine how transnational processes such as the international division of care are related to particular policy changes shaped by neoliberal values.[2] According to advocates of neoliberalism, economic growth is strongest when the market is unhampered by the state; therefore, they believe that economies are healthiest when labor markets are deregulated, and when the state pulls back social protections. In response to this dominant ideology, many countries in the past two decades have limited their roles in regulating markets and providing social supports for their citizens. In wealthy countries, the more generous welfare policies of the past have been replaced by market-driven approaches to provisioning, and employment regulations have also been loosened—all under the rubric of "welfare state restructuring" (Michel and Mahon 2002). In developing countries, "structural adjustment" policies, often imposed by international lending agencies such as the World Bank, have led to even more serious cutbacks in welfare programs as well as to the deregulation of labor markets, resulting in lower wages and the elimination or diminishing of health and safety standards. We argue that neoliberal economic restructuring—in the form of structural adjustment policies and welfare state restructuring—has resulted in a system that requires the emigration of poor women workers to provide low-cost care in wealthier countries in order to support their own families. Migration policies help shape these flows, while generally leading many workers to labor in the postmodern "twilight zone" of illegal and completely unregulated work (Lutz 2004).

The international division of care, and its effects on immigrant women workers and their families, must be understood within a wider political economic system that has been increasingly affected by neoliberal ideologies and policies. State policies shape both the needs and experiences of employers and careworkers in multiple ways. Recognizing the policy face of these developments allows for the potential to resist these processes, and to create more equitable care arrangements. Accordingly, we ask in this chapter how economic policies as well as immigration and emigration policies have helped shape the international division of care (Parreñas 2001a).

In the upcoming section, we explore the relationship between carework and inequality—in terms of gender, class, race/ethnicity, nationality, and citizenship status. In the section after that, we discuss the political economy of carework, examining neoliberal economic restructuring in both receiving and sending countries. Next, we look more closely at the emigration and immigration policies that help shape these flows. Finally, we suggest policy goals meant to decrease the inequalities created and maintained by these global processes.

INEQUALITY AND CAREWORK

Carework is central to the continuation of society. Capitalism as an economic system is predicated on keeping down the costs of social reproduction (e.g., the production of new workers); therefore, it relies upon a devaluing of carework and an unequal division of reproductive labor. These trends are not new—there have *always* been inequalities in the performance of carework. However, the increased mobility of workers across borders has exacerbated the global nature of such trends. In this section, we consider how inequalities of gender, class, race/ethnicity, nationality, citizenship, and immigration status are embedded in carework.

Carework clearly reinforces gender inequalities. Patriarchal ideas about women's appropriate roles in society have helped to socially construct the idea of women as caretakers. Feminist research has shown that carework is not "natural" for women; rather, women are socialized into fulfilling this role in society. At the same time, patriarchal ideas have devalued skills associated with women, such as nurturing. As a result, although women are held responsible for caretaking, both unpaid and paid carework are acutely undervalued (Folbre 1994).

Carework is also a site in which class is played out. Economic resources determine who provides care as well as the quality of the care that families receive. Employers may be reluctant to recognize their own homes as workplaces, but class and power differentials clearly exist between careworkers and employers (Rollins 1985). Although there are variations in the class levels of both employers and careworkers, the class differences *between* employers and workers are what drive the system.[3] Indeed, "a crucial determinant of the extent of employment in paid domestic labor in a given location is the degree of economic inequality there" (Milkman et al. 1998, 486).

Many immigrants come from privileged backgrounds in their home countries, inasmuch as the poorest workers usually do not have the resources to emigrate (Hondagneu-Sotelo 2001; Parreñas 2001a). There may be significant variability in the expectations of immigrant workers, depending on their backgrounds and the context of their positions (e.g., au pairs recruited legally through an agency versus undocumented workers recruited through word of mouth)—expectations that shape their relationships with employers.[4] Immigrant careworkers often confront contradictory class mobility by emigrating, experiencing downward status mobility at the same time that they experience upward financial mobility in their home country.[5] As noted before, immigrant careworkers themselves may employ careworkers for family members left in their home countries, creating complicated hierarchies of privilege (Parreñas 2001a).

Class intersects with gender, particularly in the gender relations between women who supervise careworkers and the workers themselves (Glenn 1992; Rollins 1985; Romero 1992). Gender inequality shapes the lives of women caregivers *and* women employers. Careworkers face the gendered devaluation of carework, which translates into low pay and poor working conditions. Yet, gendered inequalities also mean that women employers remain responsible for ensuring that carework is carried out, even as they benefit from class inequality by hiring other women to handle the work assigned to them. Given these class relations, women employers may deploy a sort of exploitative maternalism to ensure that the needed work is getting done (Glenn 1992; Rollins 1985; Romero 1992). Both women careworkers and employers may struggle against a sense that they are transgressing idealized gender norms (Chang 2000; Hondagneu-Sotelo and Avila 1997; Parreñas 2001b). Women employers may hope that the women they employ are responsible caregivers, but fear that these workers may replace their employers in the hearts of their family members. At the same time, women careworkers violate gendered norms when they provide care for other families rather than for their own. These women may critique their employers for *choosing* not to care for their families, but they themselves are forced to break these norms in order to provide crucial financial support for their families (Hondagneu-Sotelo and Avila 1997).[6]

Class and gender also intersect with race and ethnicity. In the United States, racial and ethnic minority women's labor has historically been appropriated for the care of white families, undermining the care of their own families (Glenn 1992). As Glenn (1992) notes, racial and ethnic minority women have moved from jobs as servants within households to low-wage service-sector jobs. In both settings, these workers lighten the more taxing aspects of carework for white and middle-class women. Employers also develop hierarchies of racial and ethnic preference, employing members of certain racial/ethnic groups for caregiving tasks, based on stereotypes of these groups' submissiveness. For example, employers may expect Latinas to care for children *and* clean but expect white workers to do one *or* the other (Wrigley 1995). Hondagneu-Sotelo (2001) further shows that careworkers themselves may deploy racial and ethnic hierarchies, preferring to work for particular groups (e.g., white Protestants) rather than for families from other racial and ethnic backgrounds (e.g., Jews, Mexicans, or African Americans).

Nationality and citizenship status are also central axes of inequality. For example, employers may rationalize paying immigrant workers less than native-born workers by arguing that immigrant workers would live in greater poverty in their home countries (Anderson 2000; Hondagneu-Sotelo 2001). Wages may even be based on wage potential in the worker's country of origin rather than on fair wages within the host country (Heyzer and Wee 1994).[7] Private employers often disregard employment laws regarding pay, taxes, working conditions, and benefits, in part due to the lack of enforcement of these laws (Chang 2000; Hondagneu-Sotelo 2001; Romero 1992). The vulnerability of noncitizen workers, particularly undocumented immigrants, allows employers greater latitude in which to exploit their workers (Cox 1999; Hondagneu-Sotelo 2001; Parreñas 2001b). Workers with legal status in the host countries may be given only tourist visas, which prohibit their employment, or work permits that tie them to a particular employer. In short, carework reinforces inequalities of gender class, race/ethnicity, nationality, and citizenship. Parreñas (2001b, 78) describes this system as follows: "The hierarchy of womanhood—involving race, class, nation, as well as gender—establishes a work transfer system of reproductive labor among women, the international system of caretaking." Bear in mind, however, that the exploitation of immigrant domestic workers must be situated in an oppressive political and economic system that squeezes families, and does not protect or recognize immigrant workers in "unskilled" and devalued jobs such as carework. Although inequalities between families shape this system, it is equally critical that we place the international division of care into its larger political and economic context. How do neoliberal economic globalization and state policies shape the pattern of carework and, in the process, reify these inequalities?

THE POLITICAL ECONOMY OF CAREWORK

Over the last several decades, neoliberalism has become the predominant economic strategy shaping policies worldwide. Neoliberalism affects the international division of care by shaping the contexts of the countries both sending and receiving immigrant careworkers. As one aspect of the withdrawal of the state and of state support for care, carework has been passed back into the private sphere, where women are expected to subsidize the economy with their caring work (Sparr 1994; Wichterich 2000).

In wealthier countries, welfare state restructuring has placed greater pressure on women to find a way to meet their family's care needs (Michel and Mahon 2002). In developing countries, neoliberal structural adjustment policies have led to serious cutbacks in welfare programs, reemphasizing women's responsibility for care needs and also deregulating labor markets. As a result of these stressful financial and social conditions, more workers are emigrating in hopes of finding greater economic opportunity (Chang 2000; Momsen 1999; Parreñas 2001a).

NEOLIBERALISM AND CARE IN RECEIVING COUNTRIES

Although neoliberal ideologies have not decimated the social welfare policies of wealthier nations, they have encouraged a greater emphasis on market-based solutions and a rolling back of the state's role in care provision (Michel and Mahon

2002). In many welfare states, the state has long played a key role in supporting carework, through subsidies for parental leave and elder care policies, as well as the provision of services, such as childcare, elder care, and care for the disabled. At the same time, welfare states have regulated employment and wages so as to ensure a certain quality of life for their citizens. Indeed, countries with more generous welfare states and lower levels of wage inequality are less likely to import high numbers of immigrant domestic workers.[8] However, welfare states are changing more dramatically in some countries than in others.

Welfare state restructuring has led to serious declines in the availability of state-provided social care services in many countries (Daly and Lewis 1998; Jenson and Sineau 2001). While not necessarily deeply cutting social welfare spending, welfare states have restructured welfare programs, creating greater decentralization, changing the welfare mix (benefits, leave, and service measures), and focusing on privatization and marketization (Knijn 2000, 2001; Mahon and Phillips 2002).[9] In particular, they have moved toward either subsidizing care that families hire or provide or withdrawing entirely from care provision. For example, the French crèche system provided high quality childcare for children under age 3 on a sliding-scale basis for decades. Although crèches still exist, the system has been weakened by new policies that encourage families to hire nannies with state subsidies (Jenson and Sineau 2001; Morgan 2002). The resulting loss of higher fees from middle-class families has meant that there are now significantly fewer crèche spaces available, to the detriment of working-class families.

The push toward privatizing care has had powerful effects on inequalities between families (Jenson and Sineau 2001; Morgan 2002). In the Netherlands, the marketization of home care has resulted in careworkers' loss of professional status, wages, benefits, and decent working conditions. Concurrently, those dependent on home care have experienced a loss in their right to receive care, and have become more dependent on their family and social networks for care (Knijn 1998). Even countries with unusually generous welfare states, such as Norway, have seen a greater privatization of care for children and the frail elderly (Waerness 1998).

At the same time that welfare states have restructured their role in the provision of care, neoliberalism has weakened worker protections and wages, such that middle- and working-class families are caught in a struggle to support themselves. Hiring low-wage careworkers allows more highly educated women to enter the workforce and substantially increase their household income. As middle-class women gain greater access to paid employment, low-wage workers replace the caretaking and housekeeping that these women previously provided (Smet 2002). By relying on a flexible and cheap labor force of immigrant women workers, reproduction in wealthy countries is then carried out despite the rollback in state provision of social services (Anderson 2000; Hondagneu-Sotelo 2001; Momsen 1999; Parreñas 2001b). Indeed, Parreñas (2001b, 33) notes that nations with low welfare provisions (such as the United States and Southern European countries) have high rates of foreign domestic work, whereas nations with large-scale institutional support for families are less likely to rely on immigrant careworkers.

The demand for careworkers in wealthy nations results from additional demographic changes such as rising divorce rates, lower marriage rates, and rapid increases in the size of the elderly population needing care. However, the care deficit results not only from a diminishing supply of family care but also from a rolling back of state provision of care (Bakan and Stanulis 1996). As Anderson (1999, 119) argues: "Caught between the declining welfare state and growth in middle class female employment outside the home, it is scarcely surprising that the employment of a migrant domestic worker is regarded as a suitable strategy for families who need full-time careers."

Neoliberalism and Care in Sending Countries

Faced with the powerful impact of structural adjustment on their economies, more and more workers in developing countries consider immigration to be a means of supporting their families. Indeed, among the international migrants in 2000, estimated at 175 million overall, 60 percent came from developing countries (United Nations 2003). In addition, more and more emigrating workers are now women. Economic pressures are a central reason for the emigration of workers.

Neoliberal structural adjustment entails (1) privatizing, limiting, or cutting social welfare programs on health, education, and welfare; (2) privatizing state enterprises and cutting subsidies on products and services; (3) limiting labor market policies such as wage minimums and cutting wages more generally; (4) liberalizing imports and easing restrictions on foreign investment; and (5) devaluing the currency in order to make export prices more competitive (Bakan and Stanulis 1996; Laurell 2000; Sparr 1994). Although these policies are meant to promote economic growth, they have led to increasing levels of unemployment, poverty, and income inequality (Sassen 2003).

Cutbacks in health services, education, and childcare have led to women's increased responsibility for caregiving (Folbre 1994). In addition, growing numbers of women are now in search of income-generating strategies, including informal sector and subsistence work as well as emigration both within and across countries (Laurell 2000; Sassen 2003; Sparr 1994). As Enloe (1989, 185) points out, the debt crisis is providing many middle-class women in Britain, Italy, Singapore, Canada, Kuwait, and the United States with a new generation of domestic servants. When a woman from Mexico, Jamaica, or the Philippines decides to emigrate in order to make money as a domestic servant, she is designing her own international debt politics. She is trying to cope with the loss of earning power and the rise in cost of living at home by cleaning bathrooms in the countries of bankers.

Remittances from immigrant workers play a key role in helping national economies service their growing debts (Parreñas 2001b; Sassen 2003). Moreover, many workers emigrate only temporarily in order to support their families at home; by sending their earnings home, they help to guarantee a smooth flow of currency for their home country (Lutz, 2002; Parreñas 2001b; Pyle and Ward 2003; Rerrich 2002).

Neoliberal strategies have contributed to care deficits across the globe and, as noted earlier, also create a situation in which more women are considering immigration as a means of meeting their family's financial needs. Rather than states taking responsibility for aiding families, neoliberal strategies have helped to create an international division of carework. According to Heyzer and Wee (1994, 44–45):

> The shifting division of responsibility between the State and the family for the social reproduction of everyday life has, thereby, been transformed into a transnational division of labour between middle class woman and working class woman.... [T]his results in hidden savings for the governments of the receiving countries, because the need for adequate state investments in child care, care of the handicapped, care of the elderly and other social services is instead provided for by the income subsidy of middle class professional women and by the labour subsidy of relatively low-paid female migrant workers.

Immigration and Emigration Patterns and Policy

A large role in shaping the international division of carework is played not only by neoliberal economic restructuring, carried out by nation-states and shaped by the priorities of international economic organizations, but also by the political economy of immigration and emigration. Immigration can be viewed as being due to "disruptions and dislocations that inevitably occur in the process of capitalist development" (Massey et al. 1993, 445; see also Massey 1999). Migration is not simply the aggregation of individual decisions; "large scale international migrations are embedded in rather complex economic, social, and ethnic networks. They are highly conditioned and structured flows" (Sassen 1998b, 62).

Economic restructuring displaces workers from their previous forms of employment, creating a mobile workforce that emigrates to different regions or countries and changes consumption patterns and gendered roles related to work by, for example, drawing young women into production (Pessar 2003; Sassen 2003). Capitalist development also creates high-paying professional jobs in wealthy nations as well as a higher demand for low-wage service workers (Sassen 1988, 1998a). Indeed, as Piore (1979) argues, immigration patterns are best explained by the fact that capitalist development creates an unavoidable demand in industrialized nations for immigrant workers. Immigrant women workers are both displaced from former modes of employment and drawn to meet the service needs generated by global capitalism.

In addition, migration policies—in both sending and receiving countries—play an important role in determining immigration patterns, though these are embedded in multilateral agreements (e.g., with the International Labour Organization) and bilateral agreements between countries (Heisler 1985). Such policies are affected by a variety of social actors (e.g., workers, capitalists, and ethnic and humanitarian organizations) and state actors (Mitchell 1989; Massey

1999). Migration choices are then shaped by their institutional context—including labor market and immigration policies, and their implementations—as well as by international legislation (Rystad 1992). For example, many countries may be interested in encouraging patterns of temporary migration as opposed to permanent resettlement. Such patterns ensure remittances and transfers of emigrants to sending countries, but they limit the costs of social reproduction for receiving countries.[10]

Immigration policies also contribute to the exploitation of immigrant workers. Since states generally do not recognize the importance of carework to the economy, work permits for careworkers are generally very constrained (Hess 2002). These policies leave many immigrant women workers vulnerable as they push many immigrants into undocumented, unprotected, and poorly paid jobs (Anderson 1997; Heyzer and Wee 1994; Mattingly 1999; Smet 2002). As Sassen (2003, 52) notes, "If [immigrant women] are undocumented, which is likely, they will not be treated as victims of abuse, but as violators of the law insofar as they have violated entry, residence, and work laws." If immigration policies recognized and provided work visas for such workers, the workers would be more effectively protected by labor laws, including minimum-wage laws, protections on hours worked, and the right to privacy (Anderson 2000).

Even documented workers are denied such protections. For example, a Bolivian live-in maid, working for a human rights lawyer in Washington D.C., was forced to work twelve-hour days for less than $1/day and was not given appropriate medical care when raped by one of her employer's friends (Zarembka 2004). And Filipina maids in Hong Kong often work longer hours than contracted and face difficult working and living conditions, in part because they may be deported within two weeks of being terminated (Constable 1997). As Anderson (1997, 37) asserts, "[T]he need for this kind of [caring] labour is not properly reflected in immigration and employment policies, making domestic workers who are already vulnerable to abuse and exploitation even more dependent on their employers by denying them an independent immigration status—or any legal immigration status at all."

In addition, in many nations, immigration policies have become more stringent while benefits for immigrants have become less generous (Ferete 1997; Jain 1997; Ugur 1995). For example, in the United States, the welfare reform legislation of 1996 made immigrants entering the country ineligible for most welfare benefits for five years, including Temporary Assistance for Needy Families (TANF), Supplemental Security Income (SSI), and Medicaid (Reese 2005). And in Germany, new legislation has made it possible to deport immigrants (even those who have resided and worked in Germany for decades) if they apply for *any* social security benefits for themselves or any family members. As Ferete (1997, 1) notes, "[W]estern Europe has sought to rid itself of settler/immigrant workers (surplus to current requirements) and replace them with temporary ad hoc labour more suited to a postindustrial economy—thereby retaining the economic benefit of migrant labour and divesting itself of its social cost—in housing, health care, welfare, education." Clearly, although immigrant women workers are needed by host countries to provide care, these countries are unwilling to reciprocate with decent wages, working conditions, and social benefits.

CONCLUSION

Across the globe, immigrant women workers are doing critical work caring for children, the elderly, the sick, and the disabled. Although immigrant women have long been involved in providing such carework, globalization has intensified the international division of care in recent decades. In addition, there have been important shifts in migration patterns, including women's increased participation in immigration for employment in domestic and caring work.

Changing migration patterns have been created by the political and economic conditions created by neoliberal policies in both sending and receiving countries. Welfare states have attempted to lower the costs of social reproduction by privatizing and marketizing care. These strategies have drawn in immigrant women workers as caregivers, exploiting these workers without recognizing the important contributions that these workers make to economic productivity and society more generally. At the same time, immigration and emigration policies help direct the flow of workers.

We have shown not only how these trends fit together but also how states have made gains by exploiting low-wage immigrant women workers, who are underpaid by their employers and unprotected by immigration policies and labor laws. By highlighting how the political economy shapes carework, this chapter demonstrates that the exploitation of careworkers is not simply the fault of those who employ careworkers and the inequalities they suffer are not simply a reflection of class conflict *between women* (e.g., Flanagan 2004). Rather, this process occurs within an oppressive political and economic system that enables this kind of abuse.

Our research suggests a variety of policy implications for both immigrant careworkers and their employers. Of course, any policy changes will be difficult to attain. Top decisionmakers have long significantly devalued carework, denying or simply failing to recognize the centrality of carework for the economy (as well as quality of life). At the same time, neoliberal values continue to shape ideas about the need to cut rather than expand spending for care. Racist and xenophobic concerns about immigration also make the expansion of immigration policies difficult to win in many contexts. In some cases, international policies, such as those put forward by the European Union, may be more likely to address these concerns; in others, domestic policies are key. Nevertheless, it is critical to recognize the policy goals we've listed below, along with their potential for lessening—rather than increasing—inequality.

1. Carework needs to be valued more highly, as central to the economy. Recognizing the value of carework would result in higher wages, better and more stable

working conditions, and benefits for workers (e.g., health insurance, pensions for the aged and disabled, and unemployment insurance). This outcome requires higher levels of state spending on care, as most families cannot afford to provide such conditions without state support. State provision of care is also more likely to reliably ensure higher wages, better working conditions, and benefits for careworkers. Public provision of care is crucial. Privatized care and marketized care may offer greater flexibility, but they provide more opportunities for exploitation.

2. Recognizing the importance of carework would also lead to more open immigration policies, resulting in the provision of work visas to caregivers and the acknowledgment that such workers deserve the pay and working conditions of legal employees. Rather than encouraging undocumented workers, who are then vulnerable to abuse, immigration policy—at both the domestic and the international levels—must recognize that careworkers are necessary to economic growth.

3. Immigrant workers, in turn, would benefit from informational campaigns clarifying their rights as workers, helping them find suitable employment, and giving them the opportunity to file grievances against exploitative employers. Indeed, careworkers must have opportunities to organize through informal forums as well as labor movements. Although carework is often done in individualized settings, careworkers benefit from being in contact with other careworkers. For example, RESPECT (2000) has worked to inform workers and employers of the rights of immigrant domestic workers, and some labor organizations, such as the Service Employers International Union (SEIU), have developed new approaches to unionizing this fragmented and diverse workforce (Walsh 2001).[11]

4. Labor regulations need to allow all families more flexibility for meeting their care needs on their own—specifically, by providing allowances for parental and family leaves, flexible schedules, and mandated shorter workweeks for both men and women (Gornick and Meyers 2003). Such policies should be instituted with an eye toward equalizing the care burden across gender lines (rather than reinforcing it, as through care leaves taken by women only), as well as mediating inequalities of class, race/ethnicity, nationality, and citizenship (Morgan and Zippel 2003).

5. Structural adjustment policies have decimated the poor in many countries. Workers must be able to *choose* to engage in carework rather than being forced into carework to sustain their families from afar. Structural adjustment policies must be evaluated from the standpoint of the poorest workers, and economic policies must be reformed to meet the needs of these groups.

6. Political and economic policies must emphasize the importance of economic survival of *all* families rather than focusing on stimulating "economic growth" in decontextualized ways. (An example of the latter would be a strategy focused on replacing subsistence farming with export-oriented crops, thereby generating greater income for a few at the expense of quality of life for many.)

Such policies must also focus on generating jobs that allow workers to support their families without traveling the globe.

Overall, we argue for better structural supports for workers *and* families, along with a greater valuing of carework more generally. Neoliberal economic strategies have led to care deficits around the globe, forcing men and women to participate in the paid labor force to provide for their families, without adequate provisions available to meet their care needs. This trend is occurring in wealthy countries as well as developing countries, and affecting middle-class as well as poor families. Although the repercussions are most severe for the poor, it is important to recognize that the devaluation of care has an impact on all families. We also argue for better supports for immigrant workers. Immigration will never simply end, as workers emigrate for a variety of reasons (Romero 1992). Therefore, it is critical to ensure that the rights of immigrant workers are protected, across the globe. Immigration policies must change to reflect the reality of the need for careworkers, just as labor organizations and other groups must work to organize and support careworkers.

As we have noted, the growing international division of care reflects inequalities of class, gender, race, ethnicity, nationality, and citizenship. These inequalities are formed and re-created in part through political and economic processes such as economic restructuring and immigration policy. By specifying how particular policies have shaped these processes, we can begin to identify concrete policy approaches aimed at lessening these inequalities.

NOTES

1. While for many years men were more likely to emigrate for work in the industrial sector, current trends emphasize informal jobs in service work and carework directed at women immigrants (Hondagneu-Sotelo 2001; Wichterich 2000). Women's immigration rates have also risen due to the adoption of family reunification policies, which allow women to join their husbands, children, and parents who have emigrated.

2. We focus many of our arguments on domestic workers who emigrate to wealthy receiving countries, such as Canada, the United States, or those in Western Europe. While we are particularly interested in what this angle of vision gives us in comparing how neoliberal economic restructuring has shaped both wealthy and developing countries, we do not mean to suggest that domestic workers emigrate to wealthy countries only. Immigration patterns are indeed more complex than this. Nevertheless, neoliberal economic restructuring has played a key role in shaping contexts around the globe.

3. Milkman et al. (1998) show that, across cities, higher levels of growth in domestic work are related to higher levels of household income inequality.

4. Indeed, au pairs who are treated as "one of the family" appear more likely to be exploited than those who are treated as workers (Hess 2002).

5. Workers may also use their positions as immigrant domestic workers as steppingstones to learn the language, gain work permits, and even receive higher levels of education (Hess 2002).

6. As Glenn (1992, 19) notes, in reviewing a wide array of research, "Perhaps the most universal theme in domestic workers' statements is that they are working so that their own daughters will not have to go into domestic service and confront the same dilemmas of leaving their babies to work."

7. For example, in Germany, Polish workers may earn twice as much as Bulgarian workers (Heubach 2002). Similar inequalities occur throughout the world (Heyzer and Wee 1994).

8. As Milkman et al. (1998, 493) note, so few women work as domestic servants in Sweden that the numbers are not published in the Swedish census—a fact that may serve as an indicator of a more equal class structure there, along with shorter work hours and more generous social policies such as universal childcare.

9. At the same time, states have expanded certain family policies that subsidize family members (often women) who provide care through care allowances, maternity, and parental leave policies (Gornick and Meyers 2003). While these policies may be heralded as recognizing care needs, they are also cost-cutting measures that reinforce traditional gender roles (Morgan and Zippel 2003).

10. Remittances from immigrant workers are "an increasingly important source of revenue for some of these governments" (Sassen 2003, 52).

11. Indeed, Walsh (2001) provides a hopeful analysis of the successful SEIU campaign to organize 74,000 home healthcare workers.

9

The Tortilla Behemoth

Sexualized Despotism and Women's Resistance in a Transnational Mexican Tortilla Factory

Carolina Bank Muñoz

A continuación entraron en pláticas acerca de la creación y la formación de nuestra primera madre y padre. De maíz amarillo y de maíz blanco se hizo su carne; de masa de maíz se hicieron los brazos y las piernas del hombre. Únicamente masa de maíz entró en la carne de nuestros padres, los cuatro hombres que fueron creados. (Popol Vuh cited in Recinos [1960])

Next they entered into discussions about the creation and formation of our first mother and father. Their flesh was made of yellow corn and white corn. Their arms and legs were made from corn dough. Only corn dough entered in the flesh of our parents, the four men that were created. (Author's translation of Popol Vuh's statement)

Tortilla making has a long and rich history within Mexico because of its ties to indigenous culture. Women have historically been the primary producers of this staple food. Although tortillas are most commonly made in the home or bought on the street, the last twenty-five years have witnessed a large-scale industrialization of tortilla production. The explosion of tortillas into the U.S. market has revolutionized tortilla manufacturing. Food giants such as Taco Bell would not be able to operate without mass-produced tortillas. In the United States, the high-volume demand from supermarkets and the fast-food industry results in a mass-produced product manufactured, predominantly, by transnational corporations. In Mexico, small tortillerias still dominate the market. However, this scenario is also rapidly changing. Tortimundo,[1] the Mexican transnational corporation under study, is trying to shift tortilla production from occurring in the home and in small tortillerias to being mass-produced. The transformation of the tortilla industry in both the United States and Mexico is connected to corporate globalization and has resulted in the erosion of Mexican culture and the exploitation of women. The company has taken advantage of the eroded rights of workers to enforce a coercive labor regime that takes explicit control of women's bodies.

In this chapter I examine the working conditions of women who work for one of Tortimundo's wholly owned subsidiaries, Hacienda Tijuana (Mexico).[2] I argue that state policies in the United States and Mexico create conditions that allow managers at Hacienda Tijuana to sustain coercive labor practices. These policies include militarization of the U.S-Mexico border, implementation of the North American Free Trade Agreement (NAFTA), and lack of enforcement of labor provisions under the Mexican constitution. Furthermore, managers create a hypersexualized and racialized work environment by pitting women workers against one another to maintain shop floor control. Yet, these women are not mere passive victims on the shop floor. Their collective and individual resistance struggles make it a bearable work environment and shape the nature of managerial control.

HACIENDA TIJUANA

Don Enrique Hernandez's lucrative tortilla manufacturing operations grew out of his corn flour empire. Tortimundo has 80 percent of the corn flour market share in Mexico. According to the company's senior vice-president of manufacturing, opening tortilla production facilities in Mexico seemed an impossibility in the 1970s and 1980s because "families would have their girls go to the corner to buy fresh tortillas or make them at home. Nobody would have bought packaged tortillas." In the early 1990s, though, the idea of opening tortilla manufacturing plants in Mexico seemed to have tremendous potential due to NAFTA, modern Mexico, and the rapid rise of the maquila industry.[3] Tortimundo's wholly owned subsidiary, Hacienda Tijuana, opened nine tortilla manufacturing plants all over Mexico, and its corn and wheat flour operations total twenty-seven plants throughout the country.

Hacienda Tijuana has had enormous success in selling their tortillas to the maquila sector and other industries. Every day, thousands of tortillas go to the lunchrooms of the maquila industry with hopes of changing the Mexican palate. The operations manager at Hacienda Tijuana commented, "People are eating our product in the maquilas, and they are getting to know us and like us. We are changing their minds about tortillas. We are proving that our tortillas are just as good as the ones from the street."

Located in the center of a lower-middle-class neighborhood surrounded by maquiladoras, Hacienda Tijuana employs 140 production workers. The production manager tells me that the building was not intended to be a factory, and that they have had to undergo numerous adjustments to make it work. As a result, there is very poor ventilation, and it is extremely hot. According to U.S. standards, there are several health and safety violations. First, many of the machines do not have side covers, and open flames are in plain view. This contributes both to the heat in the factory and to numerous minor burn injuries reported by workers. Second, the cooking oil spilled onto the floor is not frequently cleaned up, and it traps small insects in the cracks of the flooring. And, third, although workers wear hair nets, they do not wear back braces or ear plugs to protect them from noise.

Workers are employed in one of three departments: warehouse, trucking, and production. The production department is the largest part of the factory. Women work almost exclusively on the line, although there are a couple of female machine operators. Men work exclusively in trucking, warehouse, and machine operation. According to managers, over 90 percent of the workers come from somewhere other than Baja, California. Of the 140 production workers, who range from 18 to 45 years of age, 72 percent are women and only 28 percent are men. All workers at Hacienda Tijuana are from Mexico, and most are single women with no family in the area.

For many, Hacienda Tijuana represents a more stable employment opportunity than other jobs in the area. Many of the women I interviewed were former maquila workers. They left the maquilas because of long days, seven-day work weeks, and the instability of the industry in bad economic times. At the Tijuana plant, workers earn an average of 86 pesos (U.S.$9.20) per day.[4] They have a six-day work week and, although they receive paid vacations, their health insurance benefits are meager.

Hacienda Tijuana has a loose managerial structure. The operations manager regularly reports to the corporate office and is in charge of overseeing all aspects of production and quality control. Under him, a production manager oversees the daily operation of the factory. The warehouse manager is in charge of sales and overseeing the truck drivers. The top leadership structure also includes supervisors and line leaders. Supervisors (all men) report to each of their department heads. Although line leaders (mostly women) lead the assembly line on a given day, they have no real authority as the position is usually determined on the basis of those who arrive at work first, rather than through a promotion system. Only the production, operations, and warehouse managers and supervisors have decisionmaking power. All of the managers are men, and all of them have some affiliation with the Tortimundo family.[5]

FACTORY REGIME

Sexualized and Racialized Despotism

In the *Politics of Production,* Burawoy (1985) explains the shift from despotic regimes to hegemonic regimes, and finally to hegemonic despotism. Despotic regimes are coercive by nature, and are founded on workers' dependence on wage labor. In such regimes, wages are tied to performance in the workplace. Hegemonic regimes are characterized by consent instead of coercion. External intervention and regulation by the state are responsible for the shift in labor regimes. Internal labor markets and the state contribute to the sustainability of a hegemonic regime.

Hacienda Tijuana incorporates components of despotism and hegemony, but it leans more heavily toward despotism. Much like Burawoy, I argue that the state plays a critical role in shop floor politics. In the case of Hacienda Tijuana, the state gives managers the tools to enforce coercion rather than consent. I also argue that race and gender are produced at the point of production and are not merely external factors. This assertion is consistent with the analyses of Lee (1998) and Salzinger (2003), who argue that managerial hiring practices create gendered subjectivities on the shop floor.

Hacienda Tijuana is governed by what I am calling a sexualized and racialized despotism. It is sexualized because women workers in the plant work in a sexually charged environment in which male managers make advances and ask for sexual favors. Most of the women I interviewed felt as if they had to flirt with management or lose their jobs. It is racialized because male managers pit lighter- and darker-skinned women against one another. Lighter-skinned and younger women get more attention from management than older and darker-skinned women. This creates a situation on the shop floor where many women feel compelled to outdo one another in flirtatious games and in productivity. At the same time, the character of the local labor market, influenced by both Mexican economic development policies and U.S. immigration policies, creates a situation where there are many single mothers who need stable jobs. Unemployment is rising because of the instability of the maquila industry. In 2001 there were 1,235 maquiladora establishments in Baja, California, compared to only 888 in 2003. Employment in this sector in Mexico as a whole also fell (INEGI 2003, 2004). Whereas production workers in the overall maquiladora sector in Tijuana earn roughly U.S.$1.37 per hour (STPS 2003),[6] production workers at Hacienda Tijuana earn an average of U.S.$1.15 per hour. Even though the hourly wage at Hacienda Tijuana is three times Mexico's minimum wage, it does not allow women to buy the product that they produce. Indeed, since Hacienda-brand bagged supermarket tortillas cost U.S.$0.96, women in the factory would have to spend nearly one hour's salary to buy them. Many of the women I interviewed indicated that on their salary they are able to afford fresh produce, but they eat meat only two or three times a week. It is important to note that real wages have been declining in Mexico since the passage of NAFTA (Shaiken 2001, 245), contributing to a further reduction of women's purchasing power. Yet, even then, these women valued job stability over higher wages. Hacienda Tijuana provides jobs that will not move offshore.

I argue that the regime is despotic because managers discipline or fire women who directly or indirectly challenge their sexual advances. The lack of alternatives available to women in Tijuana forces them to sell their labor power with little power to negotiate with their employers over their working conditions. The Mexican government does a very poor job of enforcing the provisions against sex discrimination and other labor protection provisions under Mexican Federal Labor Law (which explicitly prohibits sex discrimination). In two different reports, Human Rights Watch found that maquiladoras consistently engaged in sex discrimination by asking women to take routine pregnancy tests (Human Rights Watch 1996, 1998). This lack of enforcement of labor law provisions makes it easier for managers at Hacienda Tijuana to enforce shop floor control through coercion.

Gender and Race on the Shop Floor

Tortilla manufacturing at Hacienda Tijuana is constructed as women's work. I asked the production manager at Hacienda Tijuana why the company hires more women than men. He responded: "Haven't you read all of the studies that prove that women are better suited for assembly line work? Women are more patient. They can stand around and do this work for hours. Men are impatient. They constantly have to do something different. Women are simply better for the job. Besides, producing tortillas has been in the hands of women for centuries."

Many of the women tend to agree with this analysis. Rosa Marta said, "I see it as women's work. Tortilla making is a tradition that women have in their blood. It doesn't make a difference if now we are doing it in a factory as well as in our homes." Hacienda Tijuana's recruitment literature is also geared explicitly toward women: "Looking for women, stable work, well paid." What is most interesting, however, is the fact that tortilla production at the Hacienda Los Angeles plant is constructed as men's work. At this factory, 75 percent of the workers are men. The managers there argue that tortilla production is men's work because it is heavy labor that involves working with many complicated machines. In terms of the local labor market, the marginalized status of men at Hacienda Los Angeles is similar to that of women at Hacienda Tijuana. The hiring of men in L.A. and of women in Tijuana is not simply a coincidence. Both groups provide cheaper labor in their respective areas. Similar to Salzinger (2003), I found that managers had a vested interest in constructing gender according to their specific needs on the different shop floors.

I asked the warehouse manager if men ever felt left out or marginalized at Hacienda Tijuana, given that so much energy was focused on women workers. He said, "The men in the factory are proud of their work. They are not tortilla makers, and they understand this. They also understand that the work they do is critical to the entire operation, and without them there would be no tortillas."

When one compares wages, it is easy to understand why the men do not feel left out of the process. Machine operators and warehouse workers, all of whom are men, earn a full two dollars per day more than the line workers, all of whom are women. When I asked the production manager about this differential, he replied, "Well yes, the men do earn more. Their job requires more hard labor or technical expertise with machines. Besides, many of them have families to support." I responded by asking, "Don't the single mothers also have families to support?" He replied, "Sure, but they do not have to support very many people, only themselves and their small children." His comments reflect the notion of a family wage system. The managers argue that men have more people to support than women. Even though the managers know that women workers in the factory are single mothers, they insist that their income is supplemental or that they have fewer people to feed. This is, of course, untrue. Although some women I interviewed had small children only, many also had older children, and a couple had to support grandchildren in addition to their own children.

Workers at Hacienda Tijuana are divided by skin color. As I mentioned above, lighter-skinned women are often preferred by managers. I witnessed managers and supervisors routinely walking around the shop floor. They would often stand behind the women, hug them, tickle them, and kiss them on the cheek. Many of the women workers looked uncomfortable. Maria Jimenez, a production worker, said: "It's part of the work culture. If we want to keep our jobs we have to go along with it. I don't like it. It makes me feel demoralized, but what can I do?" Women are caught in multiple oppressions (skin color, poverty, and gender) that intersect at the point of production. Because these women are poor, their job security is essential. If they are lighter skinned they have better job security because they are given more attention, but they also have to endure more sexual harassment. If they are darker skinned, they face less sexual harassment but have less job security. Although sexual harassment makes all of these women feel uncomfortable, they are forced to compete for attention. I asked the production manager what he thinks about how women respond to his advances. He said, "It doesn't matter. In Tijuana we have a very unique situation. There are many single women, and many single mothers. These women need a stable job, and since they do not have husbands, they do whatever we want." Managers at the plant feel very confident in their actions because of women's vulnerable position in the local labor market.

The women made it very clear to me that sexual harassment is not limited to the work day. Managers and supervisors have also harassed women after hours. Lupe said, "One time a supervisor told me that I had to go to dinner with him. I told him that I could not, that I had to go home and feed my children. He said that if I didn't he would have to let me go. I was terrified of losing my job, so I went. I don't want to talk about what happened after that." I asked her why she did not try to find other work. She replied, "Despite the advances, this is a good job, a stable job. Before coming here I worked in a garment maquila. There, I was not paid for over three weeks. The working conditions were terrible, and I was screamed at. I cannot afford to wait three weeks for my paycheck. Here, at least I have friends. The women have similar experiences and so we bond."

Several of the women at Hacienda Tijuana did not feel the same way that Lupe did. Some did not feel a common bond with other women. Gloria said, "Sure, we all have some common experiences. But the younger, lighter-skinned women get more attention. This is difficult for the rest of us because we are forced to work harder while those women have it easier on the line. I don't mean to sound like I want the manager's attention. It's just that when they [the supervisors] like you, you are guaranteed a stable job. Sometimes I am afraid of not getting attention, because maybe they will fire me." Supervisors at Hacienda Tijuana are aware of this dynamic and are particularly adept at fostering favoritism since they have the most contact on the shop floor. I asked Oscar, a supervisor, what he thought of the competition between women for his attention. He responded, "A little competition is always a good motivator. We feel it keeps productivity levels up. We try to be fair when we are giving women compliments, so that they all feel good about themselves. But you know women. They can never get enough." Why does management at Hacienda Tijuana use the sexualization of women as the main form of coercion? The answer has to do with the complex relationship between state policies and the local labor market. To this issue I turn next.

State Policies on the Shop Floor

The multifaceted relations between the U.S. state and the Mexican state play an important, though indirect, role in shaping shop floor politics at Hacienda Tijuana. Specifically, U.S. immigration policies and Mexican economic development policies and practices interact in such a way as to allow managers in the Tijuana plant to maintain a regime of sexualized and racialized despotism.

The United States and Mexico have had a long and complex relationship negotiating foreign capital and emigration. Over the last hundred years, Mexico has fluctuated between economic nationalism with complete state sovereignty and the attraction of foreign capital, on the one hand, and privatization of certain national industries, on the other (Caulfield 1998, 18). The United States, for its part, has fluctuated between opening and closing its doors to Mexican immigrants. The Bracero Program, Operation Wetback,[7] the Immigration Reform and Control Act (IRCA), and Operation Gatekeeper are examples of this fluctuation (Bank Muñoz 2004a, 2004b). However, in the last thirty years, Mexico has maintained a consistent process of export-led development highlighted by Mexico's participation in the General Agreement on Trade and Tariffs (GATT) in 1983 and NAFTA in 1994. Both of these policies have situated Mexico firmly in neoliberal strategies, forcing Mexico to open its doors and to support a climate of foreign investment in Mexico.

Globalization has led to serious social problems in developing countries by increasing the "proletarianization" of indigenous and rural peoples who relied mainly on subsistence agriculture (Lee 1998). Studies also predicted that the liberalization of corn prices would displace thousands of small farmers (Hinojosa-Ojeda and Robinson 1992, 73). The resulting shift from subsistence agriculture to wage labor has led to internal and external migration, deterioration of the culture, erosion of the countryside, and superexploitation of workers.

Because corn and tortillas are essential to the Mexican economy and diet, tortillas have long been subsidized by the Mexican government. Food agencies were created in postrevolutionary Mexico as part of the welfare state. These agencies, such as the Compañía Nacional de Subsistencias Populares (CONASUPO), ensured that producers were given a good price for their harvest and that staple foods, such as tortillas, were available to consumers at affordable prices (Ochoa 2000, 4).

From the mid-1980s onward, Mexico pursued a neoliberal strategy to end its economic problems. This included attracting foreign investment, opening Mexico to the world market, and rapid privatization. As a result, the operations of CONASUPO began rapidly to decline. Many of CONASUPO's industries were privatized and others were eliminated altogether. The elimination of price controls on corn forced CONASUPO to purchase imported corn at higher levels in order to continue subsidizing tortillas and other food products (Ochoa 2000). NAFTA has facilitated the importation of U.S. corn to Mexico. In fact, the United States is the largest producer and exporter of corn in the world, and 25 percent of the corn consumed in Mexico comes directly from the U.S. market (Ribeiro, *La Jornada,* January 17, 2005). After the passage of NAFTA and the complete dismantling of CONASUPO in 1996, the Mexican corn market was privatized and flooded by firms such as Arthur Daniels Midland (ADM) and Cargill-Monsanto (Mendoza 1996; Pujol 1996; Ribeiro, *La Jornada,* January 17, 2005; Torres 1996). The results have been disastrous. Not only have hundreds of thousands of Mexican corn farmers been displaced and migrated (Malkin, *New York Times,* March 27, 2005), but privatization also has taken a serious toll on the economy.

Many of the displaced corn farmers migrated to work in maquiladoras along the border or in large cities in the interior of Mexico. Others moved to work in the tortilla corn flour industry, which employs over 225,000 people (and is one of Mexico's largest industries). This was certainly the case for Margarita, a production worker at Hacienda Tijuana. "My family," she said, " has a long history in the corn industry. My entire family used to grow corn. In 1998 my father had to abandon the farm that we all grew up on. He could no longer compete with the cheap U.S. corn that was coming into Mexico. We [the children] moved to Tijuana to find maquila employment. I worked as a garment worker for two years, but then the factory closed. So that is how I came to work for Hacienda Tijuana."

Margarita is not the only worker who experienced such circumstances. Most of the women I interviewed said they had to migrate because there were no opportunities for their families in their home towns. In fact, maquila employment rose dramatically after the passage of NAFTA. In 1995 the industry employed 648,263 people; at its peak in 2000, it employed 1,291,232 (INEGI 2003; Pastor and Wise

2003). All but one of the women I interviewed had migrated to Tijuana with their husbands and small children. Half of these women came from rural areas, and the others came from small cities. Many had been planning on crossing the border with their families. However, because of U.S. immigration policies, such as Operation Gatekeeper, the women decided to stay in Tijuana with their children and to let their spouses cross alone. Operation Gatekeeper is a policy that was implemented in 1994. Its intent was to "restore integrity and safety to the San Diego border crossing." The initiative increased the number of border patrol agents from 980 in 1994 to 2,264 in 1998 (Immigration and Naturalization Service 1998). This policy did not stop immigration (as noted, although the women decided to stay in Tijuana, their partners continued to cross the border); it only made it harder for people to cross the border at relatively safe places, leading them to cross in more dangerous places such as the Arizona desert. Since its implementation, there have been over 200 deaths at the San Diego border crossing alone. Many of the women I interviewed were left as single mothers in Tijuana with no familial networks. Some of their spouses are missing, others are dead, and yet others cannot afford to bring their families to the United States. Rosa said, "I haven't been in communication with my husband for five years. When he crossed to the other side, our daughter was 6 months old. I stayed here in Tijuana without any family, waiting for him."

Mexican elites have been trying for many years to attract foreign capital to the border region in the name of development. The state has played an ambivalent role in this process. They have had to succumb to pressures by Mexican elites, the United States, and supranational institutions such as the IMF and the World Bank. U.S. corporations have had the most to gain from foreign investment in Mexico because they have been able to avoid many of the provisions protecting workers under the Mexican constitution. U.S. foreign capital along the border, along with restrictive immigration policies and the militarization of the border, has created a local labor market of single women, particularly single mothers. Hacienda Tijuana has been able to attract these single women into its factory because of the stability of the tortilla industry in comparison to maquilas. Since these women prize stable jobs above wages and other working conditions, managers and supervisors can be unscrupulous in their exploitation of women.

NAFTA—in combination with the liberalization of the corn market, the militarization of the U.S.–Mexico border, and the instability of the maquila industry (as it moves to Asia or other developing countries)—has created a system whereby capital is extremely mobile and flexible, while labor has become increasingly less mobile and workers have fewer options. On the one hand, the Mexican state is weak because it has succumbed to structural adjustment policies, and U.S. pressures are increasingly liberalizing its market. In significant ways, the Mexican economy historically has been, and continues to be, shaped by U.S. imperialism (González 2004). On the other hand, the Mexican state acts as a strong and powerful institution in relation to the regulation of poor women's bodies and lives. Such policies impact both the shop floor and the ability of managers to enforce coercion. I turn to this issue next.

THE STATE, UNIONS, CONSTITUTIONAL RIGHTS, AND ENFORCEMENT

Another way in which the state plays a role in giving Hacienda Tijuana managers the tools to maintain a despotic regime is through lack of enforcement of the Mexican constitution. On paper, this constitution is one of the most progressive in the world. Written in 1917 during the Mexican Revolution of 1910–1920, it affords workers unprecedented labor protections. Article 123, the provision that delineates workers' rights, includes minimum-wage standards, the right to form a union, nondiscrimination (including sexual harassment), health and safety, overtime pay, health insurance, and paid vacation, among other benefits. However, it is often not enforced. Hacienda Tijuana is located in a border zone aimed at attracting foreign capital. As Ong (1999) notes, border zones are often zones of graduated sovereignty. The border in Mexico is a place where the Mexican state gives up some of its sovereignty in order to attract foreign capital. This results in both a loosening of labor laws and a lack of enforcement of constitutional provisions. Many government officials turn a blind eye to such violations. Location in this zone benefits not just maquilas but national industries as well, because the latter receive some of the same benefits and compete with the maquilas.[8]

Hacienda Tijuana uses its advantageous location in the free trade zone to maintain a regime of sexualized despotism. The company has a very close relationship with national leaders and the local government. There is also a strong relationship between the union and the company. During my first visit to Hacienda Tijuana, I asked the production manager if there was a union in the factory. Looking at me suspiciously, he replied, "Yes and no. The CTM [Confederación de Trabajadores Mexicanos][9] represents the factory in Monterrey [headquarters for Hacienda], and supposedly this union also has jurisdiction over the Tijuana factory, but not really. In any case, we like it this way because if anyone tries to start something I can show him that a union represents him. If anyone ever started making trouble and tried to get a union, I would kill them [signaled with a hand to the throat]. We are a business, not a charity, and I am the only one who controls these workers."

When I observed sexual harassment on the shop floor, I asked the women why they didn't file a grievance with their union. Most of them rolled their eyes at me. Marta said, "The union is not a union for workers. They are always on management's side. They are sympathizers of the same political party as the owners of the company, so they help each other out. We don't go to the local arbitration boards, because we know that the state will also protect the union and the company, since they helped them [the ruling political party] get into power." Ximena said, "There was a girl who worked with us, Juana was her name. She went to the union once to complain about the harassment. The very next day she was fired. What kind of confidence does that give us?" Managers at Hacienda Tijuana can count on the union siding with the company. They can count on the state siding with them. The women in the factory are forced by their economic circumstances to sell their labor power, and they are coerced by managers to flirt with them and to perform sexual favors. Although there are constitutional provisions that supposedly protect them, they are not enforced. This leaves no buffer between women and the corporation. Furthermore, the economic instability of the area, owing to the cheaper production sought by maquilas in the interior of Mexico and other developing regions, limits the options for work in the surrounding maquilas.

RESISTANCE

Despite serious oppression on the shop floor at Hacienda Tijuana, the workers are not passive victims. They engage in acts of both collective and individual resistance. As indicated in my interviews with several managers, when the Tijuana plant opened in 1994 management at Hacienda headquarters in Mexico signed a contract with the CTM before the workers even started working at the factory. This collective bargaining agreement covers all employees in the factory, including the truck drivers. The contract is renewed every three years without worker input or knowledge of negotiations. Union leaders who are not part of the workforce negotiate contracts behind closed doors. According to the production manager, in 1996 a few production workers started talking about unionization during a particularly bad month in which five workers were injured on the job and management did nothing for them. When the workers threatened to unionize, the plant manager told them that they could not because they were already represented by the CTM. When the workers tried to contact their union to file a grievance against management, they were told that the union was based in Monterrey. Although there were many attempts to file a grievance, the union never responded to the workers. As a result, 50 percent of the workers in the factory participated in a walkout that lasted several days. When they returned to work, managers still had not met the workers' demands for better health and safety. Accordingly, many women workers left to go work in the maquila industry, which at that time offered better wages and benefits.

There has been no mass-scale worker movement inside the factory since that time, nor have attempts been made to organize an independent union. Josefina said, "It's not that we don't want an independent union. We do. We want a union that will fight for our rights. We don't want to live in constant fear. But we will have to be patient and wait to organize. Times have changed, and the situation for women workers is much more difficult today than eight years ago."

Nonetheless, workers do resist in both individual and collective ways. The women I interviewed cited various individual actions that they engage in to make the day pass faster. One example was provided by Marta: "I take many bathroom breaks during the day. This bothers the managers because they have to move someone from another part of the factory to keep my place on the assembly line while I go to the bathroom. I do this because it makes the day go faster. I get more chances to rest. They [managers] complain that I use the bathroom too much. What will they do? People have to use the bathroom." Taking bathroom breaks is not uncommon among the women I interviewed. Many of them told me that they did the same thing, and that other women in the factory also engaged in this activity.

Women also viewed getting to work late as an act of resistance. They know that they will not be penalized for arriving late, so they take their time getting to work. Ximena and Rosa said, "Why should we give them [managers] an extra fifteen minutes of our sweat, when we get paid the same if we come on time or are fifteen minutes late? We are so busy that it is hard to get to work on time. This way we have a little extra time. We can't leave the factory early, so we take advantage of the fact that we can come late." Occasionally women will engage in spontaneous collective action inside of the factory: A small group will all take a break, drink water, or go to the bathroom at the same exact time. When this occurs managers slow down the machines for a few minutes until everyone is back in their places. However, this kind of action is rare.

Aside from the more general matter of having a legitimate union that represents their rights, the women in the factory were particularly interested in organizing around health and safety issues, including sexual harassment, in order to work in a cleaner and safer environment. However, any kind of collective organizing is viewed as threatening by management. In order to launch an effective campaign the women need to fight the company, the union, and the local state. But doing so is extraordinarily hard for workers in Tijuana who are single mothers with little support. This is not to say that organizing has not been done or could not be done.

There are community organizations in Tijuana such as the Centro de Información para Trabajadoras y Trabajadores (Information Center for Workers) and the Factor X-Casa de la Mujer (Woman's House) that are actively working on campaigns in the maquila sector. They organize around environmental justice, sexual harassment, and independent union organizing. The Environmental Justice Coalition and the Maquiladora Solidarity Network also engage in active campaigns along the U.S.–Mexico border. However, many of these organizations focus on the maquila sector and not on national industries or Mexican corporations. Places like Hacienda Tijuana can slip through the cracks. Furthermore, organizing in Mexico remains an extraordinarily difficult venture. Mexican labor law makes it nearly impossible for independent unions to win recognition and collective bargaining. Although there are some successful independent union campaigns in Mexico, there are none, to my knowledge, in Tijuana specifically.

NOTES

1. All names (including that of the company) have been changed to protect confidentiality.

2. This chapter is part of a larger project that compares the labor regimes of two tortilla factories owned by the same Mexican transnational corporation on both sides of the U.S.–Mexico border. For more details, see Bank Muñoz (2004a).

3. "Maquilas" (also known as "maquiladoras") are export processing factories that assemble parts produced in Mexico for the U.S. consumer market. Some examples of maquilas in Mexico are garment, electronics, and food processing factories. Since the passage of NAFTA, much of Mexico's industries have turned to production processes that are similar to maquilas. While Hacienda Tijuana is not a maquila in the traditional sense, it does have components that function like maquilas.

4. I calculated this dollar amount using the nominal exchange rate.

5. The operations manager is the son of a close family friend of the the Tortimundo family, the production manager went to school with one of Don Hernandez's sons, and the warehouse manager is an in-law. All of these managers have college educations. Two of them graduated from universities in the United States.

6. I used the average exchange rate for the year 2003 to calculate the average hourly dollar wage.

7. The Bracero Program (1942–1964) was initiated by the U.S. and Mexican governments to solve a labor shortage in the United States and an agricultural crisis in Mexico. Experienced agricultural workers in Mexico abandoned their farms in hopes of earning significant money in the United States. Anti-immigrant sentiment reached new heights in this country during the time of the Bracero Program. In fact, nativist feelings among the U.S. population led to the development of Operation Wetback in 1954. Operation Wetback was concerned with "illegal" Mexican immigration to the United States. In 1954 border patrol agents raided Mexican barrios in the Southwest and deported anyone who looked Mexican. Operation Wetback deported thousands of Mexican immigrants, including a sizable number of U.S. citizens of Mexican descent.

8. This information was gathered during interviews with several managers at Hacienda Tijuana and with one manager from an apparel maquiladora.

9. The CTM is considered a "charro" union. It is tied to both the company and the ruling party of Mexico.

10

Roses, Thorns, and Seven Dollars a Day

Women Workers in Colombia's Export Flower Industry

Cynthia Mellon

❀

The growing, harvesting, transporting, and marketing of cut flowers on the world market is an international industry in which billions of dollars change hands each year.[1] In the United States alone, consumers spend close to U.S.$15 billion per year on flowers and plants—about four times more than one generation ago.[2] Since the early 1980s, the international cut flower industry has grown by about 15 percent every five years (Brassel and Rangel 2001a, 5). In recent years, the world trade in floriculture products has averaged $7.9 billion annually, with cut flowers accounting for about 50 percent of sales (Government of British Colombia 2003).

The world's biggest flower-producing country is the Netherlands, which represents about 50 percent of the world market (Brassel and Rangel 2001b, 5; Campos 2002, 2). The Netherlands has shaped the flower industry with technology and seed stock that have been developed over centuries, and its international flower auction sets the world standard for price and quality. The second-largest flower-producing country is Colombia, with about 7.5 percent of world flower sales (Government of British Columbia 2003). Other important flower-producing countries are Kenya, Ecuador, Zimbabwe, Tanzania, and Zambia (Brassel and Rangel 2001a, 5). In all of these countries, conditions for flower workers are exploitative, and the people who plant, tend, and package the plantation-grown flowers for worldwide shipping are placed at the lowest rung of a complex system of production, vending, and distribution.

Flower production is a labor-intensive activity that requires a large workforce. Around the world, the majority of flower workers are women. Unlike many agricultural crops, floriculture is not mechanized and involves numerous precise steps that must be carried out by hand. As the demand for cut flowers grows, the trend is shifting toward producing them in developing countries of the global South, where the hours of sunlight are long, labor costs are low, and enforcement of labor and environmental standards tends to be weak or nonexistent (Campos 2002, 2). These factors shape the current profile of the flower industry.

In this chapter I examine the effects of the cut flower industry on Colombian workers, along with some of the factors that helped the industry to gain the place it currently holds in the global flower market. I also explore some of the strategies that are being used in the struggle to gain improved conditions for workers. In doing so, I draw on field observations and unstructured interviews with flower workers and the lawyers and organizers who have supported them in their decades-long struggle for better wages and working conditions. The information contained in this chapter was gathered over a period of nine years and was especially facilitated by my work as coordinator of women's programs at a legal services and human rights center in Colombia that collaborates with flower workers and their allies in research, outreach, and other kinds of technical support.

A LUCRATIVE AND PROTECTED INDUSTRY

Cut flowers have been produced on the *Sabana de Bogotá*—a high plain of prime farmland lying to the west of the capital city of Colombia—since the late 1960s. Ideal natural conditions for flower cultivation, combined with access to the necessary infrastructure and favorable tax and legislative conditions, have made the industry highly competitive in the world market. The *sabana* has a cool, stable climate that is ideal for flower cultivation. Over the years, it has been possible for flower companies to acquire land at low prices and in sufficient quantities to construct the greenhouses, packing facilities, and refrigeration structures that are needed for the various stages of production. The flower-growing zone is close to Colombia's main international airport, and there is a large, readily available labor force living on the outskirts of nearby Bogotá and the towns that dot the *sabana*. Coupled with the Colombian government's favorable attitude toward the industry, these factors led to the development of a sector that is highly productive and profitable for its owners and investors.

Following several decades of slow growth, flowers became one of Colombia's main export products (Cactus 2005). In 2003, Colombia's export flower sales were U.S.$682 million dollars, showing a growth rate of 6.5 percent since 1999. Eighty-four percent of Colombia's exported flowers are destined for North America (Asocolflores 2004). Colombia's biggest market is the United States, where 60 percent of all flowers sold are from Colombia (Asocolflores 2004). The next biggest market is the European Union (EU), which imports only about 11.5 percent of Colombia's flowers (Campos 2002, 3; ILO 1998b, 3). The countries of the EU prefer to buy flowers from Kenya, Uganda, and other African countries, which are geographically closer and with which it has maintained trade agreements for the last forty years.[3] Roses, carnations, and chrysanthemums are Colombia's most popular export crops, but large quantities of astromerias, lilies, daisies, and other varieties are grown in Colombia as well. Virtually all carnations sold in the United States and Canada are produced in Colombia.

Cut flower production, which, as suggested earlier, is technically known as floriculture, has been promoted by the World Bank and the U.S. Agency for International Development (USAID) as a suitable industry for some of the weak and in-debt economies of the so-called Third World (Cactus 2000, 9; Campos 2002, 2). However, the introduction of floriculture has brought its own set of problems to countries where the flower industry has, in some cases, supplanted local food production (Mena 2002, 2).

Labor conditions for flower workers are bad in most parts of the world, and Colombia is no exception. In most cases in Latin America and Africa, flower workers are employed on short, fixed-term contracts, or as "temporary" or "casual" workers, even though they may work at the same farm for years. Colombian flower workers generally earn minimum wage, which hovers at around U.S.$154 per month, leaving workers and their families with about $7 per day to live on.

Flower workers, often without adequate protection, are exposed to numerous pesticides and other toxic chemicals. The excessive use of agrochemicals—sometimes of varieties banned in Europe and North America—is creating environmental problems as well. Both the subsoil and the water table of the *sabana* are contaminated, perhaps irreversibly (Campos 2002, 10–12; Utría 2002, 48–52).

The phenomenal growth of the flower industry in recent years is due to several factors, including ongoing protection by successive Colombian government administrations.[4] Commercial flowers are produced through a labor-intensive process in which each bloom receives individual attention throughout the growing cycle. However, despite the factory-like organization and discipline of the plantations, and the fact that the flowers are grown in an artificially controlled, indoor environment, the Colombian government classifies flower production as an agricultural rather than industrial activity, making it eligible for the types of concessions that agricultural producers receive. Perhaps the most important of these is exemption from the high value-added tax that is paid on all goods and services in Colombia. In addition to the economic breaks the industry receives at home, Colombian flowers enter the United States duty-free under the Andean

Trade Preference and Drug Eradication Act (ATPDEA). All of these factors helped the Colombian flower industry to become very competitive in northern markets. However, the industry's greatest advantage is the large pool of available labor and the low wages and scarce benefits that flower workers receive.

THE MAQUILA OF COLOMBIA

Unlike some of the other countries of Latin America and the Caribbean, Colombia does not have a developed, multinationally owned export processing sector specializing in garments or electronic components. These types of factories, which generally operate under transnational ownership, are sometimes referred to as "sweatshops" in the North, but are known in Spanish by the name originally applied to them in Mexico—the maquiladora or maquila.[5] Since its beginning in 1965 on the U.S.–Mexico border, the maquila industry has been an important source of jobs for women from poor urban and rural regions and a significant source of dollars for the host countries, with earnings going disproportionately to company owners. Maquila factories are characterized by low wages, long hours, fairly low-skilled and repetitive work, and a lack of job stability due to heavy use of short, fixed-term contracts, a lack of opportunities for job advancement or pay raises, pressure and surveillance while on the job, and, frequently, suspension of national labor laws. Union organizing is strongly discouraged by industry owners, and efforts to form unions in the maquilas have led to workers' dismissal and sometimes even plant closure. Many maquila factories also violate environmental laws with impunity.

The flower industry in Colombia has many of the characteristics of the maquila. It has long preferred to hire women for the work that is directly related to flower growing and handling, reserving supervisory, construction, and some of the other heavier jobs for men. This preference for women workers is based on the social assumption that women are better than men at detailed work requiring manual dexterity and a delicate touch. Like many maquila workers, women employed in the flower industry enter the workforce at a young age and are often single mothers with sole responsibility for their families (Brassel and Rangel 2001a, 21; Campos 2002, 4).[6] They are poor urban or landless rural women seeking work in a society where the real rate of unemployment may be as high as 29 percent (Godoy 1999).[7] Work in the flower industry is often their first waged job, and the only one available to them.

As in the maquila industry, wages are disproportionately low when compared to the price for which the finished, exported product sells and the volume of dollars floriculture brings into Colombia each year. Regardless of how many years they may work in the industry, flower workers do not earn more than minimum wage—a figure so low that it places workers in this wage bracket considerably below the poverty line.[8] The flower industry is a mass employer of women at low wages in a job where high demands are made on them in terms of quality of work and output, and where there is no opportunity for professional advancement or of gaining a share of the wealth that the industry generates.

Nevertheless, the Colombian flower industry differs from the maquila in two important ways. First, unlike the transnationally owned maquila factories, the flower companies have, until quite recently, been largely owned by Colombian producers. Second, the product that is produced—fresh, cut flowers—is not usually associated with any brand name or labeled as originating in any specific country. This has meant that strategies for pressuring companies to improve their labor practices, such as boycotts or negative publicity campaigns, must be organized differently from those designed to bring pressure on large, multinational (or U.S.-owned) companies selling easily recognized brand-name products.

A LABOR-INTENSIVE PROCESS

About 163,000 workers are employed, directly or indirectly, in the Colombian export flower industry (Silverman 2005). Approximately 60–70 percent of flower workers are women who work at growing, sorting, and packing the flowers for shipment (Brassel and Rangel 2001b, 16; Ismi 2000, 35; Rangel et al. 1996, 56). Indirect jobs in the industry mainly involve the production of plastics for greenhouse production, packing boxes, pesticides, and other inputs.[9]

There are about 500 flower companies in Colombia, producing on 4,900 hectares of land (Brassel and Rangel 2001b, 15). Between 400 and 500 people are generally working at any given time at an average-sized flower farm. This number, and the number of hours worked, increase at peak seasons, especially just before Valentine's Day and Mother's Day, when more workers are required in order to meet higher production quotas with a tight deadline. Failure to get the crop out of the plantation and onto the planes at the right time can result in loss of profits, so workers experience great pressure during these times.

Flower production takes place in a series of well-defined steps, beginning with steam disinfection and chemical fumigation of the soil in which seedlings imported from the United States, Germany, and the Netherlands are planted. Women plant the seedling while kneeling on damp, chemically treated soil contained in raised wooden platforms that are referred to as "beds." Planting dates are calculated and computer-monitored right down to the ideal date for supplying specific market destinations. At subsequent stages during the growing cycle, workers string netting to support the plants, pinch back lateral buds, "comb" the plants to ensure uniform growth, and then cover them with plastic to prevent early blooming. After harvest, flowers are selected and graded individually in refrigerated packing rooms that are located on the plantations (Acosta 1995, 176; Campos 2002, 6). The workers who perform these tasks may be paid on a piecework basis and, if hired through a labor contractor, generally do not receive benefits (Brassel and Rangel 2001b, 16; Rangel et al. 1996, 58–61).

As the industry has become more competitive, the intensity of the work has increased. In the early days of the flower industry in Colombia, each worker was normally responsible for eight beds of flowers, which vary in length from about 98 to 130 feet. During the 1980s, that number increased to between twelve and twenty-four beds per worker. Today, workers are expected to care for forty to forty-two beds each (Ortiz 2000). Workers have raised complaints that, at some facilities, they are expected to handle an even greater number of beds and are being pressured to further increase their productivity and output (Cactus 2001).

Flower workers are on the job approximately forty-eight hours per week and must meet required output quotas or they will be fired. During peak seasons, hours worked per week can climb to around sixty, frequently without overtime pay (Cox 2002, 17).[10] In addition to the pressure to increase their output, workers are subject to sanctions in the form of suspension without pay for perceived infractions, which include low productivity, unreliability, absence, or "bad behavior" (Rangel et al. 1996, 64).

The long hours that workers put in during peak seasons often amount to forced overtime. Since most of the women have children, the many hours spent away from the home are a particular burden. Many flower workers feel they do not have enough contact with their children and are concerned that they are not adequately supervised during the week. The fact that women often return home late at night and must then spend time catching up on cooking and other housework is a cause of considerable stress, and leaves them with little time to rest or relax. Women flower workers often refer to this problem when speaking about their lives.

HEALTH AND SAFETY PROBLEMS THREATEN WORKERS' HEALTH

The greatest health and safety problem confronting flower workers is exposure to toxic pesticides and other agrochemicals. Flowers exported to Europe and North America must be completely free of pests and disease, and failure to meet these standards will result in customs officials' refusal of an entire shipment (Acosta 1995, 176; Maharaj and Hohn 2001, 67). In order to provide insect- and disease-free flowers, the industry relies heavily on pesticides, which are applied several times per week (Cox 2002, 1). Numerous chemical substances are used in flower production, including fertilizers, insecticides, fungicides, nematocides, and plant growth regulators (PANUPS 2002, 2). One-fifth of the chemicals used in the Colombian flower industry are carcinogens or toxins that are restricted or prohibited in Europe and North America (Maharaj and Hohn 2001, 67).

The Colombian flower industry uses 200 kilos of pesticide per hectare of land, which is double the amount used in the Netherlands (Ismi 2000, 36). Seven of the 134 pesticides approved for use in the Colombian flower industry are designated by the Colombian government as "extremely toxic." At least twelve of the pesticides in use were singled out as possible or probable carcinogens by the U.S. Environmental Protection Agency (Cox 2002, 19).

The large quantities of toxic materials used inside the greenhouses are a source of health problems for workers. Dust from fumigation causes dizziness, headaches, cramps, and other symptoms (Acosta 1995, 176). Longer-term symptoms, such as numbness of limbs and partial paralysis, are present as well (Anonymous flower worker 2002; Mellon 1996). A further serious health hazard for workers is related to the fact that pesticides designed for use in the open air are being applied inside closed plastic greenhouses where residues cling to the interior walls long after fumigation is over (Cox 2002, 21). Workers, as well as eyewitnesses who visited plantations, testify that greenhouses are not always cleared of people during fumigation and that workers return to them too soon following fumigation (Anonymous interviewees 1997, 2002). Although attempts are now being made to remedy this situation, unsafe and negligent use of toxic chemicals is an ongoing problem. Moreover, although training in proper handling and application of pesticides has recently improved on some farms, it is still often inadequate, and safety equipment for workers is not always complete (Anonymous interviewee 1997).[11]

On November 25, 2003, 200 flower workers were poisoned in a chemical accident at the Flores Aposentos plantation in the municipality of Sopó, about forty minutes' drive north of Bogotá. In this instance, at least nine chemicals were mixed together and applied in unsafe circumstances. Twenty ambulances were needed to transport the workers to hospitals around the region, and although none died, a number of them remained under observation for several days. In seeking the cause of the accident, investigators discovered that the lack of record keeping and the unprofessional way in which the chemicals were mixed and stored made it impossible to draw a clear conclusion about what really took place before the workers became sick. There are no statistics on pesticide poisonings in the Colombian flower industry. However, the World Health Organization and the UN Environment Programme reported in 1990 that pesticides cause 20,000 deaths and poison 3 million people worldwide each year (Cox 2002, 1).

Constant exposure to toxic chemicals poses special problems for women, especially during pregnancy. A study carried out by the Colombian National Institute of Health in 1990 found a higher-than-average rate of miscarriages, premature births, and congenital malformations among the offspring of pregnant flower workers (Cox 2002, 20). No new study has taken place in Colombia to date.

Flower workers frequently suffer from respiratory infections caused by the drastic temperature changes and high humidity levels in the greenhouses. They also experience back and muscle pain and a variety of leg and knee problems caused by kneeling for long hours on damp ground (León and Luna 1996, 31; Mellon 1996). Carpal tunnel syndrome, brought on by constant, repetitive use of certain muscle-tendon groups, is not uncommon (Anonymous interviewees 2002). In addition to the threats to physical health cited above, workers often complain of verbal abuse and insulting behavior by supervisors. Sexual harassment of women workers by male supervisors is sometimes mentioned, but, to date, there is a lack of documented case studies for Colombia.[12]

An Industry Built on Worker Exploitation

The flower industry is an important indicator of downward changes in labor practices that have taken place in Colombia over the last fifteen years. Beginning in the 1980s, the industry played a key role in introducing flexible labor practices when it began hiring workers on short, fixed-term contracts, negotiated through labor contractors that specialized in providing temporary workers to the flower industry.[13] At that time, the practice was illegal under the Colombian labor code, but it was generally overlooked by the Ministry of Labor. In 1990, the labor code was changed with the introduction of Law 50/90, one of several pieces of legislation designed to encourage flexibilization of wage and hiring practices in Colombia (Cactus and Mesa de Trabajo 1999, 14; Rangel et al. 1996, 60–61).

Under this system, workers are not formally hired by the company they work for. The contracted flower workers strike individual bargains for their labor and may be paid at a piecework or per-job rate (Brassel and Rangel 2001b, 16). Short contracts of between one and six months are the most common. During peak seasons, there are also very short contracts of fifteen to twenty days, depending on the workload (Cox 2002, 17). One of the main reasons the industry prefers to hire short-term, contracted labor is because it is nearly impossible for workers to organize unions under such conditions (Rangel et al. 1996, 60–61).

In the past, a fair number of Colombian workers employed in the formal labor market enjoyed benefits, including retirement pensions and health and injury insurance, which were paid for through contributions by employers and workers to a national social security system.[14] These protections were put in place in earlier decades when unions in Colombia were considerably stronger and the labor movement had influence in Colombian society. Short-term contracts like those now used in the flower industry help employers avoid responsibility for contributing to workers' benefits (Cactus 1996, 13). Frequently, even the longer-term, six-month contracts have a probation period during which no benefits are paid. At the current time, downward changes to Colombian labor laws are leaving large numbers of workers virtually unprotected. Like other poor workers, flower workers are particularly vulnerable, as an already fragile social safety net is dismantled.

By law, Colombian women in the paid labor force have the right to twelve weeks of maternity leave, which is in keeping with the standard set by the International Labor Organisation (ILO). Like other social security benefits, maternity leave is paid for through worker and employer contributions to the system. However, flower workers generally cannot access this right. The illegal, though pervasive, use of obligatory pregnancy testing in order to get a job is still practiced in Colombia (Mellon 1995; Ridgeway 2004, 148; Rangel et al. 1996) and women who become pregnant while employed are often fired or their contracts are not renewed. Cases challenging these practices have nearly always resulted in a Ministry of Labor ruling against the worker.

A further setback for flower workers took place in 2003 with the introduction of Law 7-89. This reform essentially eliminated overtime pay by legislating changes that both lengthened the work day—making it much harder for workers to accrue overtime hours—and substantially lowered the hourly overtime rate. Under the new law, the long hours that flower workers must put in during peak seasons are not reflected in their paychecks.

Recent sweeping downward changes to Colombian labor law under the right-wing administration of President Álvaro Uribe Vélez created even greater problems for flower workers. One of the new laws, which came into effect in 2004, updates earlier legislation permitting the establishment of workers' cooperatives (Cooperativas de Trabajo Asociado) through which workers can contract themselves to an employer as a group. In practice, there is little that is cooperative about the new work associations. Observers of the flower industry have discovered that some of the new workers' cooperative associations were actually organized by labor contractors or by the flower companies themselves.

Workers who belong to the new cooperative associations essentially become their own employers, thus entering into the practice of exploiting themselves. They are not covered by the few protections still provided by national labor law, and they receive no benefits. They are prohibited from forming unions.

The cooperative association system is being strongly criticized by many people in Colombia, and pressure from within Congress has resulted in new legislation to guarantee at least minimal benefits for the association members. Nevertheless, the introduction of the cooperative associations represents yet another step in the process of increasing profits by lowering standards for the already superexploited flower industry workforce.

CHALLENGING THE FLOWER INDUSTRY: DEFENDING WORKERS' RIGHTS

For years, workers in the flower industry were largely ignored, or at best overlooked, by Colombian society. Disadvantaged by their sex and social class, they were a sector without influence in a setting where repeated erosion of national labor law succeeded in disabling workers' rights over a period of two decades.

During the early 1980s, some headway was made toward organizing flower workers into unions. However, plantation owners responded with violent repression and the movement was essentially broken.[15] To this day, the only unions tolerated by the industry are company unions that serve owners' interests but do nothing to protect workers' rights.

It is widely recognized that Colombia is the world's most dangerous country for unions. Unions are viewed by conservative social sectors as subversive, and their leaders and activists have long been targets in a social conflict played out at every level of society. A total of 94 Colombian trade unionists were murdered in 2004, with over 2,100 assassinated since 1991 (U.S. LEAP 2005). In recent months, leaders in agricultural workers' unions were particularly targeted (IUF 2005). At the plantation level, companies deal with union organizing by firing workers and circulating the names of people who are considered troublemakers, so they will not be able to find work in other companies (Mellon 2003, 41).

Given the lack of strong, independent unions in the sector, support and advocacy for flower workers has been carried out by local community and church-based groups that provide education in labor rights, health and safety information, and legal advice to workers and attempt to draw international attention to conditions in the industry. Since the mid-1990s, most efforts at seeking improvement for flower workers focused on attempts to persuade the industry to agree to a voluntary code of conduct that was designed by European pressure groups.[16] However, despite a long-term campaign, the Colombian flower industry refused to participate in the program since little or no pressure came from its biggest market, the United States.

The purchase of Floramérica, the largest flower production and export company in Colombia, by the U.S.-owned Dole Food Company, the world's largest distributor of fruits and vegetables, has introduced a new element into the struggle for flower workers' rights. With this acquisition, Dole became a major employer of flower workers and an active member of Ascolflores (Cox 2002, 17; Maharaj and Hohn 2001, 66; Pacific Business News 1998). Dole keeps a low profile at its Colombian flower farms. It did not change the names of the plantations it owns and continues to operate them under Colombian management (Cactus 2001). However, Dole's presence in the industry gives rise to new possibilities for applying international pressure to the industry—a factor that labor rights groups are exploring.

In late 2004, the International Labor Rights Fund (ILRF) began its Fairness in Flowers campaign—the first effort organized in the United States to support Colombian flower workers. The Washington D.C.–based ILRF has a long history of supporting labor rights and is staffed by a team of lawyers and researchers that supports campaigns around the world. In February 2005, a representative of Cactus, the most visible of the Colombian flower worker support groups, traveled to Washington where he met with members of the U.S. Congress International Workers' Rights Caucus. Although this work is still in the early stages, once again it has become clear that Dole's industry presence is providing a lever for U.S. groups to begin working on the issue of labor rights for flower workers.

In the meantime, union organizing for flower workers recently gained new life when new independent unions began organizing workers at three Dole-owned flower farms. Although the new unions were recognized by the Colombian government, the company is doing everything it can to oppose them and to promote the company unions it supports (ILRF 2005). At Splendor Flowers, where the independent Sintrasplendor Union is organizing workers, the company fired eleven union activists in May 2005. On June 2, workers responded with a lively demonstration in front of the company's head office in Bogotá in an upsurge of a type of union militancy that has not been seen in the industry in decades. The ILRF is helping the process by encouraging an international letter-writing campaign urging the company to recognize the union's legal status and to respect its employees' right to freedom of organization. The new union gained certification in August 2005 and, at the time of this writing, is preparing to negotiate its first contract.

For the last four years, Colombian flower workers' organizations have declared Valentine's Day (a holiday that is not celebrated in Colombia) to be National Flower Workers' Day, applying a creative media strategy that is beginning to show some positive results. Flower workers have been profiled in the local and national media, and worker organizers have debated industry representatives on national television and in the municipal councils of the towns in the flower producing region. These activities not only represent an important step in applying pressure locally to industry owners but also serve to increase worker pride, identity, and solidarity. Like the latest union mobilizations, they are creating a level of visibility for flower workers that, until now, has been lacking. They represent home-grown efforts as well as a commitment to flower workers' efforts to take control of their destiny in a long-term battle against extreme exploitation.

NOTES

1. I wish to thank Angélica Chaparro, Nora Ferm, and Ricardo Zamudio for their help with this chapter.

2. The increase in flower purchases in the United States can be attributed to several factors. The flower industry spent huge sums on advertising and marketing in an effort to promote the giving of flowers on as many occasions as possible. The new marketing strategy makes flowers available in many nontraditional venues, including supermarkets, in emulation of the European custom of buying fresh flowers with the weekly groceries. The ease with which flowers can be ordered on the Internet is also a factor in the recent growth in sales.

3. The Lomé Convention, adopted in 1975, provides for trade preferences between European countries and their former colonies in Africa, the Caribbean, and the Pacific.

4. As one of the most economically powerful sectors in the country, the Colombian flower industry wields considerable economic and political influence. It is favored by the government because it exemplifies the agricultural export model officially promoted by the Colombian state and because it generates jobs.

5. The term *maquila* refers to a type of offshore manufacturing plant that operates under special programs beneficial to transnational owners and exports products assembled by local workers. While the origin of the word is unclear, in the past it referred to the charge a miller collects for processing other people's grain. Maquila plants are present in many countries of Latin America and the Caribbean, and in other parts of the world as well. However, this type of foreign investment failed to take hold in Colombia, due to the ongoing social and political unrest there as well as the civil war that has ravaged the country for decades.

6. Education in Colombia is not free, and many teens end their schooling to work. There is a strong age bias in hiring practices in Colombia, with employers preferring to hire younger people. Older workers in the industry often express concern that they will be unable to find another job if they are fired.

7. Colombia has one of the worst land distribution rates in Latin America. Over 1 million rural families own no land at all, and 64 percent of the rural population live in poverty.

8. Workers in the flower industry suddenly gained worldwide visibility with the 2004 release of the film *Maria Full of Grace,* which shows the pregnant, teenage protagonist working unhappily on a flower plantation before deciding to risk her freedom and her life smuggling heroin into the United States. When Joshua Marston, the film's U.S.-based writer and director, traveled to Colombia to carry out research for his script, local people steered him to the flower industry as an example of dead-end, low-wage, unpleasant work for women.

9. Statistical estimates of the number of flower workers, and of other industry indicators, vary considerably—depending on their source. On the world level, most of the available data are generated by the industry itself, and figures are sometimes adapted in an effort to evade taxes or to improve the industry's appearance with regard to job creation (Brassel and Rangel 2001b, 11). Until fairly recently, independent research and reporting were rare, and those researching the field today are still largely reliant on industry figures.

10. In recent years some plantations have witnessed the introduction of productivity bonus schemes, in which workers commit to work a specific number of overtime hours per month in exchange for a bonus in lieu of overtime pay. When calculated on the basis of the number of workers involved, this amounts to a tremendous savings in overtime wages paid by the company.

11. During a visit to Colombia in 1997, a delegation of Canadian trade unionists met secretly with several flower workers—in this case, male workers who carried out fumigation procedures—to discuss health and safety conditions on the plantations. They discovered that, while the company was providing a particular type of safety mask with which the Canadians were familiar, the workers were not informed that the mask requires frequent changes of an internal, removable filter in order to be effective. To their knowledge, the filters were never changed.

12. Current information on sexual harassment in the flower industry is available in a recent study carried out in Ecuador for the International Labor Rights Fund. The report, which is titled "Sexual Harassment in the Workplace: The Cut Flower Industry," can be viewed at www.laborrights. org/actions.

13. The term *flexible* refers to production and employment practices that began in the 1970s and accelerated rapidly throughout the 1980s and 1990s. In response to the increased pressures of international competition, employers boosted profits by lowering labor costs and eliminating workers' ability to organize into unions. Flexible labor practices include a decrease in full-time, permanent employment and an increase in short, fixed-term contracts, so that workers can be hired or fired depending on production needs.

14. At the time of this writing, a proposal by the current administration to privatize the social security system is being hotly debated in Colombian society.

15. The story of a union struggle by flower workers is documented in the 1988 film *Love, Women, and Flowers,* produced and directed by Marta Rodríguez and Jorge Silva.

16. The *International Code of Conduct for the Production of Cut Flowers* can be viewed at www.flowercampaign.org/english/code.pdf.

11

The Process of Exporting Neoliberal Development

The Consequences of the Growth of Export Processing Zones in El Salvador

Jill Esbenshade

❀

El Salvador's failure to safeguard workers' human rights in the private export sector not only allows local employers and multinational corporations to carry out and benefit from human rights violations but also helps create a model in which export goods are produced under abusive conditions. (Human Rights Watch 2003a)

In El Salvador, as elsewhere, maquila workers are subject to the harsh realities of export processing jobs that have become one of the principal employment "opportunities" for women around the world. Although these jobs may pay better than the existing alternatives in such areas as agriculture and domestic service, they bring with them their own complex of exploitative conditions. They have also proved to be an unsatisfactory basis for sustainable national growth, as employment moves from one country to another.

A major facet of globalization has been the proliferation of export processing zones (EPZs). EPZs are not development projects originating from local needs. Rather, they are tied in with the implementation of the neoliberal agenda promoted by the U.S. government and transnational corporations, along with multinational entities such as the World Bank and the International Monetary Fund. The adoption of export processing as a development strategy is driven in large measure by the dictates of loan programs and of repayments to these international financial institutions. This strategy adds to economic growth as measured in GDP, but it does not translate into decent working conditions or living wages for employees. Moreover, as transnational corporations move their production across the globe in accordance with relative wages, improvements in transportation technology, and changing trade benefits, factories close down and workers dependent on EPZ employment are displaced.

The present chapter tells the story of this process in El Salvador—a story that is partially based on two six-week periods of field research in El Salvador. My research included fifty-four in-depth interviews with workers, factory owners, government officials, and nongovernmental organization representatives, with additional interviews and data collection conducted in 2005. Specifically, I trace the development of EPZs in El Salvador, document the conditions in these factories, discuss them in the larger context of conditions observed elsewhere in the world, and briefly explore how workers have been affected by the termination of apparel quotas in 2005 as well as what strategies the Salvadoran government is implementing in response.

THE MAQUILA INDUSTRY IN EL SALVADOR

During the civil wars that raged in Central America throughout the 1980s, the United States complemented its strategy of low-intensity warfare with an aggressive campaign to build up capitalist economies in the region oriented toward the United States. During the height of the wars, economic development was frustrated by sabotage, insecurity, and instability. When the right-wing Alianza Republicana Nacionalista (Nationalist Republican Alliance) (ARENA) party came to power in El Salvador in 1989, it began instituting a plan of structural adjustment that included export-oriented development. However, the new government was not able to fully implement its strategy until the signing of the peace accords three years later.

Export-oriented development is largely based on maquila production, which involves the importation of unassembled parts—in the case of garments, this would be principally cloth—and the exportation of finished products. Maquilas in El Salvador are located in two areas: free trade zones, or *zonas francas* (the common Latin American term for EPZs), and *recintos fiscales*. Whereas *zonas francas* are "extraterritorial geographic spaces," *recinto fiscal* is a legal designation accorded to qualifying factories located outside the free trade zones that also produce for export and are given many of the same tax and trade benefits.

EPZs are large fenced-off areas that house several (often a dozen or so) factories, which have been built for the express purpose of export manufacturing. Many of these factories resemble airport hangars. Usually there are armed guards posted at the gates of the zones as well as at the individual factories. Factories in the EPZs are much larger than in *recintos fiscales,* averaging 400 workers. These EPZ factories are most often foreign-owned—mainly by Koreans, Taiwanese, and Americans—whereas nearly all *recintos fiscales* are owned and operated by Salvadorans (Quinteros et al. 1998). According to a survey conducted by a local labor research institute, more than 80 percent of the workers are women under 35; of these, most are younger than 25 and two-thirds are mothers (Quinteros et al. 1998).

When the Salvadoran civil war ended in 1992, there was only one export processing zone in the country, and it employed 6,500 workers. By 1998, there were 80,000 workers in the export processing plants, accounting for over one-third of the industrial workers in the metropolitan area.[1] Products resulting from the export processing of imported components surpassed the export of coffee in 2000, making maquilas the leading export sector (BCRES 2002). EPZs have continued to expand, from eight in 2000 to fifteen in 2004 (USITC 2004; U.S. State Department 2005). In El Salvador 90 percent of EPZ production is textile and apparel, the great majority of which is produced for U.S. brands and 97 percent of which is destined for the U.S. market (USITC 2004).

U.S. government funding was essential to this growth process. In 1988, as part of Reagan's "Trade not Aid" initiative, the U.S. government gave El Salvador $37 million to build export processing facilities (Kernaghan 1997). The U.S. government not only provided the needed infrastructure to facilitate manufacturing activities but also spent tens of millions more to promote the transfer of jobs to the region. Under Reagan, the U.S. Agency for International Development underwrote the budget of the Salvadoran Foundation for Economic and Social Development (FUSADES), whose mission was to promote U.S. investment in labor-intensive assembly production in El Salvador with a focus on apparel (Kernaghan 1997).

Programs to financially support U.S. companies producing abroad proliferated during the 1980s. In 1986, apparel was added to the list of duty-free items allowed into the United States under the Caribbean Basin Initiative (CBI) program (Safa 1994). Twenty-seven million dollars in government funds were allocated to subsidize worker training for companies moving to El Salvador (Kernaghan 1997). The U.S. government also provided U.S. companies that invested abroad with tax breaks, loans, insurance, and other incentives to move production to developing countries (Barnet 1994; Rothstein 1989; Varley 1998).

El Salvador promised cheap labor and few industrial regulations to U.S. investors, but it also gave the U.S. government a chance to consolidate its political influence in the region. As the current Salvadoran economic attaché to Washington put it, "The whole maquila thing in the case of El Salvador became popular in the 1980s under [the] CBI promoted by Ronald Reagan to create economic opportunities because countries were facing the menace of communism and instability that could lead these countries to change to autocratic or socialist governments. So those countries could believe in democracy, that's the bottom line."[2] Thus, for the U.S. government there was a confluence of opposing leftist guerrillas in Central America and supporting multinational companies moving jobs to the region.

The Salvadoran government has also been integrally involved in attracting investors. Maquilas in El Salvador are exempt from income, municipal and other taxes such as sales and rent tax. In addition, they are able to import necessary equipment (machinery, tools, furniture) and materials duty-free (BCRES 2002; Quinteros et al. 1998; USITC 2004). And in 2001, El Salvador stabilized its currency by replacing it with the U.S. dollar, simultaneously creating the lowest interest rates in Central America (USITC 2004).

The Salvadoran government, like the governments of many developing nations, is caught up in the neoliberal economic order, which virtually requires it to offer such benefits to investors. Indebted Third World countries are required by loan conditions to engage in export manufacturing and to offer favorable conditions to foreign investors. Third World governments are thus able to gain the hard currency with which to make payments on international loans. The implementation of export-oriented economic growth is part of a complex of neoliberal policies that debtor countries are required to adopt. Central to such structural adjustment programs are the privatization of government operations (in El Salvador, these consist of telephone service, medical care, and electricity), curtailment of social programs, and removal of trade barriers.

The most important attraction offered by Third World countries is easily available, cheap, and docile labor. The benefits associated with Salvadoran workers are publicized in U.S. trade journals, where these workers compete with millions of under- and unemployed people around the world. FUSADES, funded by U.S. tax dollars, placed an advertisement in the early 1990s that featured a photo of a young woman and a caption reading "You can hire her for 57 cents an hour. Rosa is more than just colorful. She and her coworkers are known for their industriousness, reliability and quick learning. They make El Salvador one of the best buys" (reprinted in Kernaghan 1997). In a later version of the ad, Rosa was available for only 33 cents. And Rosa's "industriousness" and "reliability" are enforced by factory discipline, high unemployment, and the government, which keeps workers in line through bureaucratic channels and security-force interventions in labor disputes.

In 1997, the Center for the Study of Work (CENTRA), a research institute in El Salvador, surveyed 750 workers from thirty-seven factories. The results indicated the occurrence of widespread violations in the EPZs. Forced overtime was rampant, with over 45 percent of workers saying they never had a choice about working overtime and another 18 percent reporting that they only sometimes had a choice. High production quotas and very little rest time were other commonly reported problems. Additionally, 44 percent of the women and 28 percent of the men reported earning less than minimum wage (Quinteros et al. 1998). And even if workers were paid properly, the minimum did not provide for basic subsistence. For example, in 1999, the minimum industrial wage was U.S.$144 per month (the same as in 2005) but basic monthly food expenditures for a family of five in the urban area were U.S.$547 dollars per month, excluding the costs of rent, medical expenses, childcare, and so on (Molina and Quinteros 2000). According to the U.S. State Department, maquila workers in El Salvador also regularly report verbal, physical, and sexual abuse (U.S. State Department 2001, 2002, 2003, 2004, 2005).

In fact, the export processing sector of the Salvadoran economy generates the largest number of officially registered worker complaints. In an interview, the chief inspector at the Ministry of Labor estimated that in 1999 approximately 30 percent of all complaints were from the maquila sector, and that in 1995 and 1996 that figure was as high as 70 percent. The chief inspector emphasized that this is true even though most workers do not complain unless they have already been fired or left their jobs.[3]

However, the Ministry of Labor in El Salvador is ineffective at enforcing local labor laws, largely due to a lack of resources. In 1999 the Ministry had only nineteen inspectors for the entire country. Inspectors were not given vehicles but, instead, had to travel to distant worksites by public transportation or to use their own cars and pay for gas themselves.[4] In 2003 there were thirty-seven inspectors, a ratio of one inspector per 70,000 workers (HRW 2003a). Another contributing factor has been corruption. In 2001, five Ministry inspectors (including a senior staff member) were fired for taking bribes from export producing companies (U.S. State Department 2002). Despite this cleanup effort, subsequent State Department reports have noted continuing allegations of corruption (U.S. State Department 2003, 2004, 2005).

Beyond logistical constraints and corruption, there is also the issue of the Ministry's political will to enforce laws and to protect workers' rights to organize. In its Country Reports, the U.S. State Department commented five years in a row that "[t]here were repeated complaints by workers, in some cases supported by the ILO Committee on Freedom of Association (CFA), that the Government impeded workers from exercising their right of association," and that "[t]he Ministry often sought to conciliate labor disputes through informal channels rather than attempt to enforce regulations strictly" (U.S. State Department 2001, 2002, 2003, 2004, 2005). For instance, although there is a statute guaranteeing that, during their year-long tenure, these union leaders "cannot be fired, transferred nor downgraded in their conditions of work, nor disciplinarily suspended," the Ministry regularly interprets this law as allowing firms to prohibit leaders from coming to work as long as they are paid. The result is that leaders are effectively banned from their place of work and thus cannot continue to organize or agitate. Although workers argue that this constitutes a de facto suspension, firms have been supported by the Ministry in their claim that, since there is no interruption in salary, union leaders have not been "disciplined." In fact, the Ministry sometimes pays out wages to barred unionists for the export processing companies (Anner 1998).

The Ministry directly contributes to union repression in a number of ways. As a matter of long-established practice, the Ministry forwards the approval of a duly registered union to the factory owner, including the names of all union officers—often resulting in the de facto suspension of these leaders. A common employer practice is to force unionists to resign, and the Ministry participates by withholding severance pay until resignation papers have been signed (HRW 2003). U.S. Country Reports consistently found that although the Ministry required severance to be paid to fired unionists, "in most cases, the Government did not prevent their dismissal or require their reinstatement" (U.S. State Department 2001, 2002, 2003, 2004, 2005). Thus, despite formal union protections, the Ministry of Labor allows illegal suspensions, forced resignations, and outright firings as well as the compounding problem of blacklisting.

Blacklisting refers to factory owners' circulation of the names of fired unionists, who are then unable to secure employment. The Ministry has failed to combat this practice (U.S. State Department 2002, 2003, 2004, 2005) and, at times, has even contributed to it. For example, in the past it has issued letters to workers to prove that they have not been registered union members, thus prejudicing workers who are unable to provide employers with such affidavits.[5] In 2000 the Ministry acknowledged the practice of blacklisting in a report. However, the report was retracted immediately after publication due to the negative reaction of the business community in the country, and no significant changes were ever made (WRC 2003).

In 2003, Human Rights Watch (HRW) released an extensive report titled *Deliberate Indifference: El Salvador's Failure to Protect Workers' Rights*. Besides the Ministry of Labor's failure to enforce laws, HRW found many other instances in which workers' rights were being undermined. In particular, it exposed a number of weaknesses in Salvadoran labor law including no right to reinstatement after retaliatory firings, no explicit protections for hiring discrimination against labor activists, and barriers to legal registration of unions. HRW also found serious obstacles in the processing of worker claims through the judicial system. Workers generally do not have the time and resources to pursue the lengthy procedures involved. They are often unable to present the requisite witnesses, given that there is no protection for retaliatory firings and co-workers fear for their jobs. And even when workers do win judgments, the actual collection of wages is often impossible.

Yet, despite the impediments just described, EPZs became a focus of union organizing due to rapid industry growth and high rates of violations. Organizing campaigns strove for higher wages and better conditions, but were often compromised by resentment over abusive and/or disrespectful treatment on the part of managers. However, organizing campaigns generally ended in firings and layoffs. CENTRA documented twenty-eight efforts to unionize maquila factories between 1993 and 1998, twenty-five of which resulted in firings or factory closures and none of which brought about a collective bargaining agreement (Quinteros et al. 1998). In a particularly active organizing period, from 1994 to 1995, more than 4,000 workers were fired or lost their jobs when plants closed in response to organizing drives. A decade later there were eighteen active unions in the maquila industry but still not a single collective bargaining agreement in the EPZs (U.S. State Department 2005).

The case of Tainan Enterprises, which has been well documented by various international solidarity organizations, offers a recent illustration of continuing problems involving the firing of unionists and their subsequent blacklisting. In the spring of 2002, union membership at the Tainan factory in the San Bartolo Free Trade Zone reached over 50 percent of the workforce in one sector known as "TS2." The union proceeded to assert its right to negotiate a collective bargaining agreement (CBA) according to Salvadoran law. However, as in other cases, management quickly closed the facility and laid off all the workers. The closure followed months of efforts by management to prevent union organizing through dismissals of leaders and other tactics. In addition, before and after the closing of Tainan an international campaign was being led by students and other antisweat-shop activists. Activists sent delegations to the headquarters of U.S. brands that sourced from Tainan (e.g., Gap, Kohl's, and Target), picketed outside their stores, and generated media attention. In Taiwan, where Tainan Enterprises' headquarters is located, a local NGO called Focus on Globalization also led a campaign, and Tainan workers in Cambodia threatened a sympathy strike.[6]

An extensive investigation by the Worker Rights Consortium, a U.S.-based nonprofit monitoring organization, determined that other factories in the same EPZ as Tainan (particularly Primo) had then blacklisted former Tainan workers. This investigation revealed that the Ministry of Labor did not fine a single factory in the EPZs for *any* labor code violations in 2002, despite the Ministry's own withdrawn report about the widespread nature of such violations. In fact, the State Department has noted that, despite the fact that El Salvador adopted a law in 1996 making it possible to revoke EPZ privileges if companies violate labor laws, "there have been no instances in which this has been used or even publicly threatened" (U.S. State Department 2001, 2002). Thus, workers are not only subject to underpayment and illegal conditions but are effectively prevented from legally organizing to protest such violations.

CONDITIONS AROUND THE WORLD

As we have seen, El Salvador provides an example of how the processes of globalization have produced exploitative jobs for women. Women in EPZs in other countries suffer much the same treatment.[7] The garment industry super exploits workers by avoiding even the low labor costs that are legally required. Reports from around the world reveal that the legal minimum wage and overtime premiums are frequently not paid, and that workers are further cheated through deductions of "fines" or penalties for refusal to work overtime, not meeting quotas, being out sick, or other perceived violations. Moreover, workers' checks are sometimes reduced by deductions for transportation, food (usually insufficient), and lodging (often overcrowded and unsanitary).

In addition, employers save money by failing to provide a safe and healthy workplace. For example, work areas often lack potable water, clean bathrooms, and clear and functioning fire exits and extinguishers. Machine guards and ergonomic seating are rarely provided. And workers are subject to chemical exposure and unhealthy levels of particles in the air they breathe. Employers are also reluctant to let workers interrupt their productive activity, thus sometimes causing or worsening their health problems. It is not uncommon for employers to restrict workers' access to toilets or to deny permission to leave work to visit a doctor, leading in some cases to serious medical problems, miscarriage, and even death.

Employers also keep costs down by evading the payment of required social security and health benefits. In many countries, employers are required to pay social security and health insurance and to provide maternity benefits such as employer contributions to necessary pre- and postnatal care, arrangement of physically nonstrenuous work tasks, and paid maternity leave. Many employers deduct for such costs but never pay them. They also avoid government-mandated maternity benefits by forcing women to take preemployment and/or regular pregnancy tests, using these tests as a basis for not hiring and for firing pregnant women, often in contravention of protective legislation. There are cases of pregnant women being beaten, of women being injected with hormonal contraceptives under threat of firing, and of women being forced to take birth control pills, which they are sometimes told are "vitamins" (Pearson and Seyfang 2002; Varley 1998). Pregnancy tests are regularly required of new and continuing employees in El Salvador, and pregnant women continue to be fired in violation of the law (U.S. Department of State 2005).

The garment industry pushes down costs not only by locating in the lowest-cost countries but also by utilizing the workers in those countries with little bargaining power: women and immigrants. Globally, women workers predominate; they account for 74 percent of workers, although there is variation by country (ILO 2000). Women workers face more barriers to organizing because of the "double day" in which they are required to perform household chores and childcare duties after work hours and on weekends. They are thus less able than men to attend union meetings and activities. Moreover, women are more vulnerable to such common societal abuses as pay discrimination, physical mistreatment, and sexual harassment, which abound in the garment industry. There are endless reports of supervisors yelling at, swearing at, hitting, and groping workers as well as scattered reports of much more severe physical abuse. Also, the ubiquitous policy of forced overtime has graver consequences for women, as they are responsible for childcare and may be endangered by nighttime travel. As the well-publicized case of Ciudad Juarez on the U.S.–Mexico border made clear, maquila workers returning home at irregular hours after working overtime have been among the 300 women who disappeared or were murdered in the past decade.

Migrant workers—as the mainstay of the industry in most industrialized and newly industrialized countries—are also particularly vulnerable to exploitation. The women among them often have fewer rights by law or are afraid of and/or threatened with deportation if they attempt to exercise the rights they do have. In developing countries like El Salvador many workers are internal migrants from rural areas. Although in most countries this scenario does not pose particular legal disadvantages for workers, it does so in China, which is the world's largest producer of apparel. In China female migrants, many of them in their teens, make up the vast majority of EPZ workers (Ross 2004). They are required to have resident permits that allow Chinese from rural areas to work and reside in the "special economic zones" where EPZs are located. In the case of both immigrants and Chinese internal migrants, employers often curtail workers' ability to travel freely or to find other jobs by confiscating the workers' travel documents.

Labor costs can also be slashed through forced labor. Debt peonage and prison labor have been used from California to Saipan to China. Recent lawsuits have brought to light what U.S. Attorney General John Ashcroft described as "nothing less than modern-day slavery."[8] Even now, at the dawn of the twenty-first century, modern-day slaves—or, more accurately, indentured servants—count among their numbers the tens of thousands of workers from China, the Philippines, Bangladesh, and Thailand who in the 1990s paid fees of up to $7,000 to be transported to supposedly well-paid garment jobs in the United States and ended up behind barbed-wire fences in Saipan (a U.S. territory in the North Pacific). Many worked seventy-hour weeks in unhealthy and dangerous conditions, paid high prices for horrendous living quarters and unhygienic food, were regularly cheated out of overtime pay, and spent years trying to repay their debt.[9] Seventy-two Thai immigrants suffered under extraordinarily similar conditions in a guarded compound in El Monte, California (Su 1997). In American Samoa (a U.S. territory in the South Pacific), an FBI investigator testified that the factory owner "defrauded, failed to pay and at times deprived of food, beat and physically restrained these workers to force them to work."[10] Dozens of companies, from J.C. Penney' to Wal-Mart to the Gap, sold clothes from these factories with "Made in the USA" labels. In a few cases, lawsuits have brought some compensation for the women involved, but in many other, less publicized cases elsewhere in the world the situation has gone unaddressed.

Like "homework," the various forms of forced labor not only reduce labor costs but are also a means of thwarting unionization.[11] To ensure maximum labor availability and minimum interference, employers often condition work upon compliance with coerced agreements. In the case of Saipan, workers were required to sign "shadow contracts" that prohibited them from unionizing, as well as attending, religious services, marrying, or quitting. Moreover, immigrants are especially vulnerable to antiunion tactics when both their job and their residence depend on the company. In American Samoa, where employers own both the factories and migrants' living quarters, they simply turned off the electricity in stifling buildings when workers struck for unpaid wages.[12]

As in El Salvador, direct repression of organizing efforts in the apparel industry is a common practice around the world (Armbruster-Sandoval 2000; Fuentes and Ehrenreich 1983; Quinteros et al. 1998; Varley 1998; Yimprasert and Candland 2000). In 2001 alone, the International Confederation of Free Trade Unions (ICFTU) reported garment workers who had been fired for union organizing in such places as Burma, Cambodia, Kenya, Lesotho, South Africa, Mexico, Nicaragua, and Malaysia; activists from Kenya to Mexico to Thailand were arrested; and there were documented cases of unionists being beaten in Iran and Thailand (ICFTU 2002).

Although employers around the globe usually play the primary role in repressing organizing efforts, government regulations or practices often thwart unionization. As discussed in relation to El Salvador, local governments sometimes participate in repression of worker rights in order to attract foreign investment. In some countries, such as Bangladesh, Namibia, Pakistan, and Panama, union activity is prohibited or restricted specifically in export processing zones as a matter of law (ILO 2000). In other countries, such as Mexico and China, the only unions in the export processing zones are official unions traditionally allied with the government. Such unions have assumed a nonadversarial role vis-à-vis employers, professing a commitment to the government's development plan that requires continued investment.[13]

THE DISTRIBUTION OF THE GLOBAL APPAREL INDUSTRY

This intense competition for investment among countries, based in large part on exploited workers, is indicative of neoliberal globalization. The garment industry was the first one to globalize its production and has often been the first one a country turns to when adopting the export-oriented economic model. Very little capital or technology is needed to participate in garment production. Until recently, countries became competitive based on cheap labor alone. This situation is now changing somewhat with the advent of "full package" production, whereby countries that produce cloth or make it easily available have an advantage. The labor-intensive nature of the industry has contributed to enormous instability as factory owners, who have invested little or no capital, easily move around the world searching for cheaper labor and more profitable overall conditions. The shifting nature of the industry will only increase in coming years as quotas and tariffs that benefited certain areas are eliminated under World Trade Organization (WTO) rules and as regionally based trade agreements proliferate. In this section I describe the distribution of production in the global apparel industry and discuss how recent changes threaten the participation of countries like El Salvador.

Clothing is an enormous industry, accounting for 22 percent of the worldwide trade in consumer goods in 1997. (During the same year, textiles and clothing together made up over two-fifths of all exports of consumer goods.) Clothing production and, especially, trade increased dramatically from 1980 to 1998. In fact, the value of clothing *made for export* increased 335 percent, a figure nearly ten times greater than the increase in the value of production generally (ILO 2000). The trend continued at a breakneck pace; apparel imports to the United States alone rose another 34 percent to more than $67 billion between 1997 and 2001.[14] U.S. imports from El Salvador rose 78 percent during the same period (USITC 2004).

In addition to substantial growth in the amount of export production, the location of production underwent a major geographical shift—generally from more industrialized to less industrialized countries, with Asia experiencing by far the largest growth. Employment in the clothing sector in such countries as Bangladesh, Mexico, Indonesia, Thailand, and China increased considerably, whereas the United States, Europe, Japan, and Hong Kong lost jobs (ILO 2000). As the search for cheaper labor continued, and as quota regimes drove companies to spread out production in order to avoid tariffs, more and more countries were drawn into the contest. By 2004, 130 countries were producing clothes for export (Appelbaum, Bonacich, and Quan 2005). However, many countries that gained production during the last two decades have subsequently seen factories leave. As a researcher at the UN International Labor Organization noted, "[J]obs created in any one country cannot be regarded as long-term gain.... [C]enters of development, production and trade are constantly shifting and taking jobs with them" (ILO 2000, section 1.2.3). Even more dramatic shifts are expected over the next few years.

On January 1, 2005, the Multi-Fiber Arrangement (MFA) quotas were eradicated, such that production from any given country was no longer limited to a certain amount. As expected, this liberalization has led to more significant shifts in production from developed to developing countries. The United States lost 17,000 garment and textile jobs in January and February of 2005 alone.[15] Researchers have also predicted the occurrence of shifts between developing countries, with Asia increasing its percentage of worldwide production and Mexico and the Caribbean decreasing theirs (Diao and Somwaru 2001). China is expected to receive the biggest influx of new production, given such characteristics as very low wages, a stable investment environment, a highly controlled labor force with the largest reserve army of labor in the world and, most important, the ability to provide "full package" production (Ross 2002). The *Washington Post* reported that up to 30 million jobs might shift to China.[16] Indeed, in just the first three months of 2005 the growth of exports from China was so dramatic that the United States invoked temporary "safeguard" quotas on certain Chinese products.

Central America is generally expected to lose production, and reports from the field show this has already begun to happen.[17] It is uncertain how much production Central America will ultimately lose. On the one hand, Central America is relatively close to the United States. With the current model of lean production, where as little as possible is warehoused, proximity to market continues to matter. On the other hand, Central America not only has higher wages and formal recognition of the right to unionize, but, equally important, it lacks significant textile production—an industry that requires far more capital inputs (Appelbaum 2005). The U.S. International Trade Commission (USITC) reported that 50 percent of the Salvadoran apparel industry may disappear with the end of the MFA quota system, unless other trade advantages are instituted (USITC 2004). The Reserve Bank of El Salvador reported a 19 percent decline in maquila activity in February 2005 as compared to February 2004 (BCRES 2005).

The distribution of production is influenced, among other factors, by proximity to markets, trade restrictions, ready supply of materials, and labor costs. However, as transportation technology advances and trade restrictions are liberalized, labor costs play an increasingly important role. The disparity in wage levels and other associated labor costs is striking. In the United States in 1995, labor costs (including wages and benefits) in apparel were officially $9.53 per hour compared to an average of only $1.25 in Latin American countries. Similarly, labor costs in Japan were $16.45 per hour versus an average of $2.78 elsewhere (ILO 2000). There are, of course, differences among developing countries as well. Currently El Salvador has the second-highest labor costs in Central America—after Costa Rica, which has lost much of its industry. There now appears to be a shifting of production to Nicaragua from El Salvador. At about 40 cents an hour, China's wages are currently lower than the wages in Mexico and Central America but higher than those in many nearby Asian countries such as Sri Lanka, Vietnam, Pakistan, and India, where wages range from 13 to 22 cents an hour.[18] However, as previously stated, China has production capabilities that far outstrip those of its neighbors.[19]

As quotas are phased out, wages may be driven down even further by increased competition; conditions may worsen as well. Analysts expect growing subcontracting and homework as well as a flight to areas where workers' rights are least protected. Even before the MFA phaseout was complete, it was being used to justify a weakening of the protections that workers had. In Sri Lanka, a high-ranking government official called for changing the overtime legislation from 100 allowed hours a year to 100 hours a month in order to maintain the country's international competitiveness when the MFA quotas were removed (Dent 2002). In an attempt to remain competitive with China, the Salvadoran business community has proposed lowering that country's current maquila minimum wage in parts of the country. And in the Philippines there is a proposal under consideration to exclude apparel workers from the minimum-wage guarantees altogether.[20]

SURVIVING THE GLOBAL GAMBLE

In the face of a decline in the export processing sector, the Salvadoran government is working on several strategies to bolster the economy. First, it has negotiated the Central American Free Trade Agreement (CAFTA) in order to gain tariff advantages that might counteract the loss of quota. Second, it is lobbying for other types of investment, such as call centers. Workers in such centers sit at telephones making airline reservations or answering customer-service questions concerning anything from computer software problems to banking overdrafts. Third, the government continues to actively work toward legal status for Salvadoran immigrants in the United States, who provide billions of dollars in remittances to the Salvadoran economy. Unfortunately, however, none of these strategies would improve the pervasively poor working conditions discussed in this chapter.

In fact, all three strategies—free trade agreements, exporting services, and ensuring continued remittances from immigrants—tie the economy of El Salvador more closely to the United States. As El Salvador loses the pay of garment workers sewing Gap T-shirts, it scrambles to find other means of accruing dollars, whether through women continuing to toil in light manufacturing, bilingual college graduates answering questions for disgruntled U.S. customers, nannies in Los Angeles, day laborers on Long Island, or hotel workers in Washington D.C. wiring money home. El Salvador, like a growing number of countries, is indeed becoming increasingly dependent on the wages of empire.

NOTES

1. Interview, economist Gilberto Garcia of the Center for the Study of Work, July 22, 1999.
2. Interview, economic attaché from Salvadoran Embassy, February 10, 2005. Also see BCERS 2002.
3. Interview, Ronoél Vela Cea, San Salvador, July 28, 1999.
4. Interviews, labor inspectors Carlos Zuniga and Marisol Henriquez, July 28, 1999.
5. Several informants reported this in interviews in 1996.
6. This international pressure, along with negotiations with the WRC and affiliated universities, prompted Tainan to finance a new factory, Just Garments, which opened in 2004 as a unionized factory. The results of this novel experiment are tentative.
7. Descriptions of all these conditions can be found in Bonacich 1994, BSR 2000, Chapkis 1993, Fuentes 1983, Klein 1999, Kwan 2000, Ross 1997, Varley 1998, and Verité 2000, as well as at the websites of various NGO organizations including Women Working Worldwide, Sweatshop Watch, National Labor Committee, Maquila Solidarity Network, Labor Rights in China, and COVERCO.
8. Quoted in David Fickling, "Misery of Rag-Trade Slaves in America's Pacific Outpost," *The Guardian*, March 1, 2003.
9. These complaints were alleged and documented in a lawsuit (*Doe I v. The Gap*) filed against eighteen retailers and their contractors in Saipan in the Commonwealth of the Northern Mariana Islands on January 13, 1999.
10. Quoted in Mary Adamski, "Feds Uncover American Somoa Sweatshop," *Honolulu Star Bulletin*, March 24, 2001.
11. Homework occurs in two main ways: Factory workers take unfinished garments home to fulfill their quota or to make extra money, or women are hired specifically to sew at home, creating yet another tier of subcontracting. In either case, homework in the garment industry is considered problematic (and in many countries, including the United States, illegal) because it cannot be regulated. Homework lends itself to violations not only of child labor laws, since children often help their mothers but also health, safety, and minimum wage laws, as workers are only paid by the piece.
12. Fickling, "Misery of Rag-Trade Slaves in America's Pacific Outpost."

13. In 2000 Mexico's ruling party, the PRI, was replaced by a more right-wing party. Although the main union, the CTM, is allied with the PRI, both parties strongly support foreign investment, export processing, and free trade.

14. These figures are available online at www.dataweb.usitc.gov.

15. David Armstrong, "A Question of Quotas," *San Francisco Chronicle,* April 4, 2005.

16. See Peter Goodman and Paul Blustein. "A New Pattern Is Cut for Global Textile Trade," *Washington Post,* November 17, 2004.

17. Interview, WRC Latin American field staff, January 21, 2005; Interview, economic attaché from Salvadoran Embassy, February 10, 2005.

18. This was the hourly wage range in 2005. Calculated on the basis of data collected by the Workers Rights Consortium, it represents both legal minimum and actual wages.

19. Trends do quickly change, and recent reports have indicated that there may be some movement from China to lower-wage Asian countries—particularly Viet Nam, which also places extreme legal restrictions on the right to freedom of association. See Don Lee, "Chinese City's Allure Fades for Some Firms," *Los Angeles Times,* July 3, 2005.

20. Marshall Tyler, Evelyn Iritani, and Marla Dickerson, "Clothes Will Cost Less, But Some Nations Will Pay," *Los Angeles Times,* January 16, 2005.

IV

War and Military Repression

Bacteria, Bioterrorism, and the Geranium Ladies of Guatemala

Caitilyn Allen

❁

This is the story of how the politics of American anxiety about terrorism combined with trade protectionism by one U.S. commodity group to destroy the livelihoods of hundreds of women in a small Guatemalan town.[1] This outcome was no less devastating for being unintended and unforeseen. In a larger sense, however, it demonstrates that relatively minor U.S. domestic policies can cause disasters in distant villages that often go completely unnoticed at their source in the United States, the largest player in the global economy.

To understand this story, we must first learn something about the global horticulture industry. This is a booming area of business: The value of cut flower and nursery stock imports to the United States jumped from U.S.$171 million in 1981 to U.S.$1.2 billion in 2001, driven by the growth of the so-called Green Industry, which includes bedding plants, ornamental trees and bushes, and turf (Anonymous 2004). The growth of this industry parallels that of American suburban sprawl with its extensive lawns, gardens, and golf courses. Most ornamental plants sold in the United States are grown vegetatively, from cuttings, because they are then uniform and predictable in appearance and because they will grow much more quickly than if the same plants were cultivated from seed. The highland tropics offer ideal conditions for large-scale vegetative cutting production: The day length, which controls some aspects of plant development, is fairly constant year round; the plants thrive in the moderate temperatures that prevail there; and labor is both abundant and cheap. Most of the flower farm workers in both Africa and Central America are women because, as one Guatemalan production manager explained, they have better fine-motor skills and are generally more reliable employees. He added unselfconsciously that "the ladies are also more compliant."

The ornamental industry in the United States currently imports more than 14 billion fresh flowers and plant cuttings each year. The largest cutting producers for the U.S. market are Guatemala (245 million cuttings per year), Costa Rica (233 million cuttings), and Mexico (100 million cuttings) (Anonymous 2004). Most ornamental cuttings sold in Europe come from highland Africa and Israel, although China is rapidly becoming an important plant cutting producer as well.

Geraniums are the single most popular bedding plant in the United States, and, like most ornamental plants, they are grown from cuttings, about 110 million of which are imported each year (Schmale 2004). Until 2004, 25 million of those geranium cuttings were produced at a single facility called Esquejes S.A. (*esquejes* means "cuttings"), which was located just outside of the small town of Jalapa in the eastern highlands of Guatemala. Esquejes employed over 600 people, mostly Maya women,[2] to work in their sixty-three large greenhouses tending the thousands of large geranium "mother plants" that are the source of the cuttings. During the busy season from August to April, several thousand chilled and packaged cuttings were shipped out by Federal Express trucks and planes each day, arriving in the Port of Miami just hours after they were harvested in the Guatemalan mountains. Following U.S. Department of Agriculture (USDA) inspection and customs clearance, the cuttings were shipped to rooting facilities, where they were kept moist and warm for several weeks while they grew roots and were transplanted into pots for eventual retail sale at outlets ranging from small family greenhouses to WalMart.

Esquejes paid its entry-level workers the minimum wage, between U.S.$5 and U.S.$6 per day. This was actually considered a good salary, since many Guatemalan employers, such as sweatshops and plantation farms, pay well below the official minimum wage. In addition, Esquejes treated its workers well. The company had onsite childcare and a small grade school for workers' children; these were free except for a 12-cents-per-day charge for lunch. Workers had access to a weekly free medical clinic, and there were also free evening literacy classes. This last is an especially valuable benefit for Guatemalan women, many of whom have only a few years of formal education and whose first language is often Mayan rather than the Spanish that is required for success in the formal national economy. Thus, working at Esquejes producing geranium cuttings was by local standards a desirable job, and those who worked there considered themselves fortunate.

However, trouble was brewing for the offshore geranium industry, and it would come from a totally unexpected source. In a seemingly completely unrelated matter, the U.S. potato lobby took advantage of the legislative response to the

Figure 12.1. Workers at Esquejes S.A. in Jalapa, Guatemala filling plastic bags with sterilized volcanic rock. This inert "scoria," which is mined nearby and steam-sterilized onsite, is used as a potting medium for geranium mother plants. Over 600 workers, mostly women, were employed producing geranium cuttings at this site.

2001 anthrax letters to engage in a bit of old-fashioned trade protectionism. Since a single plant disease is common to both potatoes and geraniums, ornamental producers and their workers in the global South were the inadvertent victims of the potato industry's successful lobbying effort. To understand how and why this happened, we must first learn a little bit of plant pathology, which is my own area of expertise. For the past sixteen years I have studied a soilborne bacterium named *Ralstonia solanacearum,* which causes bacterial wilt disease of diverse crop and native plant species. Because of my familiarity with *R. solanacearum* and bacterial wilt, I became an (unpaid) consultant for both the U.S. Department of Agriculture and the geranium industry when this pathogen became a problem on geraniums. I

Figure 12.2. A geranium cutter at Esquejes S.A. in Jalapa, Guatemala. Shoots from a large "mother plant" are planted in volcanic scoria and kept moist until they form roots and can eventually grow into new full-sized plants. This delicate work requires skill and patience, and was reserved for the more experienced workers.

traveled to Guatemala to inspect offshore geranium production facilities and have done considerable research on bacterial wilt of these plants.

R. solanacearum is primarily a tropical pathogen, most likely to cause disease and serious economic losses when soil and air temperatures are high. The bacterium enters host plants through wounds, usually through the roots, and spreads quickly into the plant's vascular system where it blocks water transport. If the host is susceptible, the result is yellowing, wilting, and rapid death. This pathogen has an unusually wide host range, attacking plants in more than fifty different families, including high-value cash crops like tomatoes, ginger, and tobacco, as well as plants such as plantains and potatoes, which are important carbohydrate foods for subsistence farmers. *R. solanacearum* is distributed around the world between the Tropics of Cancer and Capricorn, and since it has been found in virgin jungle soils in both Asia and the Americas, its origin is believed to predate the geological separation of the continents (Hayward 1991; Prior, Allen, and Elphinstone 1998). Because of its destructiveness, broad distribution, and large host range, *R. solanacearum* is considered the world's single most important bacterial plant pathogen (Elphinstone 2005).

There are many different strains of *R. solanacearum,* and they are subdivided into races and biovars based on physiological and pathogenic traits. One subgroup known as Race 3, biovar 2 (hereafter R3b2),[3] is best known as a pathogen of potatoes in the tropical highlands, though it also infects several other hosts. R3b2 is tolerant of the cooler temperatures prevailing in the mountains, and it is believed to have originated in the South American Andes, possibly having co-evolved along with the ancestral potato. In addition to killing potato plants outright when temperatures are warm, R3b2 can also form symptomless (or latent) infections so that farmers unknowingly spread the pest when they plant apparently healthy potato tubers that are infected with *R. solanacearum* (Allen, Kelman, and French 2001). It is difficult to estimate potato crop losses to bacterial wilt because many of the people affected are subsistence farmers in the developing world, where disease losses are not tabulated, and because farmers often abandon cultivation of the crop altogether after their fields become infested. Nonetheless, the International Potato Center in Lima, Peru, estimates that the disease causes more than U.S.$950 million in losses each year (Elphinstone 2005). Certainly bacterial wilt is one of the most serious threats to potato growers in the developing world, notably in the South and Central American highlands, the central African highlands, India, Nepal, and northern China, where potatoes form a key part of the diet.

Bacterial wilt has not caused much damage to potatoes in cold temperate climates, however, because the temperatures are too low for good disease development and the pathogen overwinters poorly there. *R. solanacerarum* is not ecologically adapted to survive the subzero temperatures common in temperate winters, and its populations decline dramatically under such conditions (van Elsas et al. 2000). R3b2 became established in Western Europe in the early 1990s, and although the ensuing quarantine and eradication efforts were disruptive and expensive, it has wilted potatoes only rarely, during unusually hot summers (Elphinstone 2005; Janse et al. 1998). Designated as a quarantine pest in both the United States and Canada, R3b2 is not believed to be established in North America.[4]

The USDA's Animal and Plant Health Inspection Service (USDA-APHIS) is responsible for detecting and excluding quarantine pests from the United States. Before September 11, 2001, *R. solanacearum* R3b2 was not a high-priority quarantine pest. The organism had been introduced repeatedly on geranium cuttings from the tropics as early as 1981, eliciting little or no interest from APHIS (Kim et al. 2003; Strider, Jones, and Haygood 1981; Williamson, Hudelson, and Allen 2002). The most significant introduction, from Guatemala in 1999, involved over a million infected cuttings, and APHIS's only regulatory response was to convene a New Pest Advisory Group, which discussed the problem during a few conference calls (Thomas 2004; Williamson, Hudelson, and Allen 2002).

This relaxed attitude underwent a rapid change after September 11, 2001. The heightened anxiety about terrorism and biosecurity extended beyond direct human health concerns into agriculture, and USDA made improving agricultural biosecurity a priority. In December 2002, Congress passed the Agricultural Bioterrorism Protection Act, which listed ten animal pathogens and (suspiciously symmetrically) ten plant pathogens that were considered potential biowarfare agents that could "pose a severe threat to U.S. agriculture" (Lambert 2002). Among these so-called Select Agents was *Ralstonia solancearum* Race 3, biovar 2.

USDA is unwilling to discuss the process by which plant pathogens were chosen for the Select Agent list that it submitted to Congress for the Bioterrorism Protection Act. Privately, agency scientists have admitted that vigorous lobbying by the U.S. potato industry resulted in the placement of two potato pathogens on the Select Agent list: *R. solanacearum* R3b2, and a fungal pathogen called *Synchytrium endobioticum,* which causes a very minor disease called potato wart.

The likely motivation behind the potato industry lobby's pressure is a desire to avoid pathogen-based exclusion of U.S. potato exports to Canada. For decades, regulators in Canada and the United States have exchanged punitive quarantine responses to each discovery of a new pathogen on potatoes from the other country. Representatives of the U.S. potato industry apparently felt that placing these two quarantine pathogens on the Select Agents list would increase surveillance and reduce the chances that they would cause trade problems for U.S. potato exporters, even though neither pathogen could plausibly be used as a biowarfare agent.

As a result of being listed as a Select Agent, R3b2 became subject to a very strict new set of security regulations and eradication actions. These regulations not only have restricted scientific research on ways to detect and control the pathogen[5] but also have caused a major and unanticipated disaster for the geranium industry, both in the United States and offshore.

Despite its destructive effect on tomatoes and potatoes, *R. solanacearum* is not an especially good geranium pathogen, only rarely causing wilting or disease on infected plants. Unfortunately, R3b2 does easily form latent (symptomless) infections of geraniums (Swanson et al. 2005). This creates a vexing problem for regulators charged with preventing introduction of the pest into the United States. Infected cuttings are usually visually indistinguishable from healthy ones, and although there are diagnostic tests that can detect the pathogen even in the absence of symptoms, these are expensive and technically demanding. Moreover, the sheer volume of imported geranium cuttings (more than 100 million per year) makes thorough testing impractical. Since R3b2 was placed on the Select Agents list, APHIS has responded to this challenging diagnostic problem with a zero-tolerance panic-button response to any find of *R. solanacearum.*

Unhappily for all concerned, early in 2003 geranium cuttings infected with R3b2 were accidentally introduced into the United States from a production farm in Kenya. Although it now appears that only a few hundred infected cuttings were imported, APHIS placed a "hold and destroy" order on the 127 greenhouses in twenty-seven states that had received shipments that might have come in contact with the infected plants. Growers were required to incinerate over 3 million plants, with estimated losses of more than U.S.$5 million (Allen and Schmale 2004). In retrospect, it is not surprising that infected cuttings were introduced. The plants were grown in parts of the world where R3b2 is common in fields, weeds, and irrigation ditches, and such introductions had certainly happened before. However, the magnitude of the regulatory response and the cost came as a shock to Goldsmith Plants, the U.S. parent company that owned the geranium farm in Kenya as well as Esquejes in Jalapa, Guatemala. Compensating its customers for the destroyed geraniums cost Goldsmith over half its revenue in 2003 (Snow 2004).

Worse was to come. In December 2003, a single shipment of geranium cuttings from Esquejes to a New York State greenhouse was found to contain three varieties of geranium infected with R3b2. Because Esquejes had no "traceback" labeling on its plants and could not identify the infected mother plants that had given rise to the infected New York geraniums, APHIS decided to require destruction of all 2 million geraniums of these three varieties that had been shipped from the Jalapa farm since the season began in August. This cost the industry another estimated U.S.$3 million. Moreover, APHIS shut down all further shipments from Esquejes for the remainder of the 2003–2004 season, which was the final blow to Goldsmith Plants, the U.S. parent company.

On March 15, 2004, Esquejes S.A. announced it was closing the Jalapa geranium production farm. The more than 600 people who were working there immediately lost their jobs (Dardon 2004). The childcare center, the grade school, and the clinic were also closed. Esquejes had been the largest employer in Jalapa, and few options remained for its former employees beyond a handful of lower-paying sweatshop jobs without benefits. The Goldsmith geranium farm in Kenya was also closed, resulting in the loss of an additional 450 jobs.

Most of the women who lost their jobs at Esquejes understood little of what had happened. One told me that the police in the United States were afraid of a bacterium that could hurt U.S. residents but not Guatemalans; ironically, the reverse was true. Another believed that the farm went out of business so that U.S. residents could grow their geraniums at home and keep the jobs for themselves. In fact, the plant stock from Jalapa was purchased by another multinational corporation that is now paying workers near Shanghai, China, about U.S.$1 per day to grow the same geranium cuttings. But the women of Esquejes certainly understood that they no longer had work, and that this had something to do with the United States.

Figure 12.3. A worker at Esquejes, S.A. in Jalapa, Guatemala cleaning and packing geranium cuttings. Once packaged, the cuttings are chilled and exported by air, reaching customers in the United States 24–48 hours after they were harvested. Over 100 million such cuttings are imported into the U.S. each year from offshore ornamental production facilities.

In *Tangled Routes: Women, Work, and Globalization on the Tomato Trail,*
Deborah Barndt discusses the many effects on women's lives of importing tomatoes
from Mexico to Canada (Barndt 2002). She argues that although women form a
critical part of the chain of global agricultural production, they often are unaware
of the other elements in the chain, even though their lives can be drastically affected
by a change anywhere along the way from the production field to the eventual
North American consumer.

The rather convoluted story of bacteria and the Guatemalan geranium ladies
reveals the unpredictable ways in which new U.S. biosecurity laws collide with our
burgeoning outsourcing of agricultural production. These collisions often result
in unexpected hardships for the women working in the far fields of our global
farm. However, such unintended global consequences of U.S. policies are usually
invisible to people within the United States, even those who helped to make the
laws. With the advent of the North American and Central American Free Trade
Agreements (NAFTA and CAFTA), it has become increasingly difficult to trace
the effects of even minor policy changes on workers around the world. At the
same time, because women make up a majority of unskilled agricultural laborers
in many parts of the developing world, they are disproportionately vulnerable to
the ripple effects of U.S. policy changes. Anxiety about (and public accountability
for) biosecurity has arguably made the U.S. government's policies both more hyper-
responsive and less thoughtfully considered. As agricultural production systems
become more transnational in practice, every policy decision holds the possibility
of unintended consequences for the least privileged workers, who are often women.
They are remote, we do not see them, but we affect them just the same.

NOTES

1. I am grateful to the workers at Esquejes, S.A. in Jalapa, Guatemala, for their willingness
to talk to me about their jobs and their lives. For useful conversations, I also thank Don Snow and
Darryl Thomas of Goldsmith Plants, Inc., Brad Barham of the University of Wisconsin–Madison
Department of Agricultural and Applied Economics, and several USDA-APHIS scientists who prefer
to remain anonymous. My research was supported by the USDA-ARS Floral Nursery Crops Initiative
and the University of Wisconsin–Madison College of Agricultural and Life Sciences.

2. An explanatory note on racial/cultural identity in Guatemala: The vast majority of
Guatemalans are descendants of the indigenous Maya inhabitants of Central America. However,
Guatemalans generally consider themselves either Maya or *ladino,* people who, regardless of their
ancestry, speak Spanish and have adopted Western culture. During the period of my research I observed that most of the flower farm workers in the Guatemalan highlands were Maya women, while
the farm managers and supervisors whom I met were uniformly male and either *ladino* or foreigners
(U.S. citizens or Europeans).

3. Because it is a large and heterogenous group, the species *R. solanacearum* is subdivided
into races based loosely on strain host range, and also, separately, into biovars based on ability of the
strain to oxidize a panel of carbohydrates (Hayward 1991). Most of these subgroups are of limited
taxonomic utility, but molecular analyses reveal that Race 3, biovar 2, is a fairly uniform (virtually
clonal) group of strains that appear to have been distributed worldwide on infected potato tubers
by humans. Although best known as a potato pathogen, Race 3 strains can also attack eggplant and
tomato (but not tobacco), as well as diverse ornamental and native plants and weeds.

4. *Quarantine pests* are those insects, weeds, and plant or animal pathogens not present in a country that are considered a serious threat to human, agricultural, or ecosystem health. They are formally excluded from import or accidental introduction into the country.

5. Any lab wishing to work with a Select Agent must first obtain a permit from the USDA or the Centers for Disease Control (CDC), a complex, lengthy, and unpredictable process; for example, getting a final permit to continue research in my lab on R3b2 took more than eighteen months. Individual scientists in my research laboratory who work with R3b2 are required to undergo a Department of Justice personal background check before they are authorized to do research. My lab has been retrofitted with an expensive set of physical security measures, including a fingerprint-activated door lock, diverse high-security cabinet, freezer, and incubator locks, and a motion-activated videocamera that directly feeds images of our research activities to university police. In addition, we are required not only to undergo mandatory compliance training as well as site inspections (both announced and unannounced) but also to submit voluminous and exacting paperwork each month documenting our experiments. Transfer of strains between permitted researchers in the United States requires advance permission through a complex chain of command at the USDA and CDC. International strain exchanges entail USDA-CDC strain transfer paperwork; they also require negotiating a completely separate bureaucracy at the Department of Commerce, which must issue a technology transfer license for each proposed transfer. Violation of these new regulations incurs stiff personal penalties (large fines and prison time). The overall effect of these cumbersome regulations has been to discourage individual U.S. scientists from doing research on Select Agent plant pathogens, even though these pathogens often pose major threats to growers in the developing world where there are few local resources for scientific research. Thus, a second unintended consequence of the Agricultural Bioterrorism Protection Act was to effectively reduce the ability of scientists in the developed world to use their well-funded and well-equipped laboratories to address some of the most pressing problems confronting poor farmers in the tropics.

13

Globalization Denied

Gender and Poverty in Iraq and Palestine

Jennifer C. Olmsted

❀

Studies critical of corporate globalization focus primarily on how pressure is being placed on countries to open their borders, particularly in conjunction with structural adjustment policies, but it should be noted that during this period of "globalization," certain communities have been forcibly economically isolated. Two communities that have been denied the right to participate fully in the increasingly globalizing economy are Iraq and the Palestinian territories.[1] Although not diminishing the concerns of those critical of corporate globalization, I illustrate how in an era where economies are increasingly interconnected, communities that are forcibly isolated from the global economy face a particularly critical economic situation. Economic isolation suggests an inability to earn foreign exchange, which is generally needed to buy many goods that are often available only as imports,[2] as well as a loss of jobs generally linked to that sector of the economy associated with trade, which in turn leads to a downward spiraling of economic conditions, as will be discussed in more detail for the case of both Iraq and the Palestinians. In addition, I suggest that this process may have implications for gender roles.

178

Although a number of descriptive studies have documented the hardships faced by Iraqis and Palestinians, few analysts have attempted to study these cases comparatively, or to examine how gender norms might be affected by this process. I provide a preliminary exploration of these issues, with an emphasis on the question of what the impact of these hardships has been and is likely to be on gender norms and relations. Three critical questions with gender implications are whether the increased poverty that has been experienced as a result of the recent economic isolation is gendered; how economic hardship has reshaped social structures and gender norms, and what implications this is likely to have for Iraqi and Palestinian girls and women, both now and in the future; and, finally, how the two case studies detailed in this chapter can inform our understanding of the ways globalization is experienced in various communities and, in particular, by the women in those communities.

SOCIOECONOMIC CONDITIONS IN IRAQ

After nationalizing oil in the 1970s, the Iraqi government made significant investments into the health and educational systems, and girls and women were major beneficiaries of these policies. This is not to deny that Saddam Hussein spent money on arms and amassed a personal fortune, nor to argue that the government's objective was to empower women,[3] but only to point out that the situation for women improved considerably, particularly in the 1970s. In fact, Iraq was portrayed as a particularly "modern" Arab country, with a large cohort of highly educated, professional women in both the private and public sectors. As Al-Ali (2005) argues, the presence of nurseries, free transportation, and other publicly provided services contributed to Iraqi women's ability to juggle paid and reproductive labor demands.

In the 1980s Iraqis endured an eight-year war with Iran (1980–1988). Thus even before the 1990 invasion of Kuwait and the U.S.-led war and sanctions, Iraq's military policies were beginning to take their toll on the population. Following the imposition of sanctions, the economic situation became considerably worse, with Iraq's national income falling from 13,863 million dinar to 3,548 million dinar, a drop of almost 75 percent (Niblock 2001, 173) in the first year. Or as Garfield (1999, 12) points out, during "the first eight years of the embargo, Iraq estimates that it lost U.S.\$120 bn [billion] in foreign exchange earnings" but received only \$1 billion in humanitarian donations. Recent figures suggest that per capita income is now about U.S.\$255 per household (UNDP 2005, 138), less than it was in 1980. Few other countries (particularly with oil resources) are facing a level of income per household lower than it was more than twenty-five years ago.

As has been well documented by a number of authors, the lack of economic development over the past twenty years has had serious implications for Iraqis' health and well-being. Ill health, early death, and low educational attainment mark this period of Iraq's history. The life expectancy of Iraqis, for instance, has risen by only four years (from 57 to 61) in the past twenty years, whereas for other countries in the region it has risen by seventeen to twenty years (UNDP 2005, 81) during the same period.

Niblock (2001, 145) reports that in central and southern Iraq, between 1989 and 2000, deaths among children under 5 from diarrhea, malnutrition, and other easily preventable diseases and conditions rose by 1,000 percent to 2,000 percent.[4] Similarly, deaths both of children under 5 and of the elderly rose rapidly between 1990 and 1991 and continued to rise throughout the 1990s. The acute malnutrition rate rose from 3 percent to 11 percent, and chronic malnutrition increased by 12 percent (from 19 percent to 31 percent) (Garfield 1999, 17). Rates of malnourishment may have risen even further in recent years, inasmuch as the UN Development Programme (UNDP) estimates that almost a quarter of all Iraqi children were suffering from chronic malnutrition in 2004, with acute malnutrition affecting as many as 17 percent of children in some areas (UNDP 2005, 57).

The particularly high death rate among children and the elderly during the sanctions period is linked not only to reduced income but to other factors as well. Although, in theory, medications and certain other goods were excluded from the sanctions, Garfield (1999) points out that the international community was often slow in responding to Iraqi requests for imports. In addition, the ability of certain sectors to function under sanctions was very limited, creating severe problems. The sanitation sector, for example, was unable to maintain a water delivery system after sanctions were imposed, leading to a rapid drop in the availability of clean water, which in turn was linked to increased disease and death. Niblock (2001, 148) reports that in 1990, 90 percent of Iraqis were receiving safe drinking water, but by 1996, 25 percent of the water was contaminated and the amount of water available per capita had declined by 40 percent. The UNDP (2005, 25) estimates that access to water remains a serious problem, with about 67 percent of rural and 40 percent of urban households being unable to access safe sources. Unsafe water leads to various health problems, which, as noted, often lead to death, particularly among children and the elderly. Thus the ability of the state, as well as of individual families and institutions, to care for those who were vulnerable to disease was diminished considerably, due to both the direct and indirect impact of sanctions. And despite the official end of the sanctions, the UNDP (2005, 50–51) reported that the infant mortality rate remained around 32 children per 1,000 births in 2004; World Bank estimates were considerably higher, at over 100 children per 1,000 (World Bank n.d.).

Because the system put in place before sanctions began was quite extensive, Iraqis do report high accessibility to health facilities (UNDP 2005, 37); however, as the UNDP points out, the ability of Iraqis to obtain *quality* health care declined considerably during the sanction period. Although medications could still be imported under sanctions, other aspects of the medical system deteriorated considerably. Trained health personnel fled Iraq (UNDP 2005, 71), and it became difficult to train new personnel. Due to sanctions, much of the equipment being used in medical facilities was old and, in some cases, nonfunctional (Niblock 2001, 147).

The educational system and parents' ability to send their children to school were also considerably affected by the sanctions. Whereas in other parts of the world literacy rates have been steadily rising, literacy rates among younger Iraqis—between the ages of 15 and 24—are currently *lower* than among the 25 to 34-year-old cohort. (UNDP 2005, 91). The alarming decline in literacy is likely to have a lasting economic as well as social impact on the country. The stagnant and sometimes worsening economic, health, and education outcomes not only illustrate the hardships that Iraqis have experienced in recent years but also raise questions about how the country will be able to recover when the violence dissipates.

SOCIOECONOMIC CONDITIONS IN PALESTINE

The Palestinians have not been direct victims of sanctions, although I have argued elsewhere (Olmsted 2005) that Israeli policies are tantamount to sanctions and a number of published reports by the World Bank and United Nations have illustrated how devastating these policies have been to the Palestinian economy in recent years. The Israeli military occupation, which began in 1967, allows the Israeli military to control all West Bank and Gaza Strip (WBGS) "borders,"[5] and thus to regulate the flow of goods and humans into and out of the area. Although in the early period (1967–1991) no actual physical border existed and humans moved fairly freely in both directions, Israel did restrict Palestinian "exports" somewhat, and around the time of the 1991 Gulf War, Israel began tightening its control over the movement of both humans and goods. This process involved the construction of checkpoints and, more recently, a physical barrier.[6]

As in the case of Iraq, the Palestinian territories have at times experienced rising literacy and life expectancy, as well as improvements in health—particularly when the movement of goods and humans was fairly unrestricted. In fact, following the military occupation of the West Bank and Gaza in 1967, Palestinian income increased and living standards improved; at the same time, however, the Occupied Territories became extremely dependent on Israel, in terms of both labor and goods markets. At the height of the occupation, between 30 percent and 40 percent of Palestinian workers were working in Israel (Farsakh 2002), with rates as high as 70 percent being observed in communities in Gaza, according to Roy (1995). In addition to the many (male) workers who were employed in Israel directly, many Palestinian women worked out of their homes, as subcontracted labor to Israeli firms (Olmsted 2001).

Access to Israel began to be reduced in 1991, leading to increased economic hardship, but in 2000 the Israeli government implemented a more extreme "closure" policy with respect to the Palestinian territories that disrupted their economic situation even more severely. For much of 2000, not only were Palestinian workers prevented from entering Israel (and the settlements where they began working after access to Israel was reduced), but they were also forbidden to move between communities within the Occupied Territories or even to leave their homes (as a condition of curfew). As a result, GDP per capita declined 40 percent in two years (World Bank 2003). The majority of Palestinian households saw their income cut in half during this period, and the UN Special Co-ordinator (UNSCO) estimated that almost 20 percent of households lost *all* of their income (UNSCO 2002, 4). Unemployment rates, which had been around 10 percent, rose to over 40 percent (World Bank 2004a, 1), with some areas experiencing rates as high as 70 percent (UNSCO 2002). This, in turn, led to a rapid rise in poverty, from 25 percent to almost 60 percent between 2000 and 2003 (World Bank 2003). As a result, food consumption rates declined by 25 percent (World Bank 2004b, 36). Similar to the situation in Iraq, malnutrition rates rose considerably during this period, particularly in the Gaza Strip. Whereas acute malnutrition rates in Gaza were quite low before 2000, they peaked in 2002; more than 13 percent of the children here were found to be acutely malnourished (World Bank 2004b, 37). In addition, school enrollment rates declined, from 92.2 percent to 88.4 percent between 2000 and 2004 (World Bank 2004b). It should also be noted that because of closures and various travel restrictions, even in the absence of economic constraints, pursuing education continues to be very difficult for Palestinians.

COPING MECHANISMS

One major issue of concern to households facing these types of economic shocks is how to cope with the sudden loss of income. Generally, families combine multiple strategies—reducing consumption, drawing down savings, strategizing about ways to bring household income levels back up, and, when possible, falling back on family and community members who can help. Coping mechanisms may involve not only ways of physically coping with increased economic hardship but also psychological steps individuals may take so that they can continue to function under extremely difficult economic conditions. The degree of community cohesion (with *community* being defined rather broadly to include not just immediate family members but also local and global communities) as well as the severity and duration of economic hardship are important factors contributing to individuals' and families' ability to cope.

A common strategy used by households facing temporary economic hardship is to draw down savings, or to incur debt. This was certainly a strategy used by a large number of Palestinian households during the recent economic crisis. The World Bank reported that during "2001, 70 percent of the *poorest* Palestinian families were reportedly drawing down their savings" (2004b, 38; emphasis mine); it also cited a Food and Agriculture Organization (FAO) report stating that 75 percent of *all* households sold jewelry between 2001 and 2003. If 70 percent of the poorest drew down their savings, the implication is that the remaining 30 percent didn't have any savings to draw on, and probably went into debt to survive this period of hardship.[7] Using debt to survive hard times may have long-term implications for individuals, families, and society at large, since the incurring of high levels of debt may be linked to an inability to escape poverty even after the period of economic hardship has ended.

Iraqis also drew down savings and incurred debt to survive the series of economic reversals their nation experienced, although few families had savings levels that were sufficient to sustain them for the entire twenty-five years in question. It is unclear how many families now saddled with such large debts will be able to escape the poverty that has plagued almost the entire society for a quarter of a century.

The finding that children in both Palestine and Iraq experienced acute malnutrition is evidence that families did far more than simply draw down savings and cut luxury items out of their budgets. Pulling children out of school, reducing spending on food, and forgoing medical expenses are all strategies that parents may have been forced to exercise, and which may have both short- and long-term ramifications for children, families, and society more generally. Educational expenses may be cut not only because parents are unable to afford the costs involved but also because children's labor is often used during times of hardship to augment household income. The data discussed above suggest that, in both the Palestinian and Iraqi cases, children's withdrawal from school occurred.

Although already dire, an even worse situation would have occurred had it not been for policies (initiated both by local governments and by international aid agencies) that provided households with material assistance. As Al-Ali (2005) reports, the majority (60 percent) of Iraqi families were dependent on food rations during the sanctions period. UNDP (2005, 63) figures suggest an even higher rate, with 96 percent of Iraqis receiving rations during the sanctions period. Similarly, the economic situation facing the Palestinians would have been considerably worse if per capita aid contributions had not risen to $308 per person (25 percent of GDP) in 2001–2002 (World Bank 2004b). The UNSCO (2002, 3) estimates that more than 40 percent of Gazans were "entirely dependent on food aid" during this period.

GENDERED CONSEQUENCES OF "SANCTIONS"

At least two approaches can be taken in exploring the gendered aspect of both the deteriorating economic situation in Iraq and Palestine and the adoption of various coping strategies. The first involves a closer examination of the statistics discussed earlier, which provide an indication of socioeconomic trends. Such an analysis is descriptive in nature and depends on the availability of various statistics, broken down by sex. The second approach is more qualitative and analytical in nature, using anthropological studies/forms of evidence to explore the often subtle ways that shifting economic conditions may alter gender relations and norms, sometimes in contradictory fashion. Unfortunately, the types of quantitative and qualitative information needed to address these issues are limited in the cases of Palestine and Iraq, so in addition to providing some preliminary analysis of this question, I argue that far more research must be carried out on these issues.

One hypothesis that comes out of the gender literature is the question of whether increased hardship, particularly when linked to conflict and/or war, leads families to channel increasingly scarce economic resources to boys, causing girls to suffer from various forms of neglect (Das Gupta and Shuzhuo 2000). Detailed data to address this question for Iraq and Palestine remain limited, but the economic statistics that are available suggest that although the overall situation facing Iraqis worsened considerably, females did not necessarily fare worse than males, at least in terms of general socioeconomic indicators. An examination of malnutrition rates (UNDP 2005, 61) and infant mortality rates (UNDP 2005, 51), for instance, suggests no discernable bias against females in Iraq. Iraqi women report rates of acute illness comparable to those of men and indicate they are equally likely to seek help when they are ill (UNDP 2005, 87). And one of the sad ironies of Iraq is that the literacy gap has actually narrowed in recent years, due to falling literacy rates among boys (UNDP 2005, 108).

Less is known about whether the recent economic downturn affected the health and nutrition status of Palestinian females and males differently, since most of the statistics covering the 2000–2003 period are not broken down by sex. Data that predate this period suggest that, at least in terms of infant mortality, there was no bias against female babies (PCBS 1998).

Although differences in most health indicators by sex are either unavailable or do not indicate a bias against females, one obvious difference between men and women is that the latter bear children—a condition that may be made riskier by economic hardship. Iraq has a very high maternal mortality rate, with almost 193 women out of 100,000 losing their lives, compared to rates in the rest of the Middle East in the range of 23 (Saudi Arabia) to 130 (Iran) out of 10,000. (This estimate, it should be noted, represents a significant drop in the mortality rate for Iraqi mothers, with earlier estimates of 370 deaths per 100,000 births.)

The maternal mortality rate in Palestine is not available for the most recent period, but previous to the economic downturn of 2000 it was between 60 and 140 deaths per 100,000, depending on the age of the woman (PCBS 1998). One trend documented during the 2000–2003 period is that pregnant women had considerable trouble reaching health facilities, leading to a decline in prenatal health care and to a very sharp decrease in the number of women who gave birth in the presence of a health worker (from almost 100 percent down to 67 percent) (UNIFEM 2005). This was due not so much to the increase in poverty (since many Palestinians have access to free health care) as to the extreme restrictions on Palestinian mobility related to Israeli road blocks and closures. As a result, women often are unable to get to a medical facility, and many have given birth at Israeli-controlled road blocks. Clearly these circumstances increase the chances of complications for both mothers and children. Amnesty International (2005) has documented a number of cases where women have been forced to give birth at road blocks and have lost their children as a result.

The data on poverty rates among female-headed households are ambiguous. World Bank figures suggest that female-headed Palestinian households are less likely to be poor (World Bank 2004b), although earlier studies suggest the opposite (PNA 1998). The UNDP (2005) concludes that female-headed households in Iraq are not more likely to suffer from poverty, although they report higher poverty rates (28 percent versus 20 percent) among female-headed households. Such statistics may disguise the fact that females may not have equal access to resources within households. In addition, female-headed households may be made up of some relatively well-off women who can choose to be independent, as well as some that may be particularly economically vulnerable. In fact the UNDP study indicates that this may be the case at least for Iraq, where female-headed households report being less able to mobilize economic resources than male or dual-headed households, suggesting higher rates of economic vulnerability.

Turning to the more complicated matter as to what implications these economic changes may have for gender relations, two major issues are worth noting. First, unemployment rates in both the Iraqi and Palestinian communities have been very high in recent years. Given that men in the pre-crisis period were the primary providers of income, one immediate question that arises is how men are coping with this rather extreme challenge to their male identity. Al-Ali (2005, 749) provides insight into this issue in the Iraqi case, arguing that some of the women she interviewed reported that their husbands became "more violent and abusive during the past decade." Similarly, UNIFEM (2005) reports that domestic violence has risen during the recent period in Palestine.

Not only does the high rate of unemployment have psychological implications, but it also clearly has economic ones for the household. One common strategy in times of high rates of male unemployment is for other family members (wives or children) to enter the paid (often informal) sector to help support their families. Although anecdotal evidence suggests this may be happening in some families (Amnesty International 2005), the statistics that are available do not suggest that this pattern is widespread. In fact, in both the Iraqi and Palestinian cases, women's participation in paid employment declined. Al-Ali (2005) points out that, during the sanctions period, women's paid-employment rates in Iraq fell rather precipitously, from 23 percent in 1991 to 10 percent in 1997. She argues that two major factors contributed to this trend. First, the government withdrew much of the support it had previously provided working women, such as subsidized daycare. Second, wages in government-sector jobs, which Iraqi women preferred, decreased considerably. For some women, it may no longer have made economic sense to stay in paid employment.

Earlier work by Cainkar (1993) provides insight into these statistics. She found that women in the informal sector were experiencing severe difficulties, because of the level of economic hardship they had to deal with. Some women were forced to sell the capital assets they had previously used to support their economic livelihood. For example, one woman reported selling her sewing machine to pay for food. Others stated that they could not continue working in informal production because they lacked money to buy necessary inputs. Finally, as other economic opportunities disappeared, some women were left with only their bodies to sell and resorted to prostitution to survive.

Similar changes in women's labor force participation have also been observed in the WBGS, even during the short period of economic downturn there. Amnesty International (2005) reports that the rate of paid employment among women declined from 15.8 percent to 10.5 percent in recent years. Women's employment options in both the West Bank and the Gaza Strip have thus shrunk considerably,[8] during a period when economic hardship has been on the rise. One possible explanation is that, because male unemployment is high, women are facing pressure not to compete with men—although, interestingly, some Palestinian women I interviewed in 2005 argued that the recent hardship has increased societal acceptance of working women. Why this has not led to a rise in women's actual participation remains a topic for further research. What *is* clear, however, is that the strategy of substituting women's earnings, as male income generation declines, has not been an option for most Iraqi and Palestinian households during periods of economic hardship.

Although both women's and men's access to paid employment has been declining, as documented by Cainkar (1993) and Al-Ali (2005), Iraqi women's unpaid-work burden increased during the period of sanctions—thus possibly making it more difficult for them to continue putting hours into paid employment. The increased time that women had to devote to food preparation (e.g., many women began baking their own bread, to save money)—but also to finding food during periods of shortages, and to strategizing about how to make ends meet on their limited budgets—was considerable. In many cases, goods that had previously been purchased in the market (such as bread and healthcare items) were no longer affordable (or even available), so women had to increase the provision of those goods through their unpaid-labor inputs. Women also had to make extremely stressful decisions concerning their families' budgets. Both Cainkar (1993) and Al-Ali (2005) describe how painful it was for women faced with decisions about how to allocate their food and other resources; in one especially poignant case, a woman sold her baby-formula ration to pay for food purchases for the rest of her family.

Amnesty International (2005) similarly reports that recent hardships in the Palestinian territories have increased women's unpaid-work burdens, although the circumstances there are somewhat less severe. Palestinian women not only had to replace market purchases with nonmarket production but also to budget more carefully due to increased economic hardship. In addition, they had to strategize carefully about how and when to purchase goods during periods of closure, when it was often difficult or even impossible for shops to restock their shelves. And because in the Palestinian case closure also meant extended periods under curfew, women had to be vigilant about stockpiling food and calculating how to manage the household's existing food (and other) resources, without any clear idea of when and for how long the curfews would be lifted.

Coping strategies may be gendered both in obvious and subtle ways and may have both short- and long-term implications. The World Bank (2004b, 38) points out that one of the first forms of wealth that Palestinians liquidated during the recent period of economic hardship was jewelry. Similarly, Cainkar (1993) reports that in Iraq, women sold not just their physical assets but also their gold. Given that jewelry is one of the few forms of wealth generally owned and controlled by women, the question of how such decisions are likely to affect women's longer-term economic situation and power within the household remains unanswered. If and when families recover economically, will women be able to argue that newly acquired savings should be under their control, as was the gold they sold during the economic crisis?

Finally, it is important to note a circumstance often ignored: that economic hardship impacts community cohesion and, more generally, the social fabric of a society. Consider, for example, the fact that Arabs pride themselves on their hospitality and that social visits involving food are an important way of maintaining social relations. As Al-Ali (2005) reports, many of her informants explained that they stopped visiting friends and family during the sanctions period, because they did not want to shame their hosts, whom they well knew would have no food or drink to offer their guests. This pattern suggests one way in which women's unpaid labor burden was eased somewhat. But it also illustrates the level of social unraveling that occurred, such that visits could not be maintained because of the level of poverty.

Criminal activity also rose considerably during sanctions, no doubt at least in part because of increased economic hardship. In fact, particularly in Baghdad, rape and kidnapping of girls and women has become a serious problem (Human Rights Watch 2003)—one that is likely linked not only to the current lack of security but also to the eroding of social cohesion that occurred during the previous period.

Possibly because of the shorter duration of the economic decline in Palestinian incomes, communities were able to maintain better social cohesion. The World Bank (2004b, 38), for instance, lists the "tight-knit Palestinian social structure" as one of the factors that helped poor Palestinians cope with increased economic hardship in the period from 2001 to 2003. But during my visit to the region during the summer of 2005, a number of people commented that they thought Palestinians had become more concerned about self-preservation and that there was far less of a sense of community cohesion and caring than had existed before the economic crisis. In addition, I was told, and witnessed firsthand, that religion provided one of the main coping mechanisms available to Palestinians, with a particularly conservative brand of Islam having gained popularity in recent years.

Al-Ali (2005, 751), having observed similar trends when interviewing Iraqi women, concludes that although there was a "decline in moral values like honesty, generosity and sociability," there was also an increase in "public religiosity and conservatism." The general sense of psychological and economic insecurity (which in the Iraqi and Palestinian cases is due not only to increased economic insecurity but also to the militarization that these communities are experiencing) is thus gendered in a number of ways. Because of safety concerns regarding women, their access to the public sphere may be increasingly restricted. In addition, women may feel that they have to be vigilant about watching over their children, which, as discussed in Maassarani and Olmsted (2005), may increase their unpaid-work responsibilities and their stress, and further reduce their ability to interact in the public sphere. Finally, the consequences of rape and violence may be particularly painful for Iraqi and Palestinian women, given that Arab society places a high premium on female virginity. Thus girls who are victims of rape may, at best, be socially ostracized and, at worst, killed by family members trying to uphold family honor.

CONCLUSION

In a world of increasing economic openness, little attention is paid to the fact that some communities have been deliberately excluded from this process. As both the Palestinian and Iraqi cases illustrate, the ability of outside powers to control a community's economy and restrict its ability to function can be economically devastating. Whereas in Iraq the tragic results of twenty-five years of economic hardship are becoming clear, the longer-term implications of the economic shock experienced by Palestinians are more difficult to ascertain, as not enough time has passed and it is as yet unclear what draconian policies might lie in the future. Certainly neither of these communities is "out of the woods" economically. Pfeifer (2004) argues that it will be very difficult for the Palestinian economy to recover, given the severity of the economic blow it recently experienced. In addition, Israel still maintains the ability to shut down the Palestinian economy at will (Olmsted 2005).[9]

Similarly, the economic policies implemented by the occupying "coalition" led by the United States have, to date, been far from successful (Yousif 2006). Although it is hoped that oil revenue will eventually pull Iraq out of its economic stagnation, the long-term impacts of economic hardship and literacy losses, as well as the physical and mental health impacts of sanctions, remain unclear. What is clear is that these two communities have been systematically isolated and remain economically vulnerable to the whims of outside powers. In a world of increasing globalization, economic isolation has led not only to economic deprivation, but also to very real fears among individuals that the fabric of their society is dissolving, which in turn has gender implications.

Insufficient research has been conducted to determine whether the rapid rise in poverty experienced by both these communities has caused female household members to experience higher levels of economic deprivation, but certainly widespread economic hardship has occurred, and women and men have been affected differently by the crises. Rapid rises in unemployment among men have not been matched by increased access to employment among women. The minority of women who were in paid employment have found that their ability to earn money has been greatly reduced, although the underlying reasons are not clear, nor is it clear how statistically robust this finding is. It also appears that as male identity was challenged, because men were increasingly unable to support their families, women became increasingly vulnerable to male violence. In addition, economic hardship often led to an increased unpaid-work burden for women. For various practical as well as ideological reasons, then, women's access to the public sphere appears to have been increasingly reduced during this period, despite (at least in the Palestinian case) a rhetoric that acknowledged the necessity for women to work and to actively contribute economically because of the economic hardship.

My work, though, provides only a preliminary and tentative discussion of the ways that this forced economic isolation may have both short and longer term gender implications. Clearly, the impact of economic deprivation on gender relations and norms is complex and requires further research.

NOTES

1. Other countries that have faced UN sanctions include Southern Rhodesia, South Africa, Yugoslavia, Somalia, Libya, Liberia, Haiti, Angola, Rwanda, Sierra Leone, and the Sudan (Garfield, 1999), while the United States has embargoed Iran and Cuba.

2. These may range from medical supplies and other goods requiring advanced technologies to basic goods such as food, oil, and other natural resources not available domestically.

3. For more discussion of political developments in Iraq that led to women's increased education and employment, see Joseph (1991).

4. Niblock (2001) distinguishes between central and southern Iraq, on the one hand, and northern Iraq, on the other. The latter is the Kurdish area and thus was treated differently and fared better under sanctions.

5. The terms *borders* and (in the next sentence) *exports* are in quotes, since Israel enforces the notion of borders through its control of humans and goods; but at the same time, because Israel continues to militarily occupy the West Bank and Gaza, Palestinians have no ability to act as a sovereign nation, with control over their borders.

6. This barrier is itself the subject of considerable controversy because of such issues as its legal status, effectiveness, and economic impact. In this connection, see Amnesty International (2004).

7. My fieldwork in Palestine during the 1991 Gulf War, when the Israelis imposed similar restrictions on the Palestinians, revealed that shopkeepers extended credit to families who were unable to earn income during this period.

8. The drop in the official labor force participation measure could be due to women switching from formal to informal employment, but given the increased care being taken to capture statistics on informal-sector employment in recent years, I think it is unlikely that this explains the drop.

9. In fact, as of this writing in 2006, the Palestinians are again facing economic isolation and hardship, following the victory of the Islamist party Hamas.

14

Amazons Go to War Without Weapons

Women and the Conflict in Escravos, Niger Delta

Joy Ngozi Ezeilo

⚙

Conflicts in the Niger Delta region of Nigeria have become so widespread that the area can now be described as "the conflict zone" in the country.[1] These conflicts revolve around claims for self-determination, minority rights, and insistence on the practice of fiscal federalism. Directly put, they are "oil conflicts" foregrounded by demands of the people from that region for resource and environmental controls.

Niger Delta, one of the largest wetlands in the world, comprises several distinctive ecological zones: sandy coastal ridge barriers; brackish or saline mangroves; fresh water, permanent and seasonal forests; and lowland rain forests (WACOL 2002a). The area is inhabited by long-settled communities, some claiming the status of indigenous groups. Niger Delta is also an area rich in oil, contributing about 3.2 percent of the world's oil requirement. The major multinational/transnational corporations that operate in the area include Shell Petroleum Development

Company (SPDC), Exxon Mobil, Chevron Texaco, ELF Petroleum Nigeria, and Agip Oil. The Nigeria National Petroleum Corporation is a major player in the oil sector, although through privatization it is gradually divesting itself of controlling shares. There are numerous oil companies in the region, and most serve the major oil industries.

The conflict in the area is chiefly caused by oil activity, which has become a political, economic, and social issue that overshadows all other discourses in the region. The intense violence that characterizes this conflict has claimed thousands of lives and led to the wanton destruction of property, the worst example being the Ogoni case. In Odi, spinoff events from the struggle for resource control led to an unprecedented invasion and the total destruction of the town. In the last decade, the conflict was male-dominated, with strong youth participation. The recent entry of women in conflict-making in the Niger Delta region has challenged the traditional assumption that women are the "peace-makers" and "victims" of man-made conflicts. In July 2002, the women in the Escravos area (hereafter called "the Amazons") occupied the Chevron flow stations. Their nonviolent protest added a new, but refreshing, dimension to conflict transformation in the region. Not surprisingly, in August of the same year, the Ijaws, Itsekiris, and Ilaje women took a cue from the Amazons of the Escravos and staged their own protests, acting in a similarly nonviolent manner under the umbrella of the Niger Delta Women's Association. In this chapter, I have used the Escravos women's protest of July 2002 as a case study to examine what women's involvement in these social protests portends for conflict transformation in that region. Why did the Amazons go to war with Chevron Texaco? The tactics that successfully brought Chevron to the negotiating table and the women who reaped the bounties of war by way of a signed memorandum of understanding (MOU) and immediate financial compensation demonstrate that women could become great actors in conflict transformation in Nigeria.

WOMEN AND SOCIAL PROTESTS IN NIGERIA: SOME HISTORICAL PERSPECTIVES

The Amazons' involvement in conflicts dates back to precolonial Nigeria, when Queen Amina of Zaria successfully led her army of men and women to victory. However, it was during colonial times that women's movements and social protests intensified. During this period, women in the eastern and western parts of Nigeria staged various protests that shook even the colonizers and their government. The most prominently cited example is the Aba women's protest, in which women from the east mobilized and went to war against the British colonial regime for imposing taxes on the indigenes (the colonized). In fact, this protest is recorded in history as the beginning of labor activism in Nigeria. Although some see it as a riot, many have eulogized it as the "Aba Women's War." This war was primarily a movement to protect women's economic and political interests, which were endangered by taxation, the economic crisis, and the actions of the warrant chiefs (Mba 1997, 77–87). Specifically, the women went to war because of the introduction of taxation of men, the drop in palm produce prices, the threat of taxation of women, and grievances against the warrant chiefs and the native courts. Unlike the Escravos women, the Aba women went to war with weapons. By the end of war, about fifty-five women were dead; ten native courts (colonial institutions run by those working for the British, whether local or British), including houses of personnel, were damaged; and factories were looted. The objectives of these women in going to war were partially met, as no taxation on women was ever introduced. However, the confrontation did not put a stop to male taxation, which the women claimed affected them equally. Some of the grievances against the warrant chiefs were addressed, and women not previously involved in the colonial administration received a few places in the native courts.

In southwest Nigeria, women have been recorded as playing an important role in the Yoruba wars of the nineteenth century (Mba 1997, 9). In Yorubaland, Iyalodes (a female title, indigenous to the Yoruba, that is given to honor exceptional women) were recognized for their contributions to defense and their military prowess. According to Nina Mba (1997, 7), the Iyalode title was introduced in the 1850s in Ibadan, Oyo, and Abeokuta in recognition of the contribution to the military success of the town made by a wealthy woman trader, Iyaola, who not only gave liberal credit to the war chiefs to enable them to acquire guns and ammunition but also fielded her own soldiers (Mba 1997, 7).

In the Abeokuta-Dahomey War, Madam Tinubu was largely responsible for providing the Egba Warriors with guns and ammunition. As a reward, she was given the title of Iyalode of all the Egba. While helping Abeokuta to defeat Dahomey, she was also the leader of a peace party in Abeokuta, demanding cessation of the Ijaye War and the opening of trade routes (Mba 1997, 10).[2]

In 1947–1948, Abeokuta women organized social protests, particularly against the introduction of the female flat rate tax. They used various nonviolent methods such as petitions, propaganda, legal processes, and the press to challenge discriminatory taxation, whereby only Abeokuta and Ijebu women paid poll tax in all of Nigeria. This poll tax triggered a mass movement of the Abeokuta women's union, led by Mrs. Ransome-Kuti (Mba 1997, 135). Unlike the Igbo women of 1929, the Abeokuta women never carried any instruments that could be construed as weapons.

As the foregoing demonstrates, history has recorded women's involvement in political and economic protests in Nigeria. In fact, women exhibited military prowess and contributed to many conquests before and during colonial rule, especially in southern Nigeria, despite the fact that the traditional Nigerian societies were not free from sexist bias founded on patriarchal constructions. Women's direct involvement in conflicts, whether violent or nonviolent, dwindled in postindependent Nigeria; yet the women's movement for equality and freedom from discrimination continues to strengthen. Thus, the recent advances made by the Niger Delta women in a nonviolent manner reenact the past roles that women played in conflict resolution, and they need to be studied closely as a new approach in conflict transformation in postcolonial Nigeria.

THE AMAZON'S WAR IN ESCRAVOS WITH CHEVRON TEXACO

> All along, men of the communities, leaders, elders, community chairmen and the rest have been facing the companies and been talking about the problems facing the communities, [but] women were not carried along. Women have been respecting them. They are the leaders and the oil companies kept promising them and the promises were not fulfilled. So, in turn, we gathered and planned, and said if things would not work out fine, why not the women move forward? Maybe, if they can't listen to the men, if they can't cooperate with them, they might cooperate with us sometimes. (Interview, Josephine Ogba, November 2002)[3]

The above quotation illustrates the resolve of the women of the Gbaramatu and Egbema clans in the Warri South West local government area at the time that they took over the Chevron Texaco flow stations in their communities on July 15, 2002. The women from ten coastal communities of the two kingdoms of Gbaramatu/ Egbema came together by the hundreds under the name "Gbaramatu/Egbema Clans Women Forum" to stage peaceful protests against this multinational corporation, which for about thirty-seven years had extracted oil, conservatively estimated to be worth U.S.$97.4 billion, and in the process had degraded their environment.

The women, acting in consensus, peacefully took over four flow stations (major points from which petroleum is prepared for distribution and export) at Abiteye, Makaraba/Otunana, Olero, and Dibi and for eleven days prevented employees from entering and carrying out their work. What started as a small protest of about 50 women on July 15 gathered momentum, such that by the ninth day more than 200 women were participating in this insurgency. It was a war without arms, but with people resolved to achieve a goal. Although men and youths were not involved, the women enjoyed massive male and community support. This support, in turn, reinforced their determination to continue the siege until peace was brokered. The oil company yielded to their demands on July 24, 2002.

Chevron Texaco (formerly known as Chevron Nigeria Limited) is the second-largest oil exploration and production company in Nigeria, with a daily production of more than 400,000 barrels. Over 60 percent of the company's daily output is extracted from the Ijaw communities of Gbaramatu and Egbema Kingdoms in the Warri South West and Warri North Local government areas, where Chevron maintains six flow stations—including Dibi, Opuekeuba, Otunnana, Abiteye, and Makaraba. The sixth flow station, Olero, is fed jointly by oil wells located in the Ijaw and Itsekiri communities in the Warri North Local government area. The women made their way into the Abiteye flow station by crushing the resistance of the Chevron security apparatus, remaining in various flow stations for nine days before the company invited them into a dialogue. They sat for another two days,

Figure 14.1. Children abandon school to pick periwinkles from the river.

negotiating terms to end the insurgency. It was only after an MOU was signed and 20 million naira in compensation was paid that the women evacuated the yards. (Given that 130 naira equal 1 dollar, this amount totaled about U.S.$154,000).

WHY THE WOMEN WENT TO WAR: CAUSES OF THE CONFLICT

> I don't even have work, but oil is being exploited from my fatherland. Oil activities have spoilt the periwinkles [a variety of sea snail used as food], which I depend on to take care of my family. Before the exploitation of oil in this community, I used to pick 40–50 bags of periwinkles per day but now, for three days I can't get up to 20 bags. Even my children who help me out find it difficult to pick periwinkles from the river. Oil has spoilt everything. (Interview, Grace Ogoba, November 2002)[4]

> Chevron doesn't look [at us] and treat us like human beings. Our people are suffering, our children are suffering and that's why we staged the protest. Oil activities have spoilt our rivers and there are no longer fishes. They say we are Ijaw people, but we don't have fish. When you catch any fish and open the belly you smell crude oil. We want the company to employ our husbands and children. They should also give the women work to do. People from other areas come here to work but we, the indigenes, are not employed. They can sponsor us to learn some hand works and encourage us to engage

Figure 14.2. Children helping their mother package periwinkle in bags for sale.

in productive activities and earn livelihood therefrom. (Interview, Rodina Daniel, November 2002)[5]

The bulk of the pressure falls back on the woman. When the husband does not have a job, it is the woman who feeds the house, sometimes through petty trading. When you send your children to school, and they become jobless after graduation, they're still tied to your apron. We have oil companies around us that can employ our sons and husbands, but they have not been doing this. We know that the men and the youth have tried. They usually come to tell us that they have signed an MOU with the companies and so on. None of these things come into existence. So this time around, we decided to take our destiny in our hands and march to the facilities. (Interview, Fanti Goodness Wariyai, August 2002)[6]

The ethnically fuelled conflict in the oil-rich Niger Delta is caused by several factors. According to Cyril Obi, "At the heart of the conflict is the claim of the oil minorities to the right to control oil versus the counterclaim of the State and oil multinationals to exclusively extract and control the oil found in the minority areas of the Niger Delta" (Obi 2001, 51). In addition, Rotimi Suberu has articulated the grievances and demands of Nigeria's oil-bearing areas into four broad themes: the disposition of mineral land rents, the application of the derivation principle to the allocation of federally collected mineral revenues, the appropriate institutional and fiscal responses to the ecological problems of the oil-producing areas, and the responsibility of the oil-prospecting companies to the oil-producing communities within the present federal structure (Rotimi 1996, 27).[7] Simply put, the agitations of the Niger Delta people centered on resource and environmental controls, political autonomy, and a democratic federal Nigeria that recognizes minority rights (ERA 2002).

When the Amazons of the Escravos rose to defend their interests and those of their communities, they based their action on what they perceived to be a long period of economic and environmental injustices. Thus, for example, the women demanded restitution for decades of expropriation and environmental degradation. According to the women leaders I spoke to, their mission was to press for their fundamental human rights, which they alleged had been violated by the oil giants. The Niger Delta people, the women noted, depend on farming and fishing for their living, and since oil exploration and exploitation started in the area forty-eight years ago, their environment has been devastated and their rivers polluted. This has resulted in poor crop yields as the land ceased to produce, and the fish in the rivers have been scared away to the high seas. The people are now living in abject poverty and suffering ill health from flaring gas, while the oil companies accumulate wealth.

It is interesting to note the linkage between poverty and conflicts in this region. In the case of the Niger Delta, widespread unemployment among youths, extreme poverty, frustrations, and neglect by both the government and the transnational oil corporations culminated in the women's protest of July 15, 2002, and all

Figure 14.3. Mrs. Grace Ogeba answering questions from WACOL Information Officer on impacts of oil exploration and exploitation activities on their environment.

the subsequent social protests by women. For them, the linkage between economic misfortune, environmental degradation, and oil expropriation was crystal-clear; they required no formal education and scientific proof to understand this. The number of periwinkles they pick and the amount of fish they catch are continuously declining, thereby increasing their poverty. Their health conditions, particularly eye problems and miscarriages, are clearly linked to gas flares. As the women observed, the oil blessings have turned to punishment. This is why the Escravos women, acting in concert, embarked upon the protest and seizure of the Chevron Texaco oil flow in Abitiye.[8] As one of the women leaders put it, "we're taking our destiny in our hands" (Interview, Fanti Goodness Wariyai, August 2002). The reasons behind women's social protest action in the oil delta, although varied, are mainly economic rather than political in nature. Poverty is indeed fueling conflicts in this region and contributing to the changing character of the "oil conflict."

WOMEN'S DEMANDS AND THE RESULTS

The Amazons took over the Chevron facilities and occupied them for eleven days to press home their demands and get Chevron to sign an MOU. The seventeen-point demand placed on the negotiating table with the management of Chevron Texaco included employment opportunities in the company for their husbands, brothers, sisters, and children; conversion of contract staff into permanent staff; development of their communities by means of provisions for infrastructure through specific community projects; and increased scholarship funds for their children.[9] The women also requested a skill acquisition program, micro/macro credit schemes, provisions for a healthcare system, schools, town halls, and respect for their environment. They complained that oil exploration had devastated their environment and occupationally displaced them. Therefore, they demanded that 25 million naira be paid to each community to compensate for the many years of neglect. The women listed several conditions to be fulfilled by Chevron before they would allow the reopening of the flow stations. These conditions included the payment of 4 million naira (approximately U.S.$31,000) in compensation to the women for each participating community, immediate employment of ten persons per community, immediate release of the letter of award for the cottage hospital in Oporoza, and a provision of executive boats for each of the traditional rulers in Egbema and Gbaramatu as agreed in 1998. In fact, the women questioned the company's accountability and transparency in implementing a previously signed MOU, which, under point four of their MOU, they called "unfulfilled promises/agreements." The Amazons recognized that their demands were many and might not be immediately met, but they wanted the company to make a commitment by signing the MOU and taking some other positive action. Chevron Texaco fulfilled one of their demands instantly by paying 2 million naira in compensation to each of the ten participating communities, although this amount was 50 percent less than what the women wanted.

The Amazons' war has opened up a peaceful avenue for continuing dialogue with the oil multinationals. Since the signing of the MOU on July 24, 2002, the women—previously excluded from decisionmaking—have met several times with the officials of Chevron to work out modalities for the enforcement of their demands as contained in the MOU.

AN ANALYSIS OF THE AMAZONS' STRATEGY

For eleven days the Amazons held Chevron Texaco hostage, disrupting their oil production activities. Here, I would like to examine the tactics employed by these women that allowed them to succeed where men, youths, and, later, other women failed. What really worked for these women? I have identified at least six strategic moves that made it possible for the Amazons to achieve their common objectives:

1. Unity of purpose and commitments
2. Mobilization of all women involved
3. Exclusion of men
4. Nonviolent approach
5. Rights-based approach
6. Articulation of demands in the form of an MOU

When the Gbaramatu/Egbema women gathered to start planning their war against Chevron, they had a clear sense of what they wanted to accomplish in terms of addressing their common problems. The women were united and committed to that struggle; otherwise, they would not have left their homes and camped in flow stations for eleven days. Even when the oil company sent representatives to dialogue with them and make preliminary promises on the ninth day, they remained in their occupied territories until they had collected the war bounties in the form of an MOU and a 20 million naira cash reward. As one of the women leaders noted in an interview, "we don't have a divided house . . . so we are not falling back. Every woman is committed to the struggle" (Ogoba 2002, 10–11).[10]

Five women—namely, Mrs. Lucky Lerekuma, Fanti Wariyai, Josephine Ogoba, Madam Kate, and Felicia Odu—mobilized other women, using the platform of Gberamatu/Egbema Clans Women's Forum. Overall, they mobilized ten communities within these two clans and thus had representation in their planning meetings. During the mobilization, the Amazons chartered some boats and made use of others belonging to one of the women leaders, Josephine Ogoba, without paying for the hire. They also seized boats belonging to the community, fueled them, and went around the communities to mobilize other women in support of their initiative who lived farther away. In addition, they made use of Chevron's independent contractors' radios to communicate with other women and share information. The mobilization was all-inclusive, with women representatives from all ten communities actively participating. These Amazons, without prior training in advocacy, knew that promoting popular participation was the key to success. However, they strategically excluded men from the planning and execution of this war. Their major reason for doing so was that men had been talking with these oil companies for years without involving women and, worse still, without much to show for it, inasmuch as all the promises and agreements purportedly reached with the multinationals were in breach.

Importantly, women didn't want interference by the men. They wanted space and believed that they had full agency to act for themselves. According to Fanti Wariyai:

> We did not collaborate with our husbands. We are the ones that feel the pains. Chevron has been operating in our place for thirty years, yet there is no single infrastructure. No hospital, nothing whatsoever. Take, for instance, if I am in labor, I have to ride in a speedboat to Warri before getting to hospital. Anything can happen in the process. I do not need my husband to come and engineer me to go and fight for a cause that will bring some assistance to me, my children, and even my husband. (Interview, Fanti Wariyai, August 2002)

As women who discreetly planned, they warned that any woman who leaked the information would incur their wrath. In fact, during the insurgency they ensured that no woman backed out due to the influence of their husbands. In fact, they warned the men that they had no right to ask their wives to withdraw, and they would be physically stopped if they attempted to do so. It must be observed that because of their determination and tactics, the women won the hearts of many men who supported them immensely by bringing them food, attending to their needs, and, especially, taking care of the home front while the Amazons were at war.

A winning strategy that is particularly relevant in conflict transformation is the nonviolent manner with which the protest was carried out. There was no introduction of violence, nobody was injured, and the MOU was peacefully concluded. This is quite remarkable, particularly in a region where violent conflicts are commonplace. Women clearly stated that their guiding principle was, "we will not use violence or our men, but we know what will force them to negotiate with us. It is we women" (Wariyai 2002, 12). Interestingly, the company did not respond violently, as is usually the case when they invite state security apparatus and even equip them, as Shell Oil allegedly did in Ogoni during the later women's protest of August 8, 2002, which will be discussed in the next section. The women were obviously wary of the violence in the struggle in the Niger Delta and were careful to avoid that approach. This appears, to me, to have been a compelling reason for not informing the men about their planned war against Chevron Texaco.

Another interesting and innovative approach the women used was to argue their case based on their fundamental human rights to live in a clean environment, to earn a livelihood, and to enjoy an adequate standard of living through provisions of basic amenities. The women considered it to be a violation of their human rights to live in want, "extreme poverty," in the midst of plenty. The area lacks a good network of roads, electricity, water supply, telecommunication, cottage hospitals, schools, employment, and health facilities. The women noted that their plight arose from the commencement of oil and gas exploration by multinational corporations. One woman spoke on behalf of herself and many others when she said that, since the beginning of the oil activities, "we have been deprived of our usual means of livelihood: fishing, farming, mat weaving, and preparation of native salt, and this has brought economic woe to our people."[11]

Thus, the women were able to link their human security to the development of their area, and they articulated their developmental needs in the MOU they presented to Chevron Texaco. Their demands included improvement in environmental standards, employment of their husbands and children, an increment in the scholarships given to some children from the locality by the oil companies, and financial empowerment of the women—since the rivers, which sustain their livelihood, have been destroyed through the activities of oil exploration and exploitation. These demands, as articulated by the women acting and speaking for themselves, demonstrate that the women had a clear objective and a need to constructively engage the oil company in a nonviolent manner. The women's resolve, perseverance, and nonviolent approach, coupled with the company's huge financial losses, must have forced Chevron Texaco to the negotiating table.

THE NEW WAVE OF WOMEN'S SOCIAL PROTESTS AND IMPLICATIONS FOR PEACE IN THE REGION

Since the anti-Chevron protests, women mobilized from different communities in Niger Delta to confront the "big oil companies." It appears that the Amazons of Escravos have opened up a floodgate of social protests. It is pertinent to discuss this development and its implications for conflict resolution and peace building in the Niger Delta region.

On the heels of the Escravos conflict, on August 8, 2002, women protesters arrived at the gates of the three oil companies in Warri City—Shell, Chevron, and Texaco—and took occupation of the premises. These women, operating under the banner of "Niger Delta Women," were singing, carrying placards, and demanding environmental justice and corporate responsibility from the transnational corporations. Numbering over 2,000, they were drawn from the Ijaw, Itsekiri, and Ilaje ethnic groups; it was the first social protest by women of that region that crossed ethnic borders. However, unlike the preceding Escravos women's conflict, this joint protest was marred by the violent response from the state security agents, who, presumably, were acting on the instructions of the government and the three big oil companies the women were protesting against. The peaceful demonstration of the women ended abruptly and violently due to the combined intervention of the police and soldiers who unleashed terror by using tear gas, horsewhips, butts of guns, and security dogs. In the course of the incident, many protesters were injured; fifteen women went missing and resurfaced three weeks later. The results of the protest were minimal, and the opportunity for dialogue, which the women had expected, never materialized. But, the women have resolved to continue this kind of protest with every drop of blood in their veins until the oil companies become socially responsible and contribute meaningfully to the development of the oil-producing communities.[12] Their demands were similar to those of the Escravos women, although they focused more on environmental injustice—particularly gas flaring—to which they attributed their health problems. They were prepared to work in partnership with the multinational oil companies and the government to ensure justice, peace, and development within the Niger Delta regions. However, they warned, "though these companies may import soldiers from all the countries in Africa, we will not relent in our agitation and struggle."[13]

In Rivers State, the Amazons renewed their struggle late in 2002. On October 30, more than 200 women from the Rebisi community in Ikwere clan in Port Harcourt started a protest against Ecodrill-Andrin-Schlumberger, one of the major oil companies operating in the area. This time, while singing war songs, they blocked the company's main gate with a wooden coffin for five days. Speaking through one of the leaders, Mrs. Mary Amadi, the women explained that the aim of their protest was to challenge the way the company treated them and the displacement of their farmlands brought about by the company's operations: "The main occupation of our people is farming, and with the occupation of a large portion of the very fertile lands by the company, there is no land again for us, especially women, to farm and take care of our children" (WACOL 2002a, 15). According to the women, the community had made several attempts to address the issue but were rebuffed by the management of the company. When all avenues to make the company attend to their problems and demands failed, the women had no option other than to embark on a peaceful demonstration to draw attention to their grievances. The Amazons who sat at the gate of the company for five days without food, water, or shelter maintained that they would not leave the place until they saw the management of the company. The women, through another woman leader, Chief (Mrs.) Dora Akarolu, maintained, "wherever they want the talk, we are ready, but we are not leaving the place until after the talks." In a warlike manner, the Rebisi Amazons toed the line of Escravos Amazons and had similar demands.

For the third time in the Delta state during 2002, in another social protest on November 20, women numbering about 4,000 besieged the Delta Steel Company (DSC), protesting the long-term neglect of the community and demanding employment of the indigenes. Although this protest was not targeted at an oil company, violence was again introduced by the police.

Women's insurgency in the Niger Delta has just begun and may be with us for a long time if pertinent issues concerning human security, survival, and development are not addressed (Commission on Human Security 2003, 2).[14] Increasing the access of marginalized individuals to resources and the basic necessities of life—including healthcare, adequate education, and a clean environment—is central to conflict resolution and peace-building. The emergence of women in the dynamic and high-tension oil conflicts in this region can have a positive impact if their efforts are managed properly and conducted in a nonviolent manner. It can open up an avenue for constructive dialogue, and it offers great potential for meaningful change that will protect human security. Moreover, when women are seen as nonviolent, trustworthy, traditional peace-makers, with commitment to the environment, the oil companies may be prepared to listen and, better still, negotiate with them. Of particular concern is the way in which conflict is managed. If the conflict resolution approach of a multinational oil corporation is to invite the state security in to "restore law and order" in response to the peaceful demands of host communities, open confrontation will result and inevitably lead to violence. Intervention from the police and the army, and insensitivity and unwillingness on the part of the oil companies to engage in dialogue, are some of the factors that turn peaceful agitations into violent conflicts. When they began, protests and social movements in the Niger Delta were not carried out violently. The violence seems to have been institutionalized since the late General Abacha's draconian regime and the miscalculation that beheading Movement for the Survival of the Ogoni People (MOSOP) leaders—playwright Ken Saro-Wiwa and eight others—would silence the people, preventing them from questioning the status quo and demanding redress for environmental and economic injustices (Obi 2001, 67). Women's appearance and participation in these "oil conflicts" may reintroduce a nonviolent approach and tame the raging crisis in the Niger Delta that continues to spread and grow in intensity.

CONCLUSION

In the Niger Delta, 2002 can best be described as the year of the Amazons, who, in an unprecedented manner, joined the long-drawn-out struggle for resource and environmental justice against the federal government of Nigeria and the multinational oil corporations operating in the region. Whether the emergence of women in these conflicts will solve the lingering problem here or compound it remains to be seen. Either way, however, the nonviolent approach employed by the Escravos Amazons who went to war with Chevron Texaco can be described as a "best practice." It provides a window of opportunity in conflict transformation and reinforces the fact that women could become great actors in conflict resolution and peace-building. The women's strategic insurgency brought to the fore a new, refreshing, and effective approach that forced Chevron Texaco to negotiate and sign agreements. There is a lot to learn from this approach, particularly in the search for sustainable peace in a region that has been plagued with conflicts threatening oil production, Nigeria's national economy, and the human security of the indigenes of the Niger Delta.

NOTES

1. This chapter was first presented at the International Seminar on Local Approaches to Conflict Transformation (North and South), which took place on May 27–28, 2003, at the University of Ibadan, Nigeria.

2. In the southwest, Madam Tinubu was the first woman to play a part in the resistance to British rule (Ajayi and Smith quoted in Mba 1997).

3. Mrs. Josephine Ogba is a spokeswoman for the women protesters.

4. Grace Ogoba is a widow with nine children from the Keyegnene community, Gbaramatu, who was interviewed by the Women's Aid Collective (WACOL) Team on November 10, 2002, during a fact-finding mission.

5. Mrs. Rodina Daniel is a trader and mother of four children. She made this statement during an interview with WACOL Information Officer Mr. Oliver Onwubunta on November 10, 2002.

6. Fanti Goodness Wariyai is a woman leader who helped to organize the Chevron Insurgency. She made this statement during an interview with *The Guardian*'s senior correspondent, Abraham Osgood, on August 25, 2002.

7. See, in particular, Chapter 3 on ERA (2002): "Ethnic Minority Problems and Oil Politics: A Case Study of Rivers State" (Rotimi 1996).

8. I gathered this information in the company of the WACOL Team, which met with various women actors in the conflict on October 2, 11, and 23, 2002, November 2 and 10, 2002, and May 21, 2003, in Warri, the Cheyenne community, Gbaramatu, and the Port Harcourt Office of WACOL.

9. This demand was referred to as either a thirty-six-point or thirty-nine-point demand in various interviews and newspaper reports. However, the memorandum of understanding I examined made reference in its title to a seventeen-point demand on Chevron Texaco.

10. Mrs. Josephine Ogoba is a woman leader who spoke to the *Action Woman,* a quarterly publication of WACOL.

11. I spoke to and interviewed several women involved in this conflict.

12. I met with about a thousand of these women in scheduled meetings on November 2 and 3, 2002. Representatives from the three ethnic communities were also present.

13. See also WACOL (2002b, 6).

14. The Nigerian government needs to focus attention on security for the people, not for the state. Specifically, it must think in terms of security that enhances human rights, strengthens human development, protects individuals and communities against a broad range of threats, and empowers them to act on their own behalf (Commission on Human Security 2003, 2).

15

Building Empire on the Backs of Women

U.S. Actions or the Role of the United States in Afghanistan

Sonali Kolhatkar

❇

Afghanistan is the country that the United States has most publicly talked about in recent years in terms of the liberation of women.[1] This is an area of the world that I have studied for the last four years, before many people were looking at it. Prior to 2001, most of us were not aware of Afghanistan. Some of us had begun to hear awful stories about women's oppression under the Taliban. I was shocked by the level of oppression that women were facing. My initial instinct was to think, "this can't be happening, this is just media exaggeration." But I did my own research, and I found that it was true. I was even more horrified to discover that nobody was doing anything about it outside of Afghanistan, and that nobody was hearing much about it. We started hearing a little bit more in 2001, when the Taliban was destroying the Buddha statues in Bamiyan, Afghanistan. These were absolutely beautiful statues as tall as buildings. The Taliban was proclaiming that the statues were offensive on the grounds that visual images of living beings are

204

perceived as an affront to Islam. They were also trying to gather world attention. And they did. They got world attention because world leaders begged them not to destroy these Buddha statues. I was enraged at the reaction of these world leaders. Yes, they should have been begging the Taliban not to destroy the Buddha statues, but nobody was coming forth begging them not to kill women or begging them not to insist that women hide themselves from society. Nobody was insisting that the Taliban refrain from violating every imaginable human rights standard where women were concerned.

Of course, in September 2001, when the United States itself was hit by a serious tragedy, it turned its attention to Afghanistan again and began talking about "women's liberation." You might have thought I would get very excited. Finally my country was going to do the most serious thing it could do on an international scale, which is to fight a war to save women! Instead I was very frightened. I didn't want the United States to "liberate" Afghan women. I wanted the United States to do everything it could to remove its influence from Afghanistan because it was U.S. influence that had led to Afghan women's oppression in the first place. We need to go back into the history of Afghanistan to understand the role of the United States in women's oppression.

When Condoleezza Rice testified in front of the 9/11 Commission about terrorism, the whole framework of the dialogue was about not going into Afghanistan early enough, not being tough enough on terrorism, not hitting Al Qaeda fast enough or hard enough. Nobody was talking about our role in actually *sowing* the seeds of terrorism in Afghanistan. In fact, the person who should have been on trial, instead of Condoleezza Rice, was Zbigniew Brzezinski, her predecessor under former President Carter. In the late 1970s, Brzezinski was a national security adviser responsible for the idea of going into Afghanistan and fueling a "jihad" against the Soviet Union. About six months before the Soviet Union invaded Afghanistan, the CIA began covertly funding seven different fundamentalist factions of *Mujahadeen,* which loosely translates as "warriors of God." In order to counter the Soviets, the United States turned Afghanistan into the last battleground for the Cold War.

The Soviet Union occupied Afghanistan for ten years, during which time the United States was fueling these fundamentalist groups, all of which were extremist, misogynist, and anti-American. One of these men, Gulbuddin Hekmatyar, was famous for throwing fundamentalist parties when he was at Kabul University. He was also well known for throwing acid on the faces of women who refused to cover their faces. Somehow the fight against the Cold War was too important. It didn't matter that we might be creating terrible conditions for Afghan women as long as we got the Soviets out of Afghanistan, as long as we toppled the Soviets. In fact, Brzezinski talked about giving the Soviet Union "its own Vietnam." What would that have meant for the Afghan people? How much did the Vietnamese suffer under our war there? This was essentially what the United States wanted: to drag the Soviet Union into a bloody mess and into an occupation that would drain it. That is exactly what happened.

During the ten years that the Soviet Union was in Afghanistan, tens of thousands of soldiers were lost, over a million Afghans were killed, and the United States fueled billions of dollars into the largest CIA covert operation in history—an operation that became overt under former President Reagan. The billions of U.S. dollars in weapons, training, and funding that were funneled through Saudi Arabia and Pakistan had the effect of inviting thousands of Arab and Muslim fighters from around the world to join in this "jihad" against the "godless communists." This was the fight of their lives, their dream come true: to get all of these "extremist Islamists," as they called them, to Afghanistan to fight the Soviets, to fight the atheists. Today, you see the legacy of that. These men of the *Mujahadeen*—the thousands of Arab fighters, Muslim fighters from Indonesia, the Philippines, Uzbekistan, and Afghan fighters—are very misogynist. They adhere to a very fundamentalist brand of Islam, which, like any other extremist interpretation of religion, is misogynist in nature. Look at any organized religion and you will see serious disparities in the treatment of women and men. Whether Christianity, Hinduism, or Judaism, organized religion in its fundamentalist form is misogynist.

The Soviet Union withdrew from Afghanistan in the late 1980s, leading to its eventual collapse and the end of the Cold War, with the United States as the victor. What did the United States do after the end of the Soviet occupation? Instead of disarming the *Mujahadeen,* it continued funding them for about three years after the Soviet Union pulled out. The next four years, from 1992 to 1996, were the bloodiest for Afghans, with 40,000–50,000 Afghans killed in the capital city of Kabul alone. These fundamentalist factions instantly turned upon themselves saying, "I want to be king," "I want to be president," and they fought one another in the cities. They rocket-shelled one another with U.S.-supplied weapons. The United States did not bother to disarm them after the "jihad" was over, and Afghan women paid the price. This was the beginning of the end for Afghan women, who before the Soviet invasion and occupation had a relatively decent standard of living, at least in the cities. They were university students. They were doctors and lawyers. They had decent participation in government—participation as good as, if not better than, women's participation in the top echelons in the U.S. government.

After the Soviets withdrew, there was lawlessness. This created a political vacuum into which stepped the marginalized groups of men who had been elevated to power. Imagine if, in the United States, a very powerful invader had come in decades ago and said, "We are going to give weapons and money to the Ku Klux Klan—to the KKK—and we are going to make them the most powerful group in this country at the expense of everyone else. We are going to give them billions of dollars in weapons." How different would the United States be today? That's what happened in Afghanistan. Many of the educated elites fled, but the poor people who couldn't flee are still there. Women, particularly, were trapped. Many committed suicide. Many were gang-raped. They saw the beginning of the end of their rights between 1992 and 1996. The world just turned its eyes away from Afghanistan.

In 1996, a group of very organized fundamentalists with satellite phones and pickup trucks emerged in Afghanistan. They called themselves the Taliban. They walked into villages and towns and said, "We are going to stop this madness, this instability. We are going to protect your women. We are going to help you. We are going to help you against the fundamentalists." The people who were desperate welcomed the Taliban with open arms, not realizing what was in store for them. The Taliban promised peace and stability, and, in fact, they did bring a kind of peace and stability—the kind that you would find in a prison. Afghan women didn't know what was in store for them, and they didn't have much of a choice because these men came with guns. They were ideologically similar to their predecessors, but they were more organized. They came in, and they took women's oppression a step further—they institutionalized it. Before, it was in the lawless hands of whoever was the strongest, whoever could win through guns and intimidation. Now it became part of the law, and Afghan women could not walk out uncovered or with nail polish on their fingers.

All along, the United States had its eyes turned away from Afghanistan. After many years, the Clinton administration tried to work with the Taliban to secure an oil-pipeline deal for the Unocal Corporation, which would have awarded the Taliban millions of dollars in royalties. When U.S. feminists discovered how the Taliban was treating women, they protested the pipeline deal until it eventually fell through. Former President Clinton also engaged Afghanistan by bombing it in 1998 when the U.S. embassies were bombed in Kenya and Tanzania. The U.S. response was to target missiles at Afghanistan and kill a few people—didn't matter who as long as there was some response—and then nothing. Finally, we had September 11, 2001, the big wake-up call. It's important that we understand the history of the context of the United States' role in setting up a system of oppression in Afghanistan. Whether by accident, negligence, or on purpose, the result is that for Afghan women the reality has been horrific.

After September 11th you might have seen in the media that Afghan women are now free. We have "liberated" them. Girls' schools are open. In my mind, the biggest heroes in Afghanistan today, those who have been fighting the hardest for their own freedom, are women themselves. I want to give you an example. The *New York Times* had a cover story about two Afghan women who were being called heroes because they had de-mined their village. It was the site of tons of cluster bomblets that had been dropped by the United States. We should know what cluster bombs are because our taxes pay for them. These are internationally condemned weapons, and they are called "antipersonnel devices," which is a nice way of saying that they are antihuman devices. A cluster bomb consists of 202 bomblets that detonate into separate bomblets, which are then strewn over a very large area the size of several football fields. About 10–22 percent of them do not explode on impact. The rest explode and disperse shrapnel over a large area, horribly maiming and killing people. The United States continues to use these internationally condemned bombs and has dropped 1,200 of them in Afghanistan since 2001. So 10–22 percent of these bomblets remain unexploded. This is a legacy of U.S liberation in that country. What do you think happens when a hungry young child wandering in the countryside sees a bright-yellow canister in the dirt? What do you think he or she is going to do? The child will walk over and pick it up! It looks like a shiny toy. These two women saw two young boys in their village get killed when they went to touch one of these bomblets. They took it upon themselves to de-mine their village. Risking their lives, they shoveled, gingerly picked up the unexploded bomblets piece by piece, and dumped them into a hole where they could be safely detonated. To these women, this is what U.S. liberation looks like—it means that Afghan women have to once more clean up the mess made by the United States.

It is important for us to know what is happening in the countryside. The United States, aid agencies, and NATO security forces are focusing the majority of their attention on the capital city of Kabul. They have been supposedly disarming the warlords and armed men there. Kabul is, relatively speaking, the safest city in Afghanistan. Women in Kabul have more freedom than those in the countryside. This means that some of them can walk around uncovered. Some of them can look for jobs. But, in reality, there are no jobs. There is very little opportunity for employment or even shelter. Who is back in power outside of Kabul? The United States' old friend is back in power. After the Taliban took power, the *Mujahadeen* retreated to the north. They put aside their differences, called themselves the Northern Alliance, and decided that they were going to be the counter to the Taliban.

The 9/11 Commission hearings have stressed that the United States should have armed and helped the Northern Alliance earlier. These were the very same terrorist, misogynist fundamentalists who were destroying Afghanistan in the early 1990s, and we enlisted their help in toppling the Taliban. All that we did was replace one organized, fundamentalist group with a series of disorganized fundamentalist groups, and the Afghan people are terrified because they know the legacy of the Northern Alliance. They remember the bloody history of the 1990s. Today, these Northern Alliance commanders are holding high positions in the government, thanks to the United States' intervention. It was the U.S. ambassador, Zalmay Khalilzad, who engineered high-level positions for the *Mujahadeen* warlords on the grounds that this was important for the stability of the country. In fact, he said that Afghanistan needs "first peace then justice" to justify this. Now these warlords are back in power in various parts of the country, terrorizing Afghans.

In western Afghanistan, in the province of Herat, Taliban-like restrictions have appeared once more, whereby women and men have to go to different schools. Scores of girls' schools have been burned down. Have we heard about that? No! Afghan women have been committing suicide in alarming numbers in Herat. Many have done so by setting themselves on fire. There is no way out, and they are desperate. They were promised a sort of "liberation," but have only seen one terrorist group replacing another.

Referring to both the Afghans and the Iraqis, Condoleezza Rice recently said, "Under President Bush's leadership, our men and women in uniform have delivered freedom to more than 50 million people in the space of two and a half years." This sounds very nice. It even sounds simple. We just delivered freedom like mail coming in at the door. We just delivered a little packet of freedom that every Afghan now has, thanks to the United States' intervention. But it is not so simple. In fact, the reality is very different. The reality is not being covered by the media, either. A White House press release asserted that millions of Afghan women are experiencing freedom for the first time. Very lofty words indeed! But if you talk to Afghans, you find that they have a very different picture. Amnesty International and Human Rights Watch have done many studies showing how women have continued to suffer in Afghanistan even after the U.S. "liberation." These organizations have gone in and interviewed Afghan people, and some Afghans actually say that it was better under the Taliban.

I worked with one of the most politicized women's group in Afghanistan, the Revolutionary Association of the Women of Afghanistan. RAWA is the only political and humanitarian aid organization in Afghanistan today. It was founded in 1977, the year before the Soviet Union invaded, and it consists of about 2,000 women who live in refugee camps in Pakistan as well as inside of Afghanistan. In 2001, it warned, "Do not enlist the help of the Northern Alliance! We will see chaos return"—and its prediction has come true. We didn't listen to what Afghans themselves wanted for their own country. We have not been aiding the Afghan people as much as we should have. In fact, the United States has given very little aid to Afghanistan, even though we hear all this talk about millions of dollars of aid. Afghanistan and Iraq are similar in size and have roughly the same population. But Afghanistan is decades behind in its standard of living compared to Iraq. Afghan women are three times less literate than Iraqi women. Afghan men are half as literate as Iraqi men. Life expectancy in Afghanistan is 47 years of age; in Iraq, it is 68. Yet we have seen billions of dollars of humanitarian aid go to Iraq and only a few million for Afghanistan. Afghanistan needs U.S.$28.7 billion to reconstruct itself. Recently, a donors' conference benevolently promised $8 billion in aid. At another conference in Tokyo several years ago, $4.5 billion of aid was promised. Very little, about half, actually came through. There are lots of promises being made with little delivery.

Many of us naively believed President Bush when he talked about delivering "liberation" to Afghan women. I heard many feminists saying, "For once we are going to war for the right reason—not over oil but for women's liberation and for women's freedom." But war is never interested in human rights. We can learn that by looking at the long history of imperialism and war. War has never been fought for the "right" reasons. The reasons have always been the wrong ones, but rhetoric has continually been used to convince the subjects of the Empire that it is doing the "right" thing on their behalf. How many of us would have agreed to go to war had we been told that the United States was just hitting back at *somebody* because of 9/11? Or that it was important for us to maintain our imperial credibility? Or that it was important for us to attack Afghanistan as an excuse to move into Iraq? There are even some in the Bush administration who have admitted that all along it wanted to invade Iraq.

So why did the United States attack Afghanistan? I maintain that the United States attacked Afghanistan for reasons of imperial credibility. The Empire was attacked on 9/11. Nobody ever imagined that the Empire would ever get hit in such a dramatic, drastic, tragic, horrific way. If you are the biggest bully on the street and somebody punches you out, would you just take it? You would have to punch out five random people, whether they did it or not, to prove that you are still a tough guy.

Right now, the United States is spending a little bit of what I call "P.R. money"—government officials call them "provincial reconstruction teams," and I call them "public relations teams" (PRTs). There are small groups of soldiers and military contractors going into the countryside in Afghanistan—just token groups. They will build a well in this village; they will build a school in that village. They will spend U.S.$10,000. If that money was given to Afghans, they could have built ten wells with the same money. However, the PRTs and the United States bring in foreign contractors, and they build only one well in a village.

Then they hand out pamphlets to the "grateful Afghans," pamphlets that say "Vote in the upcoming election: Vote for Karzai!" Karzai was a U.S.-backed candidate for the presidency of Afghanistan whom many have considered to be a puppet. He doesn't have very much power; he doesn't have very much popularity. He is a moderate. He is not a fundamentalist, and that is certainly good. We are deciding the outcome of the election in this country. What do you think that Afghans are going to do? These guys came and built a well. Most of these Afghans can't read or write, but they say, "Sure, these guys are good guys, and if they tell us to go vote for Karzai, maybe we should."

Women are being registered to vote in greater and greater numbers, although only 4–15 percent can read or write! Also, many women outside of Kabul are afraid to leave their homes to register. What did Karzai say? He made a statement on International Women's Day, March 8, 2004, appealing to Afghan men: "Go and let your women vote. Go and let your wives and daughters vote. Please let them vote. Go and let them register to vote, and later on you can control who she votes for!" I am not joking; this is what he said. Once more Afghan women will be used to carry out the agenda of the United States. Women have been "liberated," and the Empire has benefited from it. Once more, Afghan women will be enlisted against their will in the furthering of Empire. This is the legacy of "liberation." This is the legacy of Empire.

RAWA represents the resistance of Afghan women. These are the women who are resisting co-optation by the United States and internal fundamentalism in Afghanistan. They hold demonstrations every year, several times a year, against fundamentalism and imperialism in their country. These are the greatest heroes in Afghanistan. These are the people who should have been funded instead of fundamentalist or terrorist organizations, because RAWA *is* rebuilding against all odds.

The women of RAWA have appealed to the United Nations for years: "We need peace keeping troops," they have said. "We need to disarm the warlords."

They march with their faces uncovered, sticks in hand for self- defense (they are a nonviolent organization) and big banners that read "Down with fundamentalism," "We want human rights," and "Democracy." Most of these demonstrations are held in Pakistan, along the border of Afghanistan, because the demonstrators would be killed or jailed if they marched inside Afghanistan. They publish documentation of human rights abuses. They have political publications. They have schools. This is why they are so revolutionary. They realize that the way to change Afghanistan is through education. In fact, they have educated both girls and boys for twenty years about history, geography, human rights, women's rights, and political science. They do this with very little money. They have hospitals for women refugees, literacy classes for women and men, and rehabilitation programs for women who have been forced into prostitution—something that no aid agency would touch because of social taboos. They have a sustainable farming program in western Afghanistan, which the Afghan Women's Mission has helped fund with the donations of Americans. This sustainable farming program helped to construct a water canal that about a year and a half ago brought water to 40,000 people. All of this has been done by a group of revolutionary women who are fighting against all odds and resisting. This, to me, is the face of Afghan women that I look to for providing alternatives to what the United States could be doing in Afghanistan.

The women of RAWA are constantly at the forefront of political resistance, demanding human rights for their fellow citizens; equally important, they are members of a secular organization who believe in a secular government. They want a government that is respectful of women, and they are uncompromising in their work. This is a group of women President Bush and his administration should be looking to when they talk about "liberation." Afghan women know exactly how to liberate themselves. They have been developing methods of liberation for years. What they need from us is not liberation. What they need from us is to get *our* government off *their* backs. We need to learn a lesson from them and figure out how to liberate ourselves from this government.

NOTE

1. This chapter was first presented as a seminar lecture at the University of California, Riverside, on March 8, 2004.

Bibliography

Acosta, Gladys. 1995. Flowers that kill: The case of the Colombian flower workers. In *From basic needs to basic rights: Women's claim to human rights,* ed. Margaret A Schuler. Washington, DC: Women, Law, and Development International.

Al-Ali, Nadje. 2005. Reconstructing gender: Iraqi women between dictatorship, war, sanctions and occupation. *Third World Quarterly* 26 (4/5): 739–758.

Allen, C., A. Kelman, and E. R. French. 2001. Brown rot of potatoes. In *Compendium of potato diseases,* ed. W. R. Stevenson, R. Loria, G. D. Franc, and D. P. Weingartner. St. Paul: American Phytopathological Society.

Allen, C., and L. Schmale. 2004. The science of Ralstonia. *Greenhouse Grower,* September, 4–5.

Amnesty International. 2004. *Israel and the occupied territories: The place of the fence/wall in international law.* Available online at http://web.amnesty.org/library/index/engmde150162004.

———. 2005. *Israel and the occupied territories: Conflict, occupation and patriarchy—Women carry the burden.* Available online at http://web.amnesty.org/library/index/engmde150162005.

Anderson, Bridget. 1997. Servants and slaves: Europe's domestic workers. *Race & Class* 39 (1): 37–49.

———. 1999. Overseas domestic workers in the European Union: Invisible women. In *Gender, migration, and domestic service,* ed. Janet Henshall Momsen. New York: Routledge.

———. 2000. *Doing the dirty work? The global politics of domestic labor.* New York: Zed Books.

Anner, Mark. 1998. La maquila y el monitoreo independiente en El Salvador. San Salvador: Independent Monitoring Group of El Salvador.

Anzaldúa, Gloria, and Cherríe Moraga, eds. 1983. *This bridge called my back: Writings by radical women of color.* New York: Kitchen Table/Women of Color Press.

Appelbaum, Richard, Edna Bonacich, and Katie Quan. 2005. *The end of apparel quotas: A faster race to the bottom?* Available online at http://repositories.cdlib.org/cgi/viewcontent.cgi?article=1041&context=gis.

Armbruster-Sandoval, Ralph. 2000. Globalization and cross-border labor organizing in the Americas: The Phillip Van Huesen campaign, the battle in Seattle and beyond. Paper presented at the Latin American Studies Association Conference, March 16–18, in Miami, Florida.

Asian Foodworker. 2003. Indian tea industry crises: What will unions do next? *Bulletin of the Regional Secretariat, International Union of Food.* Available online at http://www.asianfoodworker.net/india/tea.htm.

Asocolflores. 2004. *Colombia tierra del flores.* Available online at http://www.asocolflores.org/info/info_datosin_ingles.php.

Assié-Lumumba, N'dri Thérése. 2000. Educational and economic reforms, gender equity, and access to schooling in Africa. *International Journal of Comparative Sociology* 41 (1): 89–120.

Ayres, Robert. 1985. *Banking on the poor: The World Bank and world poverty.* Cambridge, MA: MIT Press.

Bakan, Abigail, and Daiva K. Stanulis. 1996. Structural adjustment, citizenship, and foreign domestic labour: The Canadian case. In *Rethinking restructuring: Gender and change in Canada,* ed. Isabella Bakker. Toronto: University of Toronto Press.

Bales, Kevin. 1999. *Disposable people: New slavery in the global economy.* Berkeley: University of California Press.

Bank Muñoz, Carolina. 2004a. Transnational capital, transnational labor: The state and the politics of shop floor control in the tortilla industry. Ph.D. dissertation, University of California, Riverside.

———. 2004b. Mobile capital, immobile labor: Inequality and opportunity in the tortilla industry. *Social Justice* 31 (3): 21–39.

Barndt, Deborah. 2002. Tangled routes: Women, work, and globalization on the tomato trail. Lanham, MD: Rowman and Littlefield.

Barnet, Richard, and John Cavanagh. 1994. *Global dreams: Imperial corporations and the new world order.* New York: Simon and Schuster.

Bashevkin, Sylvia. 2000. Rethinking retrenchment: North American social policy during the early Clinton and Chretien years. *Canadian Journal of Political Science* 33 (1): 7–36.

Baumgardner, Jennifer, and Amy Richards. 2000. *Manifesta: Young women, feminism, and the future.* New York: Farrar, Straus and Giroux.

BCRES (Banco Central de Reserva de El Salvador). 2002. *La industria maquiladora en El Salvador.* San Salvador, El Salvador: BCRES.

———. 2005. *Bóletin estatico mensual, marzo 2005.* San Salvador, El Salvador: BCRES.

Bergeron, Suzanne. 2003a. Challenging the World Bank's narrative of inclusion. In *World Bank literature,* ed. A. Kumar. Minneapolis: University of Minnesota Press.

———. 2003b. The post-Washington consensus and economic representations of women in development at the World Bank. *International Feminist Journal of Politics* 5 (3): 397–419.

Bourne, Compton. 1993. The contemporary employment and unemployment situation in Trinidad and Tobago: Building national consensus on social policy. Report prepared for the Inter-American Development Bank.

B.P.W. (Cyprus Federation of Business and Professional Women). 2000. *Resolution.* Cyprus Federation of Business and Professional Women.

Brassel, Frank, and Cruz Emilia Rangel. 2001a. *International social standards for the international flower industry* (Draft). Bonn: Friedrich-Ebert-Stiftung, Food First Information and Action Network-FIAN, and the International Union of Food, Agricultural, Hotel, Restaurant, Catering, Tobacco and Allied Workers-IUF.

————. 2001b. *Flowers for justice: Implementing the international code of conduct.* Bonn: Friedrich-Ebert-Stiftung, Food First Information and Action Network-FIAN, and the International Union of Food, Agricultural, Hotel, Restaurant, Catering, Tobacco and Allied Workers-IUF.

Brenner, Neil, and Nik Theodore. 2002. Cities and the geographies of "actually existing neoliberalism." In *Spaces of neoliberalism: Urban restructuring in North America and Western Europe,* ed. Neil Brenner and Nik Theodore. Malden, MA: Oxford's Blackwell Press.

Brigg, Morgan. 2001. Empowering NGOs: The microcredit movement through Foucault's notion of dispositif. *Alternatives: Global, local, political* 26 (3): 233–258.

Brosch, Iris. 2004. Think pink. *Marie Claire,* July, p. 107.

BSR (Business for Social Responsibility), Investor Responsibility Research Center and Dara O'Rourke. 2000. *Independent university initiative: Final report.* San Francisco: BSR.

Bunker, Stephen. 1985. *Underdeveloping the Amazon: Extraction, unequal exchange, and the failure of the modern state.* Chicago: Chicago University Press.

Burawoy, Michael. 1985. *The politics of production.* London: Verso.

Butler, Judith. 1990. *Gender trouble.* New York: Routledge.

Byrd, Scott C. 2005. The Porto Alegre consensus: Theorizing the forum movement. *Globalizations* 2 (1): 151–163.

Cabezas, Amalia. 2005. Accidental crossings: Tourism, sex work, and women's rights in the Dominican Republic. In *Dialogue and difference: Feminisms challenge globalization,* ed. Marguerite Waller and Sylvia Marcos. New York and London: Palgrave.

Cabezas, Amalia, Ellen Reese, and Marguerite Waller. 2006. Introduction: Emerging subjects of neoliberal global capitalism. *Social Identities* 12 (5): 503–505.

Cactus. 1996. Impacto socio-económico de la floricultura en la sabana. In Cactus, defensoría del pueblo and FESCOL. *Memorias del Seminario Taller Sello de calidad para florese colombianas. Condiciones y Criterios* (agosto).

————. 2000. Informaciones varias sobre rendimientos. Unpublished report.

————. 2001. Campaña internacional de flores: Los frutos recogidos. *Boletín cactus* (junio): 9.

————. 2005. Flower workers' day 2005: Direct contracting and freedom of association—rights to be conquered again. Unpublished flyer.

Cactus and Mesa de Trabajo Mujeres y Economía. 1999. Untitled. Unpublished report.

Cainkar, Louise. 1993. The Gulf War, sanctions and the lives of Iraqi women. *Arab Studies Quarterly* 15 (2): 15–51.

Campos, Milagros. 2002. *Deceptive beauty: A look at the global flower industry.* Victoria, Canada: Victoria International Development Education Association (VIDEA).

Caulfield, Norman. 1998. *Mexican workers and the state: From Porfiriato to NAFTA.* Fort Worth: Texas Christian University Press.

CGAP. 2001. *Microfinance, grants, and non-financial responses to poverty reduction: Where does microcredit fit?* Focus Note 20, May.

Chang, Grace. 2000. *Disposable domestics: Immigrant women workers in the global economy.* Boston: South End Press.

Chaparro, Angélica. 2005. Floricultura: Quién gana con el TLC. Unpublished paper.

Chatterjee, Piya. 2001. *A Time for Tea: Women, Labor, and Post/Colonial Politics on an Indian Plantation.* Durham, NC: Duke University Press.

Chomsky, Noam. 2003. *Hegemony or survival: America's quest for global dominance.* New York: Metropolitan Books.

Christen, Robert, and Deborah Drake. 2003. Commercialization: The new reality of microfinance. In *The commercialization of microfinance: Balancing business and development,* ed. Deborah Drake and Elisabeth Rhyne. Bloomfield: Kumarian Press.

Chua, Amy. 2003. *World on fire: How exporting free market democracy breeds ethnic hatred and global instability.* New York: Doubleday.

Combahee River Collective. 2004. A black feminist statement. In *Women's lives: Multicultural perspectives,* 3rd edition, ed. Gwyn Kirk and Margo Okazawa-Rey. New York: McGraw-Hill.

Commission on Human Security. 2003. *Human security now.* New York.

Constable, Nicole. 1997. *Maid to order in Hong Kong.* Ithaca, NY: Cornell.

Coppin, Addington, and Reed Olsen. 1992. Earnings and ethnicity in Trinidad and Tobago. *Journal of Development Studies* 34: 116–134.

Cover. 2004. *Marie Claire,* November.

Cox, Rosie. 1999. The role of ethnicity in shaping the domestic employment sector in Britain. In *Gender, migration, and domestic service,* ed. Janet Henshall Momsen. New York: Routledge.

Cox, Sarah. 2002. The dark side of flowers. *Georgia Strait,* May 30–June 6, 17–22.

CSO (Central Statistical Office). 1999. *Continuous sample survey: Labor force report.* Republic of Trinidad and Tobago.

Daly, Mary, and Jane Lewis. 1998. Introduction: Conceptualizing social care in the context of welfare state restructuring. In *Gender, social care, and welfare state restructuring,* ed. Jane Lewis. Aldershot: Ashgate.

Dardon, B. 2004. "Golpe a la exportacion de Geranios" ("Blow to geranium exports"). *Prensa Libre,* March 15, 2004.

Das Gupta, Monica, and Li Shuzhuo. 2000. Gender bias in China, South Korea and India 1920–1990: Effects of war, famine and fertility decline. In *Gendered poverty and wellbeing,* ed. Shahra Razavi. Oxford: Blackwell.

della Porta, Donatella. 2005. Making the polis: Social forums and democracy in the global justice movement. *Mobilization* 10 (1): 73–94.

Dent, Kelly. 2002. The contradictions in codes: The Sri-Lakan experience. In *Corporate responsibility and labor rights: Codes of conduct in the global economy,* ed. Rhys Jenkins, Ruth Pearson, and Gill Seyfang. London: Earthscan.

Department of Social Insurance. 2001. *Social insurance in Cyprus.* Published report.

Dhar, Biswajit. 1988. *Foreign-controlled companies in India: An attempt at identification.* Institute for Studies in Industrial Development (ISID). Working Paper. New Delhi, India. Available online at http://isidev.nic.in/r&p2.html.

Diao, Xinshen, and Agapi Somwaru. 2001. *Impact of the MFA phase-out on the world economy: An intertemporal, global general equilibrium analysis* (Discussion Paper No. 79). Washington, DC: International Food Policy Research Institute. Available online at http://www.cgiar.org/ifpri/divs/tmd/dp.htm.

Dietz, Mary. 1992. Context is all: Feminism and theories of citizenship. In *Learning about women: Gender, politics, and power,* ed. J. K. Conway, S. Bourque, and J. W. Scott. Ann Arbor: University of Michigan.

Dignard, Louise, and Jose Havet. 1995. *Women in micro- and small-scale enterprise development.* Boulder, CO: Westview Press.

Dodenhoff, David. 2004. What happened to the "work" in Wisconsin works? *Wisconsin Interest* 13 (1): 31–37.

Dyer, Richard. 1997. *White.* London: Routledge.

Ehrenreich, Barbara, and Arlie Russell Hochschild, eds. 2002. *Global woman: Nannies, maids, and sex workers in the new economy.* New York: Metropolitan Books.

Eisenstein, Zillah. 2004. *Against empire: Feminisms, racism, and the west.* London/New York: Zed Books.

Elphinstone, J. G. 2005. The current bacterial wilt situation: A global overview. In *Bacterial wilt: The disease and the ralstonia solanacearum species complex,* ed. C. Allen, P. Prior, and A. C. Hayward. St. Paul, MN: American Phytopathological Society Press.

Elyachar, Julie. 2002. Empowerment money: The World Bank, non-governmental organizations, and the value of culture in Egypt. *Public Culture* 14 (3): 493–513.

Enloe, Cynthia. 1989. *Bananas, beaches, and bases.* Berkeley: University of California Press.

———. 2000. *Maneuvers: The international politics of militarizing women's lives.* Berkeley/Los Angeles/London: University of California Press.

———. 2004. *The curious feminist: Searching for women in the new age of empire.* Berkeley: University of California Press.

ERA (Environmental Rights Action). 2002. *A blanket of silence: Images of the Odi genocide.* Nigeria: Author.

EPW Commentary. 2003. Undernutrition and starvation deaths: An inquiry. *Economic and political weekly,* May 3. Available online at http://www.epw.org.in/showArticles.

Escobar, Arturo. 1995. *Encountering development: The making and unmaking of the Third World.* Princeton: Princeton University Press.

Escrivá, Angeles. 2005. Aged global care chains: A southern European contribution to the field. Paper presented at the International Conference on "Migration and Global Domestic Work," May 26–29, in Wassenaar, the Netherlands.

Everett, Jana. 1989. Incorporation versus conflict: Lower-class women, collective action, and the state in India. In *Women, the state, and development,* ed. S. E. M. Charlton, J. Everett, and K. Staudt. New York: State University of New York Press.

Farmer, Paul. 1992. *AIDS and accusation: Haiti and the geography of blame.* Berkeley: University of California Press.

———. 1996. Social inequalities and emerging infectious diseases. *Emerging Infectious Diseases* 2 (4): 259–269.

———. 2001. *Infections and inequalities: The microbial burden of poverty.* Report presented to the House Subcommittee on Biomedical Research, U.S. Congress, on September 26, 2001.

Farsakh, Leila. 2002. Palestinian labor flows to the Israeli economy: A finished story? *Journal of Palestine Studies* 32 (1).

Ferete, Liz. 1997. Blackening the economy: The path to convergence. *Race & Class* 39 (1): 1–17.

Ferguson, James. 1994. *The anti-politics machine: Development, depoliticization, and bureaucratic power in Lesotho.* Minneapolis: University of Minnesota Press.

Final report on starvation crises in the tea industry. 2004. *The Indian people's tribunal on human rights and the environment.* India: Mumbai.

Fisher, Tracy. 2001. Shifting ideologies, social transformations: Black women's grass-roots organization, Thatcherism, and the flattening of the left in London. Ph.D. dissertation, City University of New York.

Flanagan, Caitlin. 2004. How serfdom saved the women's movement. *Atlantic Monthly,* March, 293 (2), 109–128.

Flanders, Laura. 2001. Afghan feminists speak out: War on terrorism, United States. *The Progressive,* November, 36–38.

Folbre, Nancy. 1994. *Who pays for the kids? Gender and the structures of constraint.* New York: Routledge.

Food and Drink Europe. 2003. *Unilever, Pepsico join forces to meet iced tea challenge.* Available online at http://www.foodanddrinkeurope.com/news/printNewsBis.asp?id=18257.

Forster, Cindy. 2005. Death, Mayan women, and free trade. Posted on the Portside listserve on March 30.

Foucault, Michel. 2000. Governmentality. In *Foucault/Power,* ed. J. Faubion. New York: New Press.

Friere, Paulo. 1985. *The politics of education: Culture, power, and liberation.* Boston: Bergin and Garvey Publishers.

Fuentes, Annette, and Barbara Ehrenreich. 1983. *Women in the global factory.* Boston: South End Press.

Gamburd, Michele Ruth. 2000. *Kitchen spoon's handle: Transnationalism and Sri Lanka's migrant housemaids.* Ithaca, NY: Cornell University Press.

Garfield, Richard. 1999. *The impact of economic sanctions on health and well-being.* Overseas Development Institute, London. Available online at http://www.eldis.org/questioning/sanctions.htm.

Gender and Cultural Citizenship Working Group. 2003. Collectivity and comparativity: A feminist approach to cultural citizenship. Unpublished paper.

Gianturco, Paola, et al. 2004. Hanging by a thread. *Marie Claire,* February, 44–50.

Glaser, Barney G., and Anselm L. Strauss. 1967. *The discovery of grounded theory: Strategies for qualitative research.* New York: Aldine de Gruyer.

Glenn, Evelyn. 1992. From servitude to service work: Historical continuities in the racial division of paid reproductive labor. *Signs* 18: 1–43.

———. 2002. *Unequal freedom: How race and gender shaped American labor.* Cambridge, MA: Harvard.

Glenn, Evelyn Nakano. 1986. *Issei, Nisei, war bride: Three generations of Japanese American women in domestic service.* Philadelphia: Temple University Press.

Godoy, Mónica. 1999. Unemployment. *Inside Colombia.* Available online at http://www.terra.com/specials.colombianinsight/1999.

Goetz, Anne Marie, and Rina Sengupta. 1996. Who takes the credit? Gender, power, and control over loan use in rural credit programs in Bangladesh. *World Development* 24 (1): 45–63.

Goldman, Michael. 2001. Constructing an environmental state: Eco-governmentality and other transnational practices of a "green" World Bank. *Social Problems* 48 (4): 499–523.

González, Gilbert G. 2004. *Culture of empire: American writers, Mexico, and Mexican immigrants 1880–1930.* Austin: University of Texas Press.

Goodwin, Jan. 2002. War is hell on women and children. *Marie Claire,* November, 100.

Gordon, Rebecca. 2001. *Cruel and unusual: How welfare "reform" punishes poor people.* Oakland, CA: Applied Research Center.

Gore, Charles. 2000. The rise and fall of the Washington consensus as a paradigm for developing countries. *World Development* 28 (5): 789–804.

Gornick, Janet C., and Marcia Meyers. 2003. *Families that work: Policies for reconciling parenthood and employment.* New York: Russell Sage Foundation.

Government of British Colombia. 2003. *An overview of the B.C. floriculture industry.* Available online at http://www.agf.gov.bc.ca/ornamentals/overview_floriculture.html.

Grameen Bank. 2007. *Grameen Bank at a glance.* Available online at http://www.grameeninfo.org/bank/GBGlance.htm.

Grosh, Barbara, and Gloria Somolekae. 1996. Mighty oaks from little acorns: Can micro-enterprise serve as the seedbed of industrialization? *World Development* 24 (12): 1879–1890.

Gugler, Josef. 1982. Overurbanization reconsidered. *Economic development and cultural change* 31: 173–189.

Gutch, Richard. 2005. *The third-sector way.* Available online at http://society.guardian.co.uk.futureforpublicservices/story/0,8150,1606216,00.html.

Hagedorn, Jessica. 2003. *Dream jungle.* New York: Viking.

Hale, Angela. 2000. *Phasing out of the multi-fibre arrangement: What does it mean for garment workers?* (Briefing Paper). Manchester, UK: Women Working Worldwide.

Hall, Stuart, and David Held. 1989. Citizens and citizenship. In *New times,* ed. S. Hall and M. Jacques. London: Lawrence and Wishart.

Handler, Joel F. 2004. *Social citizenship and workfare in the United States and Western Europe: The paradox of inclusion.* Cambridge, UK: Cambridge University Press.

Hardt, Michael, and Antonio Negri. 2000. *Empire.* Cambridge, UK: Cambridge University Press.

Harvey, David. 2003. *The new imperialism.* Oxford/New York: Oxford University Press.

Haute Culture. 2002. *Marie Claire,* November, 181.

Hayward, A. C. 1991. Biology and epidemiology of bacterial wilt caused by *pseudomonas solanacearum. Annual Review of Phytophatholology* 29: 65–87.

Hein, Jay. 2002. Ideas as exports. *American Outlook,* Summer, 36–38.

Heisler, Barbara Schmitter. 1985. Sending countries and the politics of emigration and destination. *International Migration Review* 19: 469–484.

Help victims of domestic violence. 2004. *Marie Claire,* November, 142.

Hess, Sabine. 2002. Au Pairs als informalisierte hausarbeiterinnen. In *Weltmarkt privathaushalt,* ed. Claudia Gather, Birgit Geissler, and Maria S. Rerrich. Münster: Westfälisches Dampfboot.

Heubach, Renate. 2002. Migrantinnen in der haushaltsarbeit: Ansaetze zur verbessering iher rechtlichen und sozialen situation. In Glaudia Gather, Birgit Geissler, Maria S. Rerrich, eds., *Weltmarkt privathaushalt.* Muenster: Westfaelisches Dampfboot, 167–182.

Heyzer, Noeleen, and Vivienne Wee. 1994. Domestic workers in transient overseas employment: Who benefits, who profits. In *The trade in domestic workers: Causes, mechanisms and consequences of international migration,* ed. Noeleen Heyzer, Gerrtje Lycklama a Nijeholt, and Nedra Weerakoon. London: Zed Books.

Hill Collins, Patricia. 1999. Producing mothers of the nation: Race, class, and contemporary U.S. population policies. In *Women, citizenship, and difference,* ed. N. Yuval-Davis and P. Werbner. London: Zed Books.

Hinojosa-Ojeda, Raul, and S. Robinson. 1992. Labor issues in a North American free trade area. In *North American free trade: Assessing the impact,* ed. Nora Lustig, Barry P. Bosworth, and Robert Z. Lawrence. Washington, DC: Brookings Institution.

Hochschild, Arlie R. 2001. Global care chains and emotional surplus value. In *On the edge: Living with global capitalism,* ed. W. Hutton and A. Giddens. London: Vintage.

————. 2004. Love and gold. In *Global woman: Nannies, maids, and sex workers in the new economy,* ed. Barbara Ehrenreich and Arlie Russel Hochschild. New York: Henry Holt.

Hondagneu-Sotelo, Pierette. 2001. *Doméstica: Immigrant workers cleaning and caring in the shadows of affluence.* Berkeley: University of California Press.

Hondagneu-Sotelo, Pierette, and Ernestine Avila. 1997. "I'm here but I'm there": The meaning of Latina transnational motherhood. *Gender & Society* 11 (5): 548–71.

hooks, bell. 1984. *Feminist theory: From margin to center.* Boston: South End Press.

HRW (Human Rights Watch). 1996. No guarantees: Sex discrimination in Mexico's maquiladora sector. *Human Rights Watch Report* 8 (6b). Available online at http://www.hrw.org/reports/1996/Mexi0896.htm.

————. 1998. A job or your rights: Continued sex discrimination in Mexico's maquiladora sector. *Human Rights Watch Report* 10 (1b). Available online at http://hrw.org/doc?t=americas&c=mexico& document_limit=40,20.

————. 2003a. *Deliberate indifference: El Salvador's failure to protect workers' rights.* Available online at http://www.hrw.org/reports/2003/elsalvador1203.

————. 2003b. *Climate of fear: Sexual violence and abduction of women and girls in Baghdad.* Available online at http://hrw.org/reports/2003/iraq0703/.

Huber, Evelyne, and John D. Stephens. 2001. *Development and crisis of the welfare state: Parties and policies in global markets.* Chicago: University of Chicago Press.

Hudson Institute. 2002. *Research and projects.* Washington, DC: Welfare Policy Center of the Hudson Institute. Available online at http://www.welfarereformer.org.

ICFTU (International Confederation of Free Trade Unions). 2002. *Annual survey of violations of trade union rights.* Available online at http://www.icftu.org.

ILO (International Labour Organization). 1991. *The Challenge of employment promotion: Trinidad and Tobago in the 1990's.* Port of Spain, Trinidad.

————. 1998a. *Report on the follow-up workshop on women entrepreneurs in micro and small businesses in Trinidad and Tobago.* St. Joseph, Trinidad: ILO publications.

————. 1998b. The world cut flower industry: Trends and prospects, Working Paper SAP 2.80/WP, 139.

————. 2000. Labour practices in the footwear, leather, textiles and clothing industries. Geneva: ILO.

ILRF (International Labour Rights Fund). 2005. *Dole fires 11 unionists at flower farm in Colombia!* Available online at http://www.laborrights.org/actions.

Immigration and Naturalization Service. 1998. Operation gatekeeper: New resources, enhanced results. *U.S. Department of Justice Fact Sheet.* Available online at http://uscis.gov/graphics/publicaffairs/factsheets/opgatefs.htm.

INEGI (Instituto Nacional de Estadística Geografía e Informática). 2003. Personal ocupado en la industria maquiladora de exportación según tipo de ocupación. *Estadística de la industria maquiladora de exportación.* Available online at http://www.inegi.gob.mx.

————. 2004. Principales características de la industria maquiladora de exportación. *Estadística de la industria maquiladora de exportación.* Available online at http://www.inegi.gob.mx.

Institute for Wisconsin's Future. 1998a. *Transitions to W-2: The first six months of welfare replacement.* Milwaukee: Institute for Wisconsin's Future.

————. 1998b. *The W-2 job path: An assessment of the employment trajectory of W-2 participants in Milwaukee.* Milwaukee: Institute for Wisconsin's Future.

Ismi, Asad. 2000. *Profiting from repression: Canadian investment in and trade with Colombia.* Toronto: Americas Update.

———. 2004. *Impoverishing a continent: The World Bank and the IMF in Africa.* Available online at http://www.policyalternatives.ca/documents/National_Office_Pubs/africa. pdf.

Isserles. 1999. Self-reliance and empowerment? Exploring the rhetoric of micro-credit. Paper presented at the American Sociological Association Annual Conference, August, Chicago, Illinois.

IUF (International Union of Food, Agricultural, Hotel, Restaurant, Catering, Tobacco, and Allied Workers Associations). 2005. *Colombian army murders rural trade unionists.* Available online at http://www.iuf.org/cgi-bin/dbman.

Jackson, Cecile. 1998. Rescuing gender from the poverty trap. In *Feminist visions of development: Gender analysis and policy,* ed. Cecile Jackson and Ruth Pearson. New York: Routledge.

Jacobs, Jane. 2000. *The nature of economics.* New York: Vintage Books.

Jain, Rajendra. 1997. Fortifying and "fortress": Immigration and the politics of the European Union. *International Studies* 34 (20): 163–192.

Janse, J. D., F. Araluppan, J. Schans, M. Wenneker, and W. Westerhuis. 1998. Experiences with bacterial brown rot caused by *ralstonia solanacearum* biovar 2, race 3 in the Netherlands. In *Bacterial wilt disease—Molecular and ecological aspects,* ed. P. Prior, C. Allen, and J. Elphinstone. Berlin: Spinger-Verlag.

Jenson, Jane, and Mariette Sineau, eds. 2001. *Who cares? Women's work, childcare, and welfare state redesign.* Toronto: University of Toronto Press.

Johnson, Susan, and Thalia Kidder. 1999. Globalization and gender—Dilemmas for microfinance organizations. *Small Enterprise Development* 10: 4–15.

Jordan, Joshua. 2004. Global glamour. *Marie Claire,* March, 164–173.

———. 2005. Wild at Heart. *Marie Claire,* March, 184–191.

Joseph, Suad. 1991. Elite strategies for state building: Women, family, religion and state in Iraq and Lebanon. In *Women, Islam and the state,* ed. Deniz Kandiyoti. London: MacMillan.

Kaplan, Caren. 1999. A world without boundaries: The body shop's trans/national geographies. In *With other eyes: Looking at race and gender in visual culture,* ed. Lisa Bloom. Minneapolis: University of Minnesota Press.

Kenworthy, Lane. 1995. *In search of national economic success: Balancing competition and cooperation.* Thousand Oaks, CA: Sage Publications.

Kernaghan, Charles. 1997. Paying to lose our jobs. In *No sweat: Fashion, free trade and the rights of garment workers,* ed. Andrew Ross. New York: Verso.

Kiely, Ray. 1998. The crisis of global development. In *Globalization and the Third World,* ed. R. Kiely and P. Marfleet. London: Routledge.

Kim, S. H., T. N. Olson, N. W. Schaad, and G. W. Moorman. 2003. "*Ralstonia solanacearum* Race 3, biovar 2, the causal agent of brown rot of potato, identified in geranium in Pennsylvania, Delaware, and Connecticut." *Plant Disease* 87:450.

Kirby, D. 2000. School-based interventions to prevent unprotected sex and HIV among adolescents. In *Handbook of HIV prevention,* ed. J. L. Peterson and R. J. DiClemente. New York: Kluwer Academic/Plenum Publishers.

Klak, Thomas. 1998. Thirteen theses on globalization and neoliberalism. In *Globalization and neoliberalism: The Caribbean context,* ed. Thomas Klak. Lanham, MD: Rowman and Littlefield.

Knijn, Trudie. 1998. Social care in the Netherlands. In *Gender, social care, and welfare state restructuring,* ed. Jane Lewis. Aldershot: Ashgate.

———. 2000. Marketization and the struggling logics of (home) care in the Netherlands. In *Care work: Gender, labor, and the welfare state,* ed. Madonna Harrington Meyer. New York: Routledge.

———. 2001. Care work: Innovations in the Netherlands. In *Care work: The quest for security,* ed. Mary Daly. Geneva: International Labour Office.

Koser, Khalid, and Helma Lutz. 1998. The new migration in Europe: Contexts, constructions and realities. In *The new migration in Europe: Social constructions and social realities,* ed. Khalid Koser and Helma Lutz. London: MacMillan.

Krieger N. 2001. Theories for social epidemiology in the 21st century: An ecosocial perspective. *International Journal of Epidemiology* 30 (4): 668–677.

———. 2003. Latin American social medicine: The quest for social justice and public health. *American Journal of Public Health* 93 (12): 1989–1991.

Kyriakou, Niko. 2005. *World's women stand together for equality.* Inter Press Service, March 12. Available online at http://ipsnews.net/interna.asp?idnews=27843.

Lambert, C. D. 2002. Agricultural bioterrorism protection act of 2002: Possession, use, and transfer of biological agents and toxins; interim and final rule (7 CFR Part 331). *Federal Register* 67 (240): 76908–76938.

Laurell, Asa Cristina. 2000. Structural adjustment and the globalization of policy in Latin America. *International Society* 15: 306–325.

Lee, Ching Kwan. 1998. *Gender and the South China miracle: Two worlds of factory women.* Berkeley: University of California Press.

Lemos, Gerard. 1999. *Forgotten no longer.* Available online at http://www.guardian.co.uk/Archive/Article/0,4273,3906750,00.html.

León, Nohra, and Jairo E. Luna. 1996. Incidencia ambiental de la floricultura. In Cactus, Defensoría del Pueblo and FESCOL. *Memorias del seminario taller "Sello de calidad para florese colombianas." Condiciones y Criterios* (agosto).

Lionnet, Francoise, Obioma Nnaemeka, Susan Perry, and Celeste Schenck. 2004. Development cultures: New environments, new realities, new strategies. *Signs: Journal of Women in Culture and Society* 29 (2): 291–298.

Lipton, Michael. 1977. *Why the poor stay poor: A study of urban bias in world development.* Cambridge, MA: Temple Smith/Harvard University Press.

Lister, Ruth. 1997a. *Citizenship: Feminist perspectives.* London: Macmillan.

———. 1997b. Citizenship: Towards a feminist synthesis. *Feminist Review* 57 (Autumn): 28–48.

Lowe, Lisa. 1996. Immigration, citizenship, racialization: Asian American critique. In *Immigrant acts: On Asian American cultural politics.* Durham: Duke.

Lurie, Peter, Percy Hintzen, and Robert A. Lowe. 1995. Socioeconomic obstacles to HIV prevention and treatment in developing countries: The roles of the International Monetary Fund and the World Bank. *AIDS* 9: 539–546.

Lutz, Helma. 2002. Transnationalität im haushalt. In *Weltmarkt privathaushalt,* ed. Claudia Gather, Birgit Geissler, and Maria S. Rerrich. Münster: Westfälisches Dampfboot.

———. 2004. Life in the twilight zone: Migration, transnationality and gender in the private household. *Journal of Contemporary European Studies* 12 (April): 47–55.

Maassarani, Tarek, and Jennifer C. Olmsted. 2004. Gendered occupation and resistance in Palestine. *Middle East Women's Studies (MEWS) Review* 19 (1/2), Spring/Summer.

Maharaj, Niala, and Donovan Hohn. 2001. Fleurs du mal. *Harper's,* February, 66–67.

Mahon, Rianne, and Susan Phillips. 2002. Dual-earner families caught in a liberal welfare regime? The politics of child care policy in Canada. In *Child care policy at the cross-*

roads: Gender and welfare state restructuring, ed. Sonya Michel and Rianne Mahon. New York: Routledge.

Mandal, Kohinoor. 2002. Tea majors sip profit despite auction fall. *Hindu business line.* Available online at http://www.blonnet.com/2002/03/19/stories/2002031902440400. html.

Manhattan Institute for Policy Research. 2002. *Manhattan institute center for civic innovation program areas.* New York: Manhattan Institute. Available online at http://www. manhattan-institute.org/html/cci.htm.

Marages, Kelly. 2005. Could you live off of free samples for a week? *Marie Claire,* March, 135–140.

Marie Claire. 2005. Hearst Magazines. Available online at http://www.marieclairemk. com /r4/home.cgi.

Marie Claire Online. 2005. http://www.magazines.ivillage.com/marieclaire.

Marshall, T. H. 1950. *Citizenship and social class.* Cambridge, UK: Cambridge University Press.

Massey, Douglas S. 1999. International migration at the dawn of the twenty-first century: The role of the state. *Population and Development Review* 25: 303–322.

Massey, Douglas S., Joaquin Arango, Graeme Hugo, Ali Kouaouci, Adela Pellgrino, and J. Edward Taylor. 1993. Theories of international migration: a review and appraisal. *Population and Development Review* 19 (3): 431–466.

Mattingly, Doreen. 1999. *Making maids: United States immigration policy and immigrant domestic workers.* New York: Routledge.

Mba, Nina Emma. 1997. *Nigerian women mobilized: Women's political activity in Southern Nigeria, 1900–1965.* International and Area Studies (Research Series No. 48), University of California at Berkeley (1982). Re-published in Nigeria. Crucible Publishers Ltd.

McAfee, Kathy. 1991. *Storm signals: Structural adjustment and development alternatives in the Caribbean.* London: Zed Books.

McClintock, Anne. 1995. *Imperial leather: Race, gender, and sexuality in the colonial contest.* New York: Routledge.

McKeown, T. 1979. *The role of medicine: Dream, mirage or nemesis?* 2nd edition. Princeton, N.J.: Princeton University Press.

McMichael, P. 1996. Globalization: Myths and realities. *Rural Sociology* 61: 1.

Mellon, Cynthia. 1995. Working women face abuses. *Alerta* 4 (Fall).

———. 1996. Women and flowers: A toxic combination. *Americas Update.* March/April: 4–5.

———. 2003. International codes of corporate conduct and the Colombian export flower industry: A look at the model from a labor rights perspective. M.A. thesis, International Institute for Sociology of Law, Oñati, Spain.

Mena, Norma. 2002. Desarrollo de la floricultura en Ecuador (Draft). Instituto de Ecología y Desarrollo de las Comunidades Andinas (IEDECA). Unpublished paper.

Mendes, Philip. 2003. Australian neoliberal think tanks and the backlash against the welfare state. *Journal of Australian Political Economy* 51: 29–56.

Mendoza, Carlota F. 1996. Objetivos, alcances, y problemática de instrumentación de la política de subsidio a la tortilla en México. In *La industria de la masa y la tortilla,* ed. Felipe Torres, Ernesto Moreno, Isabel Chong, and Juan Quintanilla. México: Universidad Autónoma de México.

Michel, Sonya, and Rianne Mahon, eds. 2002. *Child care policy at the crossroads: Gender and welfare state restructuring.* New York: Routledge.

Mies, Maria. 1998. *Patriarchy and accumulation on a world scale: Women in the international division of labor.* London: Zed Books, Ltd.

Milkman, Ruth, Ellen Reese, and Benita Roth. 1998. The macro-sociology of paid domestic service. *Work & Occupations* 25 (4): 483–510.

Millennium Campaign. 2005. *International women's groups mobilize to tackle poverty.* Available online at http://www.whiteband.org/News/gcapnews.2005-06-17.7909245833.

Milwaukee Women and Poverty Public Education Initiative. 1998. *W-2 community impact study.* Prepared for the Milwaukee County Board of Supervisors. Milwaukee, WI: Milwaukee Women and Poverty Public Education Initiative.

———. 1999. *Substance abuse: The silent barrier.* Prepared for the Milwaukee County Board of Supervisors. Milwaukee, WI: Milwaukee Women and Poverty Public Education Initiative.

———. 2000. *The status of employment opportunity for W-2 participants in Central City Milwaukee.* Milwaukee, WI: Milwaukee Women and Poverty Public Education Initiative.

———. 2001. *Voices from the community.* Milwaukee, WI: Milwaukee Women and Poverty Public Education Initiative.

Mink, Gwendolyn. 2001. Violating women: Rights and abuses in the welfare police state. *Annals of the American Academy of Political and Social Science* 577: 79–91.

Mitchell, Christopher. 1989. International migration, international relations, and foreign policy. *International Migration Review* 23 (30): 681–708.

Mitchell, Timothy. 2002. *Rule of experts: Egypt, techno-politics, modernity.* Berkeley: University of California Press.

Mitchell, William. 2003. *Me ++the cyborg self and the networked city.* Cambridge, MA: MIT Press.

Moghadam, Valentine. 2005. *Globalizing women: Transnational feminist networks.* Baltimore: Johns Hopkins University Press.

Mohanty, Chandra Talpade. 1991. Under western eyes: Feminist scholarship and colonial discourses. In *Third World women and the politics of feminism,* ed. Chandra Talpade Mohanty. Bloomington: Indiana University Press.

———. 1994. On race and voice: Challenges for liberal education in the 1990's. *Cultural critique* 14 (Winter 1989–90): 179–208.

———. 2003. *Feminism without borders: Decolonizing theory, practicing solidarity.* Durham: Duke University Press.

Molina, Norma, and Carolina Quinteros. 2000. El monitoreo independiente en El Salvador. In *Codigos de conducta y monitoreo en la industria de confeccion: Experiencias internacionales y regionales,* ed. Ronald Koepke, Norma Molina, and Carolina Quinteros. El Salvador: Heinrich Böll Foundation.

Momsen, Janet Henshall. 1999. Maids on the move: Victim or victor? In *Gender, migration, and domestic service,* ed. Janet Henshall Momsen. New York: Routledge.

Moore, Sally Falk. 2001. The international production of authoritative knowledge: The case of drought-stricken West Africa. *Ethnography* 2 (2): 161–189.

Moore, Thomas, and Vicky Selkowe. 1999. *The impact of welfare reform on Wisconsin's Hmong aid recipients.* Milwaukee: Institute for Wisconsin's Future.

Morgan, Kimberly. 2002. Does anyone have a "libre choix"? Subversive liberalism and the politics of French child care policy. In *Child care policy at the crossroads: Gender and welfare state restructuring,* ed. Sonya Michel and Rianne Mahon. New York: Routledge.

Morgan, Kimberly J., and Kathrin Zippel. 2003. Paid to care: The origins and effects of care leave policies in Western Europe. *Social Politics* 10 (1): 49–85.

Mosley, Paul, and David Hulme. 1998. Microenterprise finance: Is there a conflict between growth and poverty alleviation? *World Development* 26: 783–790.

Mullard, Maurice. 2000. *New labour, new thinking: The politics, economics, and social policy of the Blair government.* Huntington, NY: Nova Science.

Naiman, R., and N. Watkins. 1999. *A survey of the impacts of IFM structural adjustment in Africa: Growth, social spending, and debt relief.* Center for Economic and Policy Research. Washington, DC, April 19.

Nandy, Vaskar. 2005. The crisis in the tea industry. In *Alternative economic survey.* New Delhi: Rainbow Publishers.

Naples, Nancy A., and Manisha Desai. 2002. *Women's activism and globalization: Linking local struggles and transnational politics.* New York/London: Routledge.

Nearchou, Lina. 1999. Women entrepreneurs in Cyprus. *The Cyprus Review* 11: 49–64.

Niblock, Tim. 2001. *"Pariah states" and sanctions in the Middle East: Iraq, Libya, Sudan.* Boulder, CO: Lynne Rienner Publishers.

Nicolaou, Andreas. 2003. *Small and medium-sized enterprises in Cyprus.* Ministry of Industry, Commerce, Trade, and Tourism.

Obi, Cyril 2001. *The changing forms of identity politics in Nigeria under economic adjustment: The case of the oil minorities of the Niger Delta.* Nordiska Afrikainstitutet, Research Report No. 119.

Ochoa, Enrique C. 2000. *Feeding Mexico: The political uses of food since 1910.* Wilmington, DE: Scholarly Resources.

Ogoba, Mrs. Josephine. 2002. *Action Woman: A Quarterly Publication of the Women's Aid Collective* (WACOL) 1(3).

Olmsted, Jennifer. 2001. Men's work/women's work: Employment, wages and occupational segregation in Bethlehem. In *The economics of women and work in the Middle East and North Africa,* ed. E. Mine Cinar. Vol. 4 of *Research in Middle East Economics.* Amsterdam: JAI/Elsevier.

———. 2005. How helpful is a sanctions model for understanding the Palestinian economy? Paper presented at the Allied Social Science Association (ASSA) Meetings, January, Philadelphia, PA, and at the Second Annual Workshop on Devastated Economies, February, UCLA.

Ong, Aihwa. 1999. *Flexible citizenship: The cultural logics of transnationality.* Durham, NC: Duke University Press.

Organization for Economic Co-operation and Development (OECD). 2001. *Employment outlook.* Paris: OECD.

Ortiz Solano, Olga. 2000. *Detrás de cada miedo hay violencia: Vida y trabajo de mujeres en la industria de flores colombianas.* Bonn: Campaña de Flores.

Ovalle, Priscilla Peña. 2005. Cosmetic borders: Collapsing oppression/opportunity into Jennifer Lopez's Hollywood. Unpublished manuscript.

Parenti, Christian. 1999. *Lockdown America: Police and prisons in the age of crisis.* New York: Verso.

Parreñas, Rhacel 2001a. *Servants of globalization: Women, migration, and domestic work.* Stanford: Stanford University Press.

———. 2001b. Between workers: Migrant domestic work and gender inequalities in the new global economy. *Concilium: Revue internationale de théologie* 5: 28–39.

Passage to India. 2003. *Marie Claire,* March.

Pastor, Manuel, and Carol Wise. 2003. *Picking up the pieces: Comparing the social impacts of financial crisis in Mexico and Argentina.* Department of Latin American and Latino Studies, University of California Santa Cruz. Unpublished manuscript.

Patomaki, Heikki, and Teivo Teivainen. 2004. The world social forum: An open space or a movement of movements? *Theory, Culture, & Society* 21 (6): 145–154.

Patriquin, Larry. 2001. The historical uniqueness of the Clinton welfare reforms: A new level of social misery? *Journal of Sociology and Social Welfare* 28 (3): 71–94.

Paul, Kathleen. 1997. *Whitewashing Britain: Race and citizenship in the postwar era.* Ithaca, NY: Cornell University Press.

PCBS (Palestinian Central Bureau of Statistics). 1998. *Women and men in Palestine: Trends and statistics.* Ramallah, Palestine.

Pearson, Ruth, and Gill Seyfang. 2002. "I'll tell you what I want … ": Women workers and codes of conduct. In *Corporate responsibility and labor rights: Codes of conduct in the global economy,* ed. Rhys Jenkins, Ruth Pearson, and Gill Seyfang. London: Earthscan.

Peck, Jamie. 2001. *Workfare states.* New York/London: Guilford Press.

Peck, Jamie, and Adam Tickell. 2002. Neoliberalizing space. In *Spaces of neoliberalism: Urban restructuring in North America and Western Europe,* ed. Neil Brenner and Nik Theodore. Malden, MA: Oxford's Blackwell Press.

Perkins, John. 2004. *Confessions of an economic hit man.* San Francisco: Berrett-Koehler Publishers.

Pessar, Patricia. 2003. Engendering migration studies. In *Gender and immigration: Contemporary trends,* ed. Pierette Hondagneu-Sotelo. Berkeley: University of California Press.

PANUPS (Pesticide Action Network Updates Service). 2002. *Floriculture: pesticides, worker health and codes of conduct.* Available online at http://panups@topica.email-publisher. com.

Pfeifer, Karen. 2004. Opportunity cost and opportunity lost: Is there hope for rebuilding the Palestinian economy? Paper presented at the First Workshop on Rebuilding Devastated Economies in the Middle East, May 2004.

Piore, Michael. 1979. *Birds of passage: Migrant labour and industrial societies.* Cambridge, UK: Cambridge University Press.

PNA (Palestinian National Authority). 1998. *Palestine poverty report* (Alternative title: *Poverty in Palestine*). National Commission on Poverty Alleviation.

Pollitt, Katha. 2005. The cheese stands alone. *The Nation,* March 21.

Portes, Alejandro. 1997. Immigration theory for a new century. *International Migration Review* 31 (4): 799–825.

Portes, Alejandro, and Lauren Benton. 1984. Industrial development and labor absorption: A reinterpretation. *Population and Development Review* 10: 586–611.

Prior, Philippe, Caitilyn Allen, and John Elphinstone, eds. 1998. *Bacterial wilt disease: Molecular and ecological aspects.* Berlin: Springer-Verlag.

Pujol, José F. 1996. Racionalización de subsidios y liberalización de precios del sector. In *La industria de la masa y la tortilla,* ed. Felipe Torres, Ernesto Moreno, Isabel Chong, and Juan Quintanilla. México: Universidad Autónoma de México.

Pyle, Jean, and Kathryn Ward. 2003. Recasting our understanding of gender and work during global restructuring. *International Sociology* 18 (3): 461–489.

Quinteros, Carolina, Gilberto García, Roberto Góchez, and Norma Molina. 1998. *Din-*

amica de la actividad maquiladora y derechos laborales en el Salvador. San Salvador: Centro de Estudios del Trabajo.

Rahman, Aminur. 1999. Micro-credit initiatives for equitable and sustainable development: Who pays? *World Development* 27 (1): 67–82.

Rai, Saritha. 2002. India's tea industry battles the blues. *Business World,* January 20.

Rakowski, Cathy. 1994. *Contrapunto: The informal-sector debate Latin American perspectives.* New York: State University of New York Press.

Rangel, Cruz Emilia, Bettina Reis, and Patricia Sierra. 1996. Forms of labor contracting in the Colombian export flower industry: The rise of "Temporary Services" companies. *Beyond Law/Más alla del derecho* 5 (14): 55–67.

Rankin, Katharine. 2001. Governing development: Neoliberalism, microcredit, and rational economic woman. *Economy and Society* 30 (1): 18–37.

Rapley, John. 2002. *Understanding development: Theory and practice in the Third World.* Boulder, CO: Lynne Rienner Publishers.

Reagon, Bernice Johnson. 1983. Coalition politics: Turning the century. In *Home girls: A black feminist anthology.* New York: Kitchen Table/Women of Color Press.

Recinos, Adrian (trans). 1960. *Popol Vuh: The sacred book of the ancient Quiche Maya.* El Fondo de la Cultura Economica.

Rector, Robert. 1997. Wisconsin's welfare miracle. *The Heartland Institute.* LEXIS-NEXIS Academic Universe, April/May.

Reddock, Rhoda E. 1993. The labour movement and the rights of the woman worker. Paper presented at the First National Women's Economic Conference, Tunapuna, Trinidad.

Reese, Ellen. 2005. *Backlash against welfare mothers: Past and present.* Berkeley: University of California Press.

Republic of Trinidad and Tobago. 1996. *Development co-operation report.*

Rerrich, Maria S. 2002. Von der Utopie der partnerschaftlichen gleichverteilung. In *Weltmarkt privathaushal,* ed. Claudia Gather, Birgit Geissler, and Maria S. Rerrich. Münster: Westfälisches Dampfboot.

RESPECT. 2000. *Migrant domestic workers in Europe: A case for action.* Available online at http://www.solidar.org/Document.asp?DocID=1994&tod=141847.

Rhyne, Elisabeth. 2001. *Mainstreaming microfinance: How lending to the poor began, grew, and came of age in Bolivia.* Bloomfied: Kumarian Press.

Ridgeway, James. 2004. *It's all for sale: The control of global resources.* Durham, N.C./London: Duke University Press.

Rodriguez, Cheryle Rene. 1995. *Women, microenterprise, and the politics of self-help.* New York: Garland Publishers.

Rollins, Judith. 1985. *Between women: Domestics and their employers.* Philadelphia: Temple University Press.

Romero, Mary. 1992. *Maid in the U.S.A.* New York: Routledge.

Ross, Andrew. 2002. China after Seattle. *Review of Education, Pedagogy and Cultural Studies* 24: 143–146.

———. 2004. Low pay, high profile: The global push for fair labor. New York: The New Press.

Rothstein, Richard. 1989. *Keeping jobs in fashion: Alternatives to the euthanasia of the U.S. apparel industry.* Washington, DC: Economic Policy Institute.

Rotimi, Suberu. 1996. *Ethnic minority conflicts and governance in Nigeria.* Ibadan, Nigeria: Spectrum.

Rowbotham, Sheila, and Stephanie Linkogle, eds. 2001. *Women resist globalization: Mobilizing for livelihood and rights.* London/New York: Zed Books.

Rowbotham, Sheila, and Swasti Mitter. 1994. *Dignity and daily bread.* London/New York: Routledge.

Roy, Ananya. 2002. Against the feminization of policy. *Wilson Center series on urban livelihoods.* Washington, DC: Woodrow Wilson Center.

———. 2003. *City requiem, Calcutta: Gender and the politics of poverty.* Minneapolis: University of Minnesota Press.

Roy, Arundhati. 2004. *An Ordinary Person's Guide to Empire.* Cambridge, MA: South End Press.

Roy, Sara. 1995. *The Gaza Strip: The political economy of de-development.* Washington, DC: Institute for Palestine Studies.

Rystad, Göran. 1992. Immigration history and the future of international migration. *International Migration Review* 26 (4): 1168–1199.

Sachs, Jeffery. 2005. *The end of poverty: Economic possibilities for our time.* New York: Penguin Press.

Safa, Helen. 1994. Export manufacturing, state policy and women workers in the Dominican Republic. In *Global production: The apparel industry in the Pacific Rim,* ed. Edna Bonacich et al. Philadelphia: Temple University.

Salzinger, Leslie. 2003. *Genders in production: Making workers in Mexico's global factories.* Berkeley: University of California Press.

Sassen, Saskia. 1984. Notes on the incorporation of Third World women into wage-labor through immigration and off-shore production. *International Migration Review* 18 (4): 1144–1167.

———. 1988. *The mobility of labor and capital: A study in international investment and labor flow.* Cambridge, UK/New York: Cambridge University Press.

———. 1998a. *Globalization and its discontents: Essays on the new mobility of people and money.* New York: The New Press.

———. 1998b. The *de facto* transnationalizing of immigration policy. In *Challenge to the nation-state,* ed. Christian Joppke. Oxford: Oxford University Press.

———. 2003. Strategic instantiations of gendering in the global economy. In *Gender and immigration: Contemporary trends,* ed. Pierette Hondagneu-Sotelo. Berkeley: University of California Press.

Scully, Nan Dawkins. 1988. Overurbanization reconceptualized: A political economy of the world-system approach. *Urban Affairs Quarterly* 23: 270–294.

———. 1997. *Microcredit no panacea for poor women.* Available online at http: www/igc.org.dgap.

Sevcik, Kimberly. 2004. Why did this woman set herself on fire? *Marie Claire,* February, 60.

Shaiken, Harley. 2001. The new global economy: Trade and production under NAFTA. *Journal für entwicklungspolitik* XVII/3 (4): 241–254.

Shiva, Vandana. 1988. *Staying alive: Women, ecology, and development.* London: Zed Books.

———. 2002. *Water Wars: Privatization, Pollution, and Profit.* Cambridge, MA: South End Press.

Siapno, Jacqueline. 2006. Bitter lessons: Aceh may have a lot to learn from East Timor. Unpublished manuscript.

Smet, Miet. 2002. Die normalisierung der haushaltsarbeit im informellen sektor. In

Weltmarkt privathaushalt, ed. Claudia Gather, Birgit Geissler, and Maria S. Rerrich. Münster: Westfälisches Dampfboot.

Smith, David A. 1996. *Third World cities in global perspective: The political economy of uneven urbanization.* Boulder, CO: Westview Press.

Smith, Jackie. 2004a. Exploring the connections between global integration and political mobilization. *Journal of World Systems Research* 10 (1): 255–85.

———. 2004b. The world social forum and the challenges of global democracy. *Global Networks* 4: 413–421.

———. Forthcoming "Social Movements and Multilateralism: Moving from the 20th to 21st Century," in *Challenges of Multilateralism,* edited by T. Newman, S. Tharoor, and J. Tirman. New York and Tokyo: United Nations University Press.

Smith, Rogers M. 1997. Fierce new world: The colonial sources of American citizenship and the America that never was: The radical hour 1866–1876. In *Civic ideals: Conflicting visions of citizenship in U.S. history.* New Haven, CT: Yale.

Smith-Nightengale, Demetra, and Kelly S. Mikelson. 2000. *An overview of research related to Wisconsin Work (W-2).* Washington, DC: The Urban Institute.

Snow, Don. 2004. Production Manager, Goldsmith Seeds, Inc. Gilroy, CA. Personal communication.

Solomos, John, and Les Back. 1995. *Race, politics, and social change.* London: Routledge.

Sparr, Pamela, ed. 1994. *Mortgaging women's lives: Feminist critiques of structural adjustment.* London: Zed Press.

Spivak, Gayatri Chakravorty. 1994. Responsibility. *Boundary 2* 21 (3): 19–64.

———. 1999. *A critique of postcolonial reason: Toward a history of the vanishing present.* Cambridge, MA: Harvard University Press.

Standing, Guy. 1999. Global feminization through flexible labor: A theme revisited. *World Development* 27 (3): 583–602.

Stefancic, Jean, and Richard Delgado. 1996. The attack on welfare. In *No mercy: How conservative think tanks and foundations changed America's social agenda.* Philadelphia: Temple University Press.

Stiglitz, Joseph. 2002. *Globalization and its discontents.* New York: Norton.

Stone, Allison. 1991. Will the real body please stand up? Boundary stories about virtual cultures. In *Cyberspace,* ed. Michael Benedikt. Cambridge, MA: MIT Press.

Stop violence against women around the world. 2004. *Marie Claire,* April, 26.

STPS (Secretaría del Trabajo y Previsión Social). 2003. Salarios medios pagados a los obreros en la industria de la maquiladora de exportación por entidad federativa. *Estadística de la maquiladora de exportación, INEGI.* Available online at http://www.stps.gob.mx.

Strider, D. L., R. K. Jones, and R. A. Haygood. 1981. Southern wilt of geranium caused by *pseudomonas solanacearum. Plant Disease* 65: 52–53.

Su, Julie. 1997. El Monte Thai garment workers: Slave sweatshops. In *No sweat: Fashion, free trade and the rights of garment workers,* ed. Andrew Ross. New York: Verso.

Sudbury, Julia. 1998. *'Other kinds of dreams': Black women's organisations and the politics of transformation.* London: Routledge.

Swank, Duane. 2001. Political institutions and welfare state restructuring: The impact of institutions and social policy change in developed democracies. In *The new politics of the welfare state,* ed. Paul Pierson. New York: Oxford University Press.

Swanson, J. K., J. Yao, J. K. Tans-Kersten, and C. Allen. 2005. Behavior of *ralstonia solanacearum* race 3 biovar 2 during latent and active infection of geranium. *Phytopathology* 95: 136–143.

Taussig, Michael T. 1980. *The devil and commodity fetishism in South America.* Chapel Hill: University of North Carolina Press.

Theodore, Karl. 1993. *An overview of social sector conditions in Trinidad and Tobago.* Republic of Trinidad and Tobago: University of West Indies Press.

Thomas, Darryl. 2004. Senior Plant Pathologist, Goldsmith Plants, Inc. Personal communication.

Tickner, Ann. 2005. Presidential Address at the Annual meeting of the International Studies Association in San Diego.

Torres, Felipe T. 1996. Antecedentes del debate actual sobre el maíz en Mexico. In *La industria de la masa y la tortilla,* ed. Felipe Torres, Ernesto Moreno, Isabel Chong, and Juan Quintanilla. México: Universidad Autónoma de México.

Trouiller, P., et al. 2001. Drugs for neglected diseases: A failure of the market and a public health failure? *Tropical Medicine and International Health* 6 (11): 945–951.

Ugur, Mehmet. 1995. Freedom of movement vs. exclusion: A re-interpretation of the "Insider"-"Outsider" divide in the European Union. *International Migration Review* 29 (4): 964–999.

UNDP (United Nations Development Programme), in conjunction with the Iraqi Ministry of Planning and Development Cooperation. 2005. *Iraq living conditions survey 2004.* Available online at http://www.iq.undp.org/ILCS/overview.htm.

UNIFEM (United Nations Development Fund for Women). 2005. *Gender profile of the conflict in the occupied Palestinian territory.* Available online at http://www.womenwarpeace.org/opt/opt.htm.

Unilever. 1999. *Unilever to acquire Indian tea gardens.* Available online at http://www.unilever.com/mediacenter/pressrelease1999/English News_874.asp.

———. 2003. *Unilver and Pepsico create "Pepsi Lipton International" RTD tea joint venture in selected international markets.* Available online at http://www.unilever.com/mediacentre/pressreleases/2003/EnglishNews_10460.asp

———. 2004a. *Unilever at a glance.* Available online at http://www.unilever.com/mediacentre/corporateinformation/factsheet/default.asp.

———.2004b. *Lipton.* Available online at http://www.unilever.com/brands/food/lipton.asp.

Unión Nacional de Trabajadores de las Flores (Untrafiores). 2003. *Demand and investigation of the poisoning of hundreds of flower workers in Colombia.* Available online at http://www.laborrights.org/urgent/intoxication.

———. 2004. *Dole subsidiary retaliates against workers at new flower union in Colombia.* Available online at http://www.laborrights.org/urgent/Flowers_Splendor_1204.htm.

United Nations. 2003. *International migration report 2002.* New York: UN Publications.

UNSCO (United Nations Special Co-ordinator). 2002. *The impact of closure and other mobility restrictions on Palestinian productive activities.* Available online at http://www.un.org/News/dh/mideast/econ-report-final.pdf.

USITC (U.S. International Trade Commission). 2004. *Textiles and apparel: Assessment of the competitiveness of certain foreign suppliers to the U.S. market.* Washington, DC: USITC.

U.S. LEAP (U.S. Labor Education in the Americas Project). 2005. *Violence against Colombian trade unionists.* Available online at http://www.usleap.org/Colombia.

U.S. State Department. 2001. *El Salvador: country reports on human rights practices—2000.*

Washington, DC: Bureau of Democracy, Human Rights and Labor, U.S. State Department.

———. 2002. *El Salvador: country reports on human rights practices—2001.* Washington, DC: Bureau of Democracy, Human Rights and Labor, U.S. State Department.

———. 2003. *El Salvador: Country reports on human rights practices—2002.* Washington, DC: Bureau of Democracy, Human Rights and Labor, U.S. State Department.

———. 2004. *El Salvador: Country reports on human rights practices—2003.* Washington, DC: Bureau of Democracy, Human Rights and Labor, U.S. State Department.

———. 2005. *El Salvador: Country reports on human rights practices—2004.* Washington, DC: Bureau of Democracy, Human Rights and Labor, U.S. State Department.

Useche, Bernardo, and Amalia Cabezas. 2004. Desigualdad social y SIDA: El contexto neoliberal de la epidemia. *Deslinde* 35: 98–112. Available online at http://www. deslinde.org.co/Dsl35/dls35_desigualdad_social_sida.htm.

Utría, Rubén D. 2002. *Hacia un desarrollo regional metropolitano concertado y democrático de la Sabana de Bogotá.* Bogotá: Friedrich Ebert Stiftung de Colombia (FESCOL).

van Elsas, J. D., P. Kastelein, P. Van Bekkum, J. M. van der Wolf, P. de Vries, and L. van Overbeek. 2000. Survival of r*alstonia solanacearum* biovar 2, the causative agent of potato brown rot, in field and microcosm soils in temperate climates. *Phytopathology* 90: 1358–1366.

Varley, Pamela. 1998. *Corporate responsibility on the global frontier.* Washington, DC: Investor Responsibility Research Center.

WACOL (Women's Aid Collective). 2002a. Environment and Niger Delta women. *Action Woman* 1 (2).

———. 2002b. Turbulence in the Niger Delta: Amazons declare war. *Action Woman* 1 (3).

Waerness, Kari. 1998. The changing "Welfare Mix" in childcare and care of the frail elderly in Norway. In *Gender, social care, and welfare state restructuring,* ed. Jane Lewis. Aldershot: Ashgate.

Walby, Sylvia. 1994. Is citizenship gendered? *Sociology* 28 (2): 379–395.

Waller, Marguerite. 2006. Addicted to virtue: The globalization policy-maker. *Social Identities* 2 (5): 575–594.

Waller, Marguerite, and Sylvia Marcos, eds. 2005. *Dialogue and difference: Feminisms challenge globalization.* New York/London: Palgrave.

Waller, Marguerite, and Jennifer Rycenga, eds. 2001. *Frontline feminisms: Women, war, and resistance.* New York/London: Routledge.

Walsh, Jess. 2001. Creating unions, creating employers: A Los Angeles home care campaign. In *Carework: The quest for security,* ed. Mary Daly. Geneva: ILO.

Walt, Vivienne. 2001. Flower trade. *National Geographic,* April, 104–119.

Wariyai, Fanti Goodness. 2002. Interview with Fanti Goodness Wariyai. *Guardian.* August 25.

Watts, Michael. 2003. Development and governmentality. *Singapore journal of tropical geography* 24 (1): 6–34.

Weber, Heloise. 2002. The imposition of a global development architecture: The example of microcredit. *Review of International Studies* 28: 537–555.

Weiss, Linda. 1987. Explaining the underground economy: State and social structure. *British Journal of Sociology* 33: 216–234.

Werbner, Pnina, and Nira Yuval-Davis. 1999. Introduction: Women and the new discourse of citizenship. In *Women citizenship and difference,* ed. N. Yuval-Davis and P. Werbner. London: Zed Books.

West Bengal Advisor to the Commissioners of the Supreme Court. 2004. *Report on hunger in tea plantations in North Bengal.* In the case of *PUCL v. UOI & Ors. Under Writ Petition* (Civil) No. 196 of 2001. India: Kolkata.

Wichterich, Christa. 2000. *The globalized woman.* New York: Zed Books.

Wilayto, Phil. 1997. *The feeding trough: The Bradley Foundation, "The Bell Curve" and the real story behind Wisconsin's national model for welfare reform.* Milwaukee: A Job Is a Right Campaign.

Williamson, L., B. D. Hudelson, and C. Allen. 2002. *Ralstonia solanacearum* strains isolated from geranium belong to race 3 and are pathogenic on potato. *Plant Disease* 86: 987–991.

Wisconsin Department of Workforce Development. 1999. *Milwaukee County: Regional workforce profile.* Division of Workforce Excellence, Bureau of Workforce Information. Available online at http://www.dwd.state.wi.us/dwelmi/.

———. 2005. *Wisconsin Works (W-2) Program: An evaluation. Report 05-6. April.* Wisconsin Department of Workforce Development, Madison, WI.

Wiseman, Michael. 1999. In the midst of reform: Wisconsin in 1997. *Assessing the new federalism, ANF Discussion Paper 99-03,* The Urban Institute. Available online at http://www.urban.org.

Women's Affairs Division. 1995. *National report on the status of women in Trinidad and Tobago.* Prepared for the Fourth World Conference on Women, Beijing, China.

Women's Co-op Bank Cyprus. 2003. *Report on female entrepreneurial activity in Cyprus.*

WorkingWomen. 1993. *Women in the search for alternative economic strategies: Conference report.* Republic of Trinidad and Tobago: Working Women. Available online at http://www.cia.gov/cia/publications/factbook/geos/cy.html.

World Bank n.d. *Iraq, data and statistics: Iraq data sheet.* Available online at http://web.worldbank.org/wbsite/external/countries/menaext/raqextn/0,,menuPK:313131~pagePK:141132~piPK:141109~theSitePK:313105,00.html.

———. 1995. Trinidad and Tobago: Poverty and unemployment in an oil based economy. Report Number 14382-TR.

———. 2003. World Bank report on impact of Intifada. *West Bank and Gaza update.* The World Bank Group, April-June. Available online at http://lnweb18.worldbank.org/mna/mena.nsf/Attachments/Update+May+2003+English/$File/may+lay-en-Blue03.pdf.

———. 2004a. *Disengagement, the Palestinian economy and the settlements.* Available online at http://lnweb18.worldbank.org/mna/mena.nsf/Attachments/Disengagement+Paper/$File/Disengagement+Paper.pdf.

———. 2004b. *Four years—Intifada, closures and Palestinian economic crisis.* World Bank, October. Available online at http://siteresources.worldbank.org/INTWESTBANKGAZA/esources/wbgaza-4yrassessment.pdf.

World March of Women. 2005. Newsletter 8 (6). Available online at http://www.marchemondiale.org/en/bulletin/06_2005.html.

WRC (Workers Rights Consortium). 2003. *Workers rights consortium assessment re primo SA de CV (El Salvador).* Washington, DC: WRC.

Wrigley, Julia. 1995. *Other people's children.* New York: Basic Books.

Yelvington, Kevin A. 1993. Introduction. In *Trinidad ethnicity,* ed. K. A. Yelvington. Memphis: University of Tennessee Press.

Yimprasert, Junya, and Christopher Candland. 2000. *Can corporate codes of conduct promote labor standards? Evidence from the Thai footwear and apparel industries.* Thailand: Thai Labor Campaign.

Young, Iris Marion. 1989. Polity and group difference: A critique of the ideal of universal citizenship. *Ethics* 99 (2): 250–274.

Yousif, Bassam. 2006. Coalition economic policies in Iraq: Motivations and outcomes. *Third World Quarterly* 27 (3): 491–505.

Yunus, Muhammad. 1999. *Banker to the poor: Micro-lending and the battle against world poverty.* New York: Public Affairs (2003 edition).

Yuval-Davis, Nira. 1997. *Gender and nation.* London: Sage.

Zarembka, Joy M. 2004. America's dirty work: Migrant maids and modern-day slaves. In *Global woman,* ed. A. R. Hochschild and B. Ehrenreich. New York: Henry Holt.

Index

Venezuela, 10
Vietnam, 6, 163, 165, 205
Vietnam War, 205
Violence, 3, 14, 17, 19, 44, 46, 48, 51, 57,
    64, 67, 70, 75, 95, 102–3, 105, 110, 181,
    185, 188–9, 191, 200, 202
VISA, 35
Visual culture, 41

Wages, 4, 9, 13, 63–5, 71, 79, 90, 92, 114–
    5, 117, 119–20, 123–4, 130–2, 135, 137,
    141, 143, 151, 157, 160, 162–5, 185
War, 3–6, 9–10, 12–14, 28, 38, 46–7, 51–2,
    64, 75, 150, 154, 179, 181, 184, 189,
    190–4, 198–201, 203, 205–6, 209; in
    Afghanistan, 7, 46, 210; in Iraq, 7, 10,
    46, 209; World War II, 3–5, 75
Wariyai, Fanti Goodness, 196–7, 203
Warri North, 193
Warri Southwest, 193
Washington, D.C., 33–4, 37–8, 164
Washington Consensus, 4, 29, 36–8
Welfare: contractors in Wisconsin, 90–1;
    and job training in Wisconsin, 91–2;
    policies in Western Europe, 88–9, 97;
    problems with access, 8, 19, 80, 83–4, 87,
    94, 101–2, 107, 122; reform in United
    States, 89–96; state and citizenship, 12,
    99–100, 104, 109; state in Great Britain,
    12, 98–100, 106; state, restructuring of
    or rollbacks in, 11, 93, 119; Wisconsin
    model of reform, 12, 86–97; Wisconsin
    Works (W-2), 86–97
Welfare-to-work policies, 87, 91–2, 94, 97.
    See also job training
West Bank, 181, 186, 189
Western Europe, 5, 8, 114, 125, 173
White space, 62, 71
Women: Afghan, 14, 44, 46, 205–11, 236;
    of color, 3, 72, 97, 102; First World, 41–
    3, 45, 50; low-income, 3, 9, 11, 13, 74–6,

84; Maya, 170, 176; microentrepreneurs,
    83–5; middle-class, 45, 114, 119–20;
    Palestinian, 181, 186, 188; superexploita-
    tion of, 3, 134; Third World, 41, 44–8,
    51, 53; unemployment of, 4, 7, 19, 25,
    74–5, 77, 79–80, 82, 84–5, 89, 103, 120,
    124, 130, 143, 155, 182, 185–6, 189,
    196; workers, 11–3, 57, 65, 80, 115, 119,
    121–3, 128, 130–1, 137, 140, 143, 159.
    See also Unemployment; Women's labor
Women in Black, 10, 14
Women in Development initiatives, 30
Women's Aid Collective (WACOL), 197,
    203, 236
Women's Cooperative Bank, 83
Women's Environment and Development
    Organization (WEDO), 11
Women's labor, 9, 71, 79, 82, 84, 114,
    116–9
Workers, migrant or immigrant, 12, 18, 88,
    97, 104–7, 112–26, 133, 139, 159–60,
    164. *See also* immigrant workers, immi-
    grants, and migrant workers
World Bank (a.k.a. International Bank for
    Reconstruction and Development), 3–6,
    10, 13, 16–7, 19–22, 24–5, 28–30, 33,
    35, 37, 45–6, 73, 76, 79–80, 115, 135,
    142, 153, 180–3, 185, 187
World Health Organization (WHO), 16–7,
    20–2, 25, 146
World March of Women, 10–11
World Social Forum (WSF), 10, 15, 29
World Trade Organization (WTO), 3, 6, 10,
    22–3, 26, 29, 36, 82, 161

Yoruba, 192
Yorubaland, 192

Zambia, 20, 141
Zapatista Movement, 14
Zimbabwe, 19, 21, 141

About the Editors
and Contributors

❊

Caitilyn Allen earned her Ph.D. in Plant Pathology at Virginia Polytechnic Institute and State University before spending two years as a research postdoctoral
fellow in Lyon, France. She is currently a professor of Plant Pathology and Women's
Studies at the University of Wisconsin–Madison, where she teaches courses in
Biology and Gender and Molecular Plant-Microbe Interactions. Her research
interests include developing sustainable strategies to control diseases caused by
the plant pathogenic bacterium *Ralstonia solanacearum* as well as understanding
the molecular basis of its virulence.

Amalia L. Cabezas is an assistant professor in Women's Studies at the University
of California–Riverside. Her research interests include sex tourism, women's human rights, and the politics of gender and sexuality in Cuba and the Dominican
Republic.

Piya Chatterjee is on the Women's Studies faculty at the University of California–Riverside. She is an activist/scholar who is committed to grassroots women's
organizing in the global South, a founding member of the Dooars Jagron collective,
and the author of *A Time for Tea: Women, Labor and Post/Colonial Politics*.

Jill Esbenshade is an associate professor at San Diego State University. She is
the author of *Monitoring Sweatshops: Workers, Consumers and the Global Apparel*

Industry. She is also on the Governing Board of the Workers' Rights Consortium, a nonprofit that monitors sweatshops around the world.

Joy Ngozi Ezeilo is an activist/feminist lawyer and scholar with a graduate degree in Law from Queen Mary and Westfield College (University of London), a B.L. from Nigerian Law School, and a diploma in Peace Studies and Conflict Resolution from Uppsala University, Sweden. She is the founder and former executive director of the Women's Aid Collective (WACOL), a nongovernmental organization that promotes the human rights of women and young people. She also has published in the areas of women's and children's rights in Nigeria.

Tracy Fisher is an assistant professor of Women's Studies at the University of California–Riverside. Her research focuses on race and gender, community activism, and citizenship. She is currently writing a book that examines the transformation of the Left in Britain from an historical as well as ethnographic perspective.

Marina Karides, an assistant professor in the Department of Sociology at Florida Atlantic University, is committed to bridging her scholarship and teaching with activist participation in the global justice movement. She is currently working on a book on race, gender, and Trinidadian street vendors' claims to city space and resistance to global capital.

Sonali Kolhatkar is host and co-producer of KPFK's *Uprising.* She has spoken widely about media democracy, women in media, U.S. foreign policy, activism, and women's rights. In addition, she is the co-founder of the Afghan Women's Mission, a U.S.-based nonprofit organization that works in solidarity with the Revolutionary Association of the Women of Afghanistan (RAWA).

Cynthia Mellon is a researcher, writer, and translator with a special interest in economic justice and women's human rights. She has studied and documented the Colombian export flower industry for more than ten years. Her publications include *Holding On to the Promise: Women's Human Rights and the Beijing + 5 Review, Deceptive Beauty: A Look at the Global Flower Industry,* and numerous articles in English and Spanish for both academic and popular readerships.

Sabine N. Merz is a Ph.D. candidate in the Sociology Department at the University of Massachusetts–Amherst. Her dissertation analyzes the gender-based division of unpaid housework in Germany. With Joya Misra, she is currently investigating the implications of the globalization of carework with a focus on OECD countries.

Joya Misra is an associate professor of Sociology and Public Policy at the University of Massachusetts–Amherst. Her research explores how various policies both mediate and reinforce inequalities by class, gender, and race/ethnicity. She has published articles in a wide range of edited volumes and journals, including *Gender*

& Society, Feminist Studies, Social Problems, Annual Review of Sociology, American Sociological Review, and *American Journal of Sociology.*

Carolina Bank Muñoz is an assistant professor at Brooklyn College of the City University of New York. A specialist in labor and work, immigration, globalization, and race, class, and gender, she was formerly a project director at UCLA's Center for Labor Research and Education. She has published articles in *Social Justice* and the *New Labor Forum,* and she is currently working on her book, *Transnational Capital, Transnational Labor: The Politics of Shop Floor Control in the Tortilla Industry.*

Jennifer C. Olmsted, having grown up in Lebanon, has long been interested in Middle East economies and, more broadly, in feminist concerns related to globalization. Her publications have appeared in various journals, including *Feminist Economics* and *World Development.* She is currently an associate professor of Economics at Drew University in Madison, New Jersey.

Ellen Reese is an associate professor of Sociology at the University of California–Riverside. Her research focuses on the politics of welfare in the United States, past and present. She is the author of *Backlash Against Welfare Mothers: Past and Present* and is currently writing *They Say Cutback, We Say Fight Back! Welfare Rights Activism in an Era of Retrenchment,* which examines efforts by low-income people and their allies to resist welfare cutbacks and shape the implementation of welfare reform.

Ananya Roy is associate professor of Urban Studies in the Department of City and Regional Planning and Associate Dean of Academic Affairs in International and Area Studies at the University of California–Berkeley. She is the author of *City Requiem, Calcutta: Gender and the Politics of Poverty* and a co-editor of *Urban Informality: Transnational Perspectives from the Middle East, South Asia, and Latin America.*

Jennifer Lynn Stoever is a doctoral candidate in the Program in American Studies and Ethnicity at the University of Southern California. Her primary research areas include twentieth-century American literature and popular culture, African American and multiethnic literatures, cultural studies, and popular music (rock, hip hop, jazz). Her dissertation, titled "Soundscapes of Blackness: Listening and the African American Novel," will present a critical cultural history of aurality in the United States.

Marguerite Waller is professor of Women's Studies and Comparative Literature at the University of California–Riverside. She has published extensively on constructions of gender and sexuality in literature (Dante, Petrarch, Shakespeare) and visual culture (Italian cinema, virtual reality, U.S./Mexico border art), and has worked creatively with the women's art-making group Las Comadres, which is active in the San Diego/Tijuana border region. She is the author of *Petrarch's Poetics and Literary History*, co-editor with Jennifer Rycenga of *Frontline Feminisms: Women, War, and Resistance*, co-editor with Frank Burke of *Federico Fellini: Contemporary Perspectives*, and co-editor with Sylvia Marcos of *Dialogue and Difference: Feminisms Challenge Globalization*.